Assertive Supervision

Building Involved Teamwork

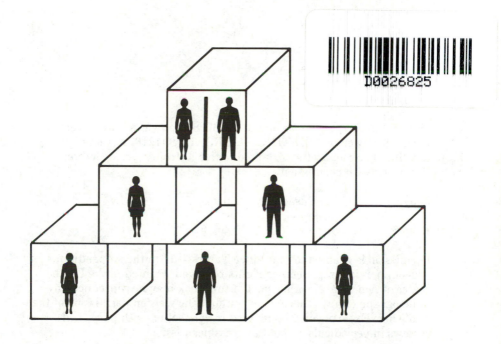

Susanne S. Drury

Research Press
2612 N. Mattis, Champaign, IL 61821

Contents

Acknowledgments

First and most important, I want to thank the workshop participants whose openness and honesty about their supervisory experiences stimulated me to create and develop this assertive supervision model. Each time I teach a workshop, I grow and learn from my participants, just as they grow and learn from me. I hope that this lively interchange can continue. I want to thank my friends Mary Schnierer for reading, critiquing, and sharpening the manuscript and Carol Marceluk for valiantly deciphering and typing my scribbles. Thanks also goes to my professional colleagues who have helped me to clarify the concepts described in this book. I would like to thank my husband and children, who were willing to support me through the struggles of building a new step-family at the same time as building a book. I also want to share my appreciation for Ann Wendel and Mary Wolf at Research Press. Their support and encouragement made the process of working on the book a nourishing experience. Mary Wolf was extraordinary in her ability to immerse herself in the manuscript until she could understand what I wanted to say even before I said it.

CHAPTER ONE

Introduction

What makes an outstanding supervisor? Although top management provides the basic structure and philosophy of an organization, the first-line supervisors make the organization work. An effective supervisor provides leadership that draws diverse employees together into a team committed to solving problems and getting the job done. Through respect for others and the encouragement of open communication, the supervisor inspires involvement and participation, while pursuing excellence by forcefully and respectfully confronting failure to perform.

This book shows you how to provide this strong leadership and at the same time create a climate of involved teamwork. It focuses on your daily interactions with your employees—*how* you can push for excellence without arousing resistance and hostility, *how* you can encourage open communication, and *how* you can inspire motivation in your employees.

Your supervisory style—what you do, when you do it, what words, voice characteristics, and body language you use—is responsible for creating a climate of leadership and teamwork. The framework of assertiveness will be used to describe and understand the impact of a supervisor's style. The concept of assertiveness has been widely used over the last 10 years to help people increase their interpersonal effectiveness. There is a large body of literature describing nonassertive, aggressive, and assertive styles of interaction, the results of each of the styles, and techniques for approaching others assertively. Some of these books include Alberti and Emmons, 1975; Bower and Bower, 1976; Cotler and Guerra, 1976; and Jakubowski and Lange, 1978. The concepts of nonassertiveness, aggressiveness, and assertiveness vividly summarize the three major approaches to supervision. This book will help you become aware of the implications of these different styles, identify your own style, and learn to respond to situations in the style that will give you the desired results. You will come to understand why an assertive supervisory style is crucial to doing your job and handling problems in a way that encourages employees, colleagues, and superiors to work with you and not against you. In each chapter you will find many case examples of the different supervisory styles in action, as well as questions, exercises, practice suggestions, and self-tests. There will be many opportunities to see how subtle or not so subtle changes in style can influence your effectiveness. The nonassertive, aggressive, and assertive styles will be explored, along with techniques for overcoming difficulties in being assertive. Assertive techniques and techniques for giving criticism and solving problems, responding to criticism, and asserting yourself with superiors and colleagues will be presented. Questions and answers about implementing assertiveness and tips for conducting assertive supervision workshops are also included.

Definitions of
Nonassertive, Aggressive, and Assertive

Words are slippery creatures; the same words often have many different meanings and connotations. The terms nonassertive, aggressive, and assertive have been used both positively and negatively. *Nonassertive* has been used to refer to both a polite, deferential style of interaction and a wishy-washy approach. The term *aggressive* has been used to describe a forceful, energetic approach to the world and to describe someone who acts in ways that infringe upon others. The word has also been used inappropriately as a criticism of anyone who strongly expresses an alternative point of view— often to disparage women who take an active role that contradicts traditional expectations for women. *Assertive* has also been used in both positive and negative ways. For some people, the term *assertive* is associated with clear, confident communication. For others, it represents a selfish, egocentric approach to life that undermines working together for common goals.

Nonassertive, aggressive, and *assertive* as they are used in this book have very specific meanings. Each of these words is a shorthand description for a whole cluster of style or approach characteristics that will be outlined in detail in Chapters Two, Three, and Four. No one responds with the same style at all times, so the terms will be used to refer to someone who predominantly uses that supervisory style. In general, someone acting nonassertively does not say what he wants or feels, speaks indirectly or apologetically, says something about a problem to the wrong person, waits too long to confront a problem, gives up too easily, and compromises without making his needs clear. Someone who is being nonassertive also tends to use words, voice characteristics, and body language that appear pleading and wishy-washy and tend to be discounted or elicit argument from others. Someone acting aggressively tends to blame and make judgmental criticisms, attribute negative intentions to others, act with too much power and too quickly, and refuse to listen or negotiate and compromise. The words he chooses and his voice characteristics and body language tend to put others on the defensive and make them feel threatened or cornered. Someone acting in an assertive way makes clear, direct, nonapologetic statements about his expectations and feelings, criticizes in a descriptive rather than a judgmental way, persists in following through on issues even if he meets resistance, listens to others' views respectfully, and negotiates and compromises. In addition, he does all of these things using words, voice characteristics, and body language that will be taken seriously without humiliating others.

The following examples illustrate how nonassertive, aggressive, and assertive styles look in practice. The first example is of a nonassertive style, the second is of an aggressive style, and the third of an assertive style.

Paul, the supervisor of the accounting department of a large company, provided very little specific direction for his staff. He delegated responsibilities in a vague way that left his employees uncertain about what they were to do and how important each task was. When someone was not doing an adequate job, Paul would postpone a confrontation and then would make some general remarks to the employee about how he hoped the employee would work harder. His lack of eye contact and his hesitant, pleading tone of voice made it difficult for employees to know when something was a serious concern. Good employees were discouraged because they had to work harder to compensate for others' poor performance, and because Paul did not seem seriously concerned about quality. Poor employees felt that they could get away with minimum performance. Everyone also knew that Paul would not fight for their concerns with management. There was no real push from Paul to build an involved work team.

Erwin, a supervisor in a chemical plant, was widely recognized as very aggressive. Since he demanded that everyone do things his way, there was little encouragement for creativity or innovation. Erwin was quick to criticize failures and slow to give credit for successes, so employees were reluctant to take any risks. When there were problems, Erwin would look for someone to blame. His impatient shouting and pounding on his desk underlined his attitude that the person who created the problem was a total idiot. His refusal to listen to explanations or to discuss the employee's view of a problem left employees more concerned about covering themselves than about exploring and preventing problems. Residual resentment over the lack of support and the employees' feelings that they were not respected as important members of the team undermined involvement and teamwork.

Milly, a nursing supervisor in a large metropolitan hospital, was respected by her employees and her co-workers. She clearly communicated her expectations about what needed to be done and how important each task was. She also made sure that employees knew why each task was important. She let others know where she stood, but would also listen to them and incorporate their ideas. When a problem did occur, she would confront it promptly by telling the employee her perceptions of the problem, asking for the employee's view, and developing a concrete plan for solving the problem. Her eye contact, her relaxed, attentive body posture, and her neutral voice tone underlined her commitment to open communication and teamwork. She pushed for excellence and was quick to recognize an employee's contribution to the team. Employees knew that they could count on Milly to take their ideas to management. By her forceful and supportive leadership, Milly created a climate of involved teamwork.

Each of the supervisors in these examples takes a different approach to assigning responsibility, attacking problems, and communicating with employees. Each style influences not only the immediate interaction with a particular employee but also the climate of the whole work unit. The supervisor, in his crucial leadership role, sets the tone for how important it is to do a good job, for how much each employee is valued by the organization, and for how people are to work together to reach organizational goals. Assertive supervision is not the best approach in every specific situation; however, an assertive approach as an overall strategy fosters the respect for others, open communication, and clear demand for competent performance that are required in building a climate of involved teamwork.

Inaccurate Beliefs about Assertiveness

You probably have been exposed to many stereotypes about assertiveness and assertiveness training. Some of these images come from popular literature, some from observing or talking to people who have attended assertiveness training workshops, and some from the assertiveness training literature itself (e.g., Smith, 1975). It is important that you see how inaccurate some of these common beliefs are.

Assertiveness is not a "do your own thing" philosophy

When someone takes a job in an organization, she agrees to provide certain services in support of organizational goals, and in return, the organization provides that person with certain benefits and with support for carrying out organizational goals. This contract implies a set of mutual rights and obligations. The supervisor carries out these obligations by translating company goals, policies, and procedures into clear expectations for the employees, and by working with employees to solve problems that interfere with accomplishing the department's objectives. Although assertiveness techniques can be used to pursue personal goals instead of organizational goals, this book describes an assertiveness model in which an assertive style is used in the service of effectively carrying out the supervisor's obligations to the organization. In the assertiveness model described in this book, insisting on "doing your own thing" and ignoring organizational priorities and the rights and needs of others is aggressive, not assertive.

> Dawn was having great difficulty with one of her tellers. The woman had attended an assertiveness training workshop and returned to work determined that "things were going to be different from now on." She applied her assertiveness by refusing to follow some personnel policies, because she thought they were unfair. She requested many exceptions from bank rules and became very angry when exceptions were not made. In her effort to take more responsibility for herself, this woman had gone from a nonassertive style to a very aggressive one. Neither style served to create effective working relationships.

**Asserting yourself doesn't guarantee
you will always get what you want**
Unfortunately, to many people, assertiveness implies getting their
own way regardless of others' needs and priorities. Not only does
this lead to unpleasant social interactions; it is also unrealistic.
There are many personal and organizational constraints on everyone. For example, political considerations, budget constraints,
others' goals and priorities, personality clashes, and organizational
conflicts may create situations in an organization in which change
will not occur no matter how much supervisors assert themselves.
Assertion often requires imaginatively looking for alternative ways
to solve a problem when personal or organizational constraints
make a particular change impossible. For example, an assertive
supervisor would look for ways to streamline time-consuming
paperwork when a tight budget makes assertion to get more staff
impractical, rather than helplessly saying, "Oh, isn't this awful?
Someone should do something." Assertiveness does not require,
however, that a supervisor continue to "beat her head against brick
walls." Continuing to push for change when constraints have been
made clear can create a great deal of frustration and therefore
damage the supervisor's effectiveness on issues where change is
possible.

Acting assertively in a situation will provide clear data about
individual and organizational constraints. When someone refuses
to comply with a request, her refusal provides a great deal of information about her position on the issue.

> Edith had been developing a plan for altering work schedules
> in her unit. When she presented the plan to her manager, he
> pointed out a number of ways in which her plan would create
> problems for the sales department. Although Edith continued
> to feel that her plan would be much better for her workers,
> she knew that pursuing the issue would not be effective at
> this point. She also knew that any workable plan would have
> to take the sales department into account.

It is also often true that not speaking out leaves an "unfinished"
feeling. Sometimes assertiveness may leave a person feeling better
about a situation even if her assertions do not lead to change. It is
often a relief just to say what needs to be said even if saying it fails
to produce the desired result. It at least creates the feeling that
everything possible has been done to correct a problem.

Ross was nearly certain that his manager would never be willing to approach upper management about the tremendous work overload in his unit. He was constantly tense and angry about the situation. When he finally confronted the manager, his guesses were confirmed. The manager refused to raise the issue. Ross found, however, that he felt less frustrated and anxious because he felt that he had done all he could.

Assertiveness is not an invitation
to be rude, obnoxious, and unpleasant

There is no incompatibility between assertiveness and courtesy; to the contrary, assertiveness requires courteous, respectful treatment of others. In one sense assertiveness is the embodiment of the Golden Rule. The Golden Rule does not say to "love others instead of yourself" or "love yourself instead of others." It implies that you should respect and value others *and* respect and value yourself. It is entirely possible to be powerful and firm and to be polite and respectful at the same time. In this book, the emphasis will be on respectful firmness.

One assertiveness trainer insisted that an assertive person should never say "I'm sorry." Even when her behavior genuinely inconvenienced someone, she refused to apologize. When someone tried to express concerns about an issue, she would say, "I can't help it if you're upset. That's your problem." Others found her disregard for their feelings quite offensive and did not like to work with her. She had confused aggressive lack of concern for others with taking an assertive stand on issues.

You don't have to be assertive all of the time

It is unlikely that anyone will be assertive all of the time. People all have strengths and weaknesses in their ability to be assertive. One supervisor may find it easy to give positive feedback but very difficult to criticize. Another supervisor may easily be clear and direct with one employee and find the same approach very difficult with someone else. Still another supervisor may find that on some days she can maintain self-control and approach things assertively and on other days tends to react in an aggressive, blaming fashion in spite of her best intentions. Assertiveness training does not pretend to create a rigid new set of rules for all behavior in all situations. Aggressive and nonassertive approaches may be the most effective responses in certain circumstances. It may not be worth the risk to be assertive. Some people will respond better to another style. Different styles of interaction tend to have specifically different effects on others; knowing potential consequences and developing alternative strategies will expand choices of behavior. The emphasis in assertiveness training is on choosing an appropriate action rather than reacting to a situation through habit or emotion.

Juanita had been told by her boss that he believed that everyone should always do things his way. He also let her know that he had fired the last three people who had suggested alternative procedures. Although she felt that another way of handling bookkeeping records would be much more efficient, she did not assert herself. Instead, she looked for ways to make her current job bearable and concentrated on looking for another job.

SELF-TEST

Pick the statements that are *not* characteristic of this book's approach to assertiveness and specify what cues you used.

1. "I want my employees to listen to what I say and respect my authority, but I also have an obligation to listen to and respect their opinions."
2. "I'm taking an assertiveness training class, and now I don't have to put up with some of those stupid company rules anymore."
3. "How dare you ask me to do that job. I won't and if you don't like it, that's too bad."
4. "I don't agree with your position on this issue, but you are the boss and you have the ultimate authority here."
5. "Assertiveness training taught me never to give up. If you bug people long enough, they are bound to give in."
6. "Now that I've learned the techniques, I'm going to be assertive no matter what."

ANSWERS

1. Characteristic—This statement reflects the respect for self and others that is involved in this approach to assertiveness.
2. Not characteristic—Assertiveness does not mean doing your own thing by placing personal goals above company procedures.
3. Not characteristic—Assertiveness does not mean being rude, obnoxious, and unpleasant to get your own way.

4. Characteristic—This statement reflects recognition that you won't always get what you want by being assertive and shows respectful treatment of others.
5. Not characteristic—This statement is based on the incorrect belief that you will always get what you want by being assertive.
6. Not characteristic—This statement is based on the misunderstanding that you must always be assertive.

Assertiveness and Human Nature

After determining which beliefs are inconsistent with this book's view of assertiveness, it is equally important to describe which beliefs about human nature and human interactions do form the basis for the model in this book. The view of assertiveness in this book has underlying assumptions that may differ from those of other approaches to assertiveness.

People want to do a good job
Theory Y, developed by McGregor (1960), takes the position that people have inherent motivation to work, have the capacity for creative problem solving, and will apply their creativity to their jobs if the conditions are right. Although not all employees fit Theory Y assumptions, one way to elicit cooperation is to approach employees as if they want to do a good job. Assuming that employees would do a good job if something were not interfering establishes a much more productive climate for problem solving than assuming they do not want to do a good job. The role of the supervisor is to uncover blocks and obstacles and to help employees get these out of the way. Among the many obstacles to an employee's performance can be inadequate understanding of the job, different values about work, different assumptions about what is expected, low self-esteem, poor work habits, limited abilities, poor skills, poor relationships with the supervisor or others, and poor design of the work place or of the job itself. When supervisors give employees the benefit of the doubt, employees are more open to letting them know what is really causing the problem so that it can be solved. On the other hand, if a supervisor approaches someone with an attitude that says "I know you really don't care about your job" or "I know you don't want to cooperate with me," he is more likely to elicit the negative attitude he imagines. Attitudes

toward others do become a kind of self-fulfilling prophecy. If you have ever worked for someone who obviously mistrusted you and your intentions, you know how undermining this attitude is. Even if a supervisor does not directly verbalize his attitude, employees or co-workers will often guess his basic assumptions about them. It will be very difficult to be assertive without some basic trust in others' willingness to cooperate with you in getting the job done.

Does this mean that there are no employees who do not want to cooperate or do a good job? Obviously not. There are clearly some employees who bring with them to the job negative attitudes that make it much more difficult to elicit their cooperation; however, the truly resistant and uncooperative employee is rare in most work settings. Giving the employee the benefit of the doubt is much less likely to lead to supervisory problems than is erring in the direction of mistrust. Approaching employees with a basically positive attitude will make it much more likely that they will respond in positive ways to supervisory interventions.

> Sue, an employee in the personnel department of a large company, had been called in to investigate complaints that the manager in one work unit would always support his supervisor even when her decisions were arbitrary and unfair. Her first approach was to point out to the manager that he did not seem to be concerned enough about what was happening in his department. The manager began to defensively describe all the ways in which he exhibited concern for the department. When Sue realized that she had put the manager on the defensive, she pointed out to him that she knew that he was trying to be supportive of his supervisory staff and that he clearly was concerned about the department, which was why she counted on his help in solving the problem. Although it took some time to overcome her initial error, Sue found that acknowledging the manager's good intentions eventually helped to lead to cooperative problem solving.

People have a powerful need to save face
A lot of people assume that getting someone to admit that he is at fault is a necessary step in getting him to change. This assumption leads to confrontations focusing on how the problems are the other person's fault. Ironically, when people feel that they are being shown as incompetent, they are most motivated to defend themselves or to berate themselves for their stupidity. Neither behavior leaves a great deal of energy for solving the problem. Also, a defensive employee is less likely to even hear what the supervisor

is saying. An employee may feel it a serious loss of face to say "You're right. I have really been doing a lousy job proofreading my reports lately." Instead, he will be likely to bluster or fume and to deny that there is a problem. If the supervisor insists on getting an employee to admit that he is wrong, the battle may be won and the war lost. The employee may change his behavior but then harbor resentment that interferes with productivity. In the assertive approach, the point is to solve the problem, not to get the other person to admit he has been wrong. If the problem is solved, the supervisor has been effective even if the employee never admits that he was at fault.

Melina had one clerk with many performance problems. She was furious because this clerk would always deny that he was doing anything wrong. Disciplinary sessions always led to an argument and left both people frustrated and resentful. Once she stopped trying to get her clerk to accept blame, she was able to focus on the behaviors she wanted him to change. Talking about behaviors allowed the clerk to change and to save face at the same time.

Failing to tell someone
about a problem is not doing him a favor
It is easy for a supervisor to believe that telling an employee about a problem is too painful and that he should only do so in dire emergencies when there is no alternative. Stop and think about this for a moment. If someone were dissatisfied with something you were doing, would you prefer that he tell you about it directly or would you rather he complain about your work to others and give you a poor performance review? By not telling an employee about a problem, a supervisor is not only depriving him of an opportunity to change, but he is also allowing the employee to continue to make more and more of the same mistakes. Therefore, the employee finds himself in serious difficulty before he even knows there is a problem. Not letting an employee know when there is a problem is a way of giving up on that person before it is clear whether he can do better. Therefore, honest feedback, although it may be painful at the time, is fairer to others in the long run.

Salvatore is especially careful to let employees know where they stand because he was the victim of a supervisor who did not confront problems. He had every reason to think that his work was satisfactory because his superior had never criticized him. When he was given an unsatisfactory rating, he felt that he had been treated very unfairly. Many of the problems

that led to an unsatisfactory rating could have been corrected
if he had known sooner that they were problems.

No one can force anyone else to change

A large part of the supervisory job is an attempt to get people to
change their behavior. Good supervision involves the ability to influence others to make productive choices of their own free will. It
is important that others feel they have some choice, however, because most people have an inherent dislike of being dominated and
controlled. A power struggle can begin if a supervisor approaches
an employee with the attitude that he can make that employee
change his behavior: the more the supervisor demands that the
employee change, the more the employee digs in his heels and
resists. Once a supervisor has begun a power struggle, the most
effective way to end it may be to say "You're right. I can't make
you do it this way. However, here is why I need to have you do it
this way. If you choose to do it another way, here are the likely
consequences." A supervisor encourages people to choose to change
by letting them know very clearly what is expected. He lets the
employees know the consequences of their failure to carry out particular tasks and listens to try to understand clearly why the employee objects to a demand. He continues to follow up and ask the
employee to do the job even when change may not occur right
away.

> Henry's major supervisory problems were connected with one
> young employee. Henry was used to issuing orders and having
> those orders followed. This new employee questioned every-
> thing. The more Henry ordered the employee to do things a
> certain way, the more the employee resisted. Henry finally
> realized that he and this employee were trapped in a power
> struggle. He decided to spend more time listening to his em-
> ployee's point of view and more time explaining his own view.
> When he stopped trying to *make* this employee change, the
> employee seemed to become more willing to change.

Everyone has more control over himself than over anyone else's
behavior. While it may be true that the ultimate goal is to influence
and change someone else's behavior, the best way to do this is for
the supervisor to focus on what he can do differently in the interaction. The belief that "if only my workers (my boss, my wife) were
different, I would not have this problem" encourages the supervisor
to fantasize about all of the ways the other person should change
rather than on what he can do to bring about change.

Assertiveness will not always work right away

An employee's initial response to an assertive confrontation is not as important as whether the employee changes his behavior in the long run. People will often respond to assertive confrontations with frustration, avoidance, or sulking and later act as if the desired change were their idea. An initial negative response does not mean that assertion will not work. There are several reasons why someone may initially respond negatively to assertive behavior. Some people feel that they will lose face by complying too easily with an assertive request. For other people, change itself is threatening. Any new idea must simmer inside for a few days before they are ready to consider it seriously. People also often like to get their own way. It may be frustrating for some people to find that they will have to take another person's point of view into account. This frustration may occur even if in the long run they would rather work with people who will stand by their own views. Most people discover in the course of their lives that certain responses tend to get others to give in and leave them alone. For example, if a supervisor gives in when an employee has a temper tantrum, he is training this employee to have temper tantrums when confronted. If a negative response to others' assertiveness has always worked before, the employee may unconsciously react this way. A supervisor may need to learn to persevere and to deal with conflict and negativity if he wants to learn to be effectively assertive.

Kara worked for a very aggressive manager. Every time she brought any problem to this man's attention, he would become very angry and would threaten and berate her. Many other supervisors simply avoided dealing with him. She discovered that he would always be very angry and upset initially, but would soften in several days and be willing to consider her ideas. In the long run, her assertiveness paid off in many productive changes in office procedures.

SELF-TEST

Pick the statements that are characteristic of this book's approach to assertiveness and specify what cues you used.
1. "I hate hassles. Everything works a lot better if you keep relations with others smooth. If assertiveness leads to conflict, it's not effective."
2. "Most employees want to do a reasonable job. If they are not doing well, there must be a problem we need to uncover and solve."

3. "My job is to make my employees do what I tell them to do. If they don't do what I say, they are questioning my authority and casting doubt on my effectiveness as a supervisor."

4. "I want my employees to change their behavior, but I realize that unless I change my approach, they are not likely to change."

5. "I try very hard not to corner people or show them up because I know that they will be less responsive to me when they are on the defensive."

6. "I don't want to upset others so it's better not to say anything unless the problem is really serious."

ANSWERS

1. Not characteristic—This statement reflects a belief that assertiveness should work right away.

2. Characteristic—This statement is based on the belief that employees want to do a good job.

3. Not characteristic—This statement is based on a belief that you should be able to make others change.

4. Characteristic—This statement reflects the belief that you can only change your own behavior and influence others to change.

5. Characteristic—This statement reflects an understanding of people's powerful need to save face.

6. Not characteristic—This statement is based on a belief that not telling someone about a problem is doing him a favor.

The Process of Changing Behavior

Every supervisor will bring with her to the supervisory job a certain style of relating to people. This style is based on her own natural temperament and on what she learned about interacting with others during childhood. A self-aware supervisor will observe her own behavior and in this process will learn which behaviors work and which do not. When she discovers that her approach does not bring the desired results, she will then choose to experiment with other approaches. With the assistance of the guidelines presented in the following chapters, you will be better equipped to observe your behavior and better prepared to understand the reactions that you get from others. The first step in the process of change is awareness and observation. This observation can then form the basis of a decision to try another supervisory approach.

Choosing, however, will not automatically produce change. Old ways of responding are often deeply ingrained habits. Anytime someone tries to change an old habit or to learn a new way of doing something, the new way will feel awkward, clumsy, and foreign. Remember the first time you learned a new skill like riding a bicycle or driving a stick shift car. The first attempt was probably clumsy and artificial. You had to think about every move. Nothing about the new behavior felt natural. However, as you practiced the new skill, the new behaviors became habits and gradually felt as natural and automatic as if you had always known that skill. Learning to be assertive is like learning any other skill. If you have always responded to employees in a nonassertive or an aggressive way, you will have to stop and think in order to respond assertively. The assertive behaviors will feel awkward and unnatural. Change is a slow step-by-step process that requires a great deal of concentration and effort. New ways of responding only begin to feel natural and spontaneous when they have been practiced often enough to be habitual. The approaches suggested in this book will become a comfortable part of your supervisory style only if you practice them.

In the process of incorporating some of the suggestions in this book into your supervisory role, you may want to elicit the help of colleagues and friends in providing feedback about your style. It may be helpful to ask for feedback directly or roleplay an interaction.

There are several other things to keep in mind about the process of change. First, there are limits to the extent of change that will occur. Although a few people make radical changes in their style, it is unlikely that a very retiring quiet person will be transformed into someone who is very outspoken and outgoing. You will always be yourself. Your supervisory style will be *your* style and will be different from someone else's style even if you are both trying to do the same things. Look for ways to shape the assertive style to fit the person you are. Second, change takes a long time. Even if you decide to handle situations in a new way, you will find old patterns returning at times. If you have been very nonassertive or very aggressive, you may find that you gradually become more assertive rather than completely changing your style all at once. Be patient with yourself and appreciate small steps toward a new style. Third, do not wait for a huge crisis to occur before practicing assertive skills. In a crisis you are likely to do the thing you do most often. To have access to new approaches in a crisis, you must practice the skills when you can take more time to think about your actions. Fourth, practice your assertive skills on simple situations first. For example, if you find asserting yourself with your superiors to be very difficult, it may be useful to practice asserting yourself with others first. Practice will increase your confidence and prepare you to be assertive in difficult situations. More about the process of changing your behavior is presented in Chapter Five.

Remember a time when you tried to change a long-term habit. How long did it take you to make the change? How did you bring about change?

EXERCISE

Over the next several weeks, observe yourself as a supervisor. You may find it helpful to keep a journal describing the situations in which you were not satisfied with the outcome of your interventions as a supervisor. This record keeping can help you to become more aware of yourself and of what you might want to work on or to change.

Sample Journal:

Situation	What did I do?	Outcome	What would I like to have done?
Late for 5th day	Didn't say anything	Late again	Confront her today.
Late again	Yelled at her	She burst into tears, sulked all day	Tell her in a calm voice how her lateness creates problems for the unit and that I want her to be on time.

Summary

Supervisory style has a powerful influence on building involved teamwork. Style consists of the actions you take, how quickly you act, and your word choices, voice characteristics, and body language. People react differently to the nonassertive, aggressive, and assertive styles. This book is designed to help you become aware of the implications of different supervisory styles, identify your own style, and learn to respond to situations in a style that will give the desired results.

The words *nonassertive, aggressive,* and *assertive* have been defined differently in different places. In this book they describe a cluster of style characteristics. No one behaves in one way all of the time, so the words refer to someone who predominantly uses that style. An overall assertive approach is the best one for building involved teamwork.

There are many inaccurate beliefs about assertiveness that people have been exposed to. One belief is that assertiveness is a "do your own thing" philosophy. Another inaccurate belief is that asserting yourself guarantees you will always get what you want. Some people also inaccurately believe that assertiveness is an invitation to be rude, obnoxious, and unpleasant. Another inaccurate belief is that you have to be assertive all of the time.

There are certain beliefs about human nature that underlie this approach to assertiveness training. One is that people want to do a good job. Another belief is that people have a powerful need to save face. This approach also holds that failing to tell someone about a problem is not doing him a favor. Another belief is that no one can force anyone else to change. Assertiveness will not always work right away is another belief of this approach.

The process of changing your behavior to become more assertive is difficult. New behaviors will feel awkward until after much practice. When trying to change your behavior, you should keep in mind that there are limits to the extent of change that will occur, change takes a long time, you should practice your assertiveness before a crisis occurs, and that you should practice on simple situations first.

Bibliography

Alberti, R. E., & Emmons, M. L. *Stand up, speak out, talk back.* New York: Pocket Books, 1975.

Bower, S. A., & Bower, G. *Asserting yourself.* Reading, Mass.: Addison-Wesley, 1976.

Cotler, S. B., & Guerra, J. J. *Assertion training: A humanistic-behavioral guide to self-dignity.* Champaign, Ill.: Research Press, 1976.

Jakubowski, P., & Lange, A. J. *The assertive option: Your rights and responsibilities.* Champaign, Ill.: Research Press, 1978.

McGregor, D. M. *The human side of enterprise.* New York: McGraw-Hill, 1960.

Smith, M. *When I say no I feel guilty.* New York: Dial Press, 1975.

CHAPTER TWO

The Nonassertive Supervisory Style

In this chapter, you will:
- Learn to identify nonassertive behavior patterns;
- Become aware of nonassertive word choices;
- Become aware of nonassertive voice characteristics and body language;
- Learn the effects of nonassertiveness on you;
- Learn others' reactions to nonassertiveness;
- Learn to recognize situations in which nonassertiveness is the best response;
- Become aware of feelings and beliefs that support nonassertiveness.

The following dialogue illustrates a nonassertive encounter between an employer and an employee. In this situation, Angela has realized that her employee George is late again in turning in his monthly report. This is the third month she has had to ask George for the report.

Angela: (With downcast eyes and a very soft and pleading voice) I was wondering about your monthly report. It's a little bit late again.

George: Boy, I have a ton of work to do. You gave me these other assignments and Mr. Washington also wants a report. It's really hard to get it all done. Don't worry. I'll get you the report as soon as I can.

Angela: Oh, I do hope you'll get to it as soon as possible. I sort of need that report sometime soon.

How effective do you think Angela will be in solving the problem?
When will she get this month's report?
Will George turn the report in on time next month?
How would you feel as Angela? How would you feel as George?
What might be the long-range consequences of this style?

In this dialogue, Angela uses minimizing words like "a little bit late," "sort of," and "I was wondering." She never says clearly what she wants, nor does she address the ongoing problem of the late reports. She has no eye contact and her voice tone is soft and pleading. George may feel temporarily guilty, and may try to do the report; however, he is likely to postpone the report again next month. Since she never says why the report is necessary, she makes it very easy for George to discount or ignore her comments and go on doing what he's doing. She has given him no compelling reason to make that report top priority in today's work schedule. This vignette illustrates some typical nonassertive behavior patterns, word choices, voice characteristics, and body language that will be described in the following sections.

Nonassertive Behavior Patterns

Nonassertive supervisors follow certain patterns of behavior. These affect their performance and the performance of their employees and co-workers.

No expression of expectations and feelings

Often nonassertive supervisors do have strong opinions about things that are going on in the unit or in the organization as a whole; they simply keep their feelings to themselves. Nonassertive supervisors will often not say no even when taking on another piece of work will disrupt the work flow in their unit. When nonassertive people need resources and support from someone, they may simply sit back and hope that the other person will see that they need help. They are prone to keep criticisms to themselves when expressing them might be an important step in solving a problem. When they feel that something will not work or is creating a problem, they may be reluctant to mention it at all.

Doreetha, office manager in an insurance company, was extremely annoyed by the way one of the secretaries answered the telephone. She felt that the person did not sound sufficiently professional for their type of office. Instead of saying something, she found herself seething every time that employee answered the phone.

Nonassertive people hold back positive suggestions for improvement in company policies and procedures as well. Organizations full of yes men tend to stagnate. Disagreement and differences of opinion give birth to new approaches and to more creative and productive ways of solving problems. Someone who holds back her point of view for fear of offending others robs the organization of everything special or unique that she might have to contribute.

Bill, the manager of a printing company, was very frustrated with one of his supervisors. Jeff was a very skilled and competent worker with many good ideas, but he was so nonassertive that he simply wouldn't speak up in meetings. When the company was buying a new printing press, Jeff would not give his opinion on the best choice of equipment even though he knew more about presses than the other supervisors. Jeff simply agreed with what had already been said when Bill prodded him to speak up. Bill did not feel Jeff could be promoted or put in charge of any major projects because of his inability to speak up.

Keeping silent may be valuable sometimes, but nonassertive supervisors carry this self-restraint to extremes. When their assertions might potentially annoy, disrupt, or inconvenience someone else, they are inclined to refrain from making them even when this reticence interferes with productivity.

———◆———

Do you find yourself holding back your views on issues, particularly when you sense that the other person might disagree or be upset by your views?

Can you think of someone who doesn't express her expectations and feelings? What is it like to interact with this person?

———◆———

Views stated indirectly or apologetically
The dialogue at the beginning of this chapter is a good example of this kind of nonassertive behavior. Angela did express her feelings

about the late report, but expressed her desire for George to change his behavior in such a low-key way that he could easily ignore her wishes. Nonassertive supervisors may use words that minimize their messages, use apologetic statements, address their concerns to a group rather than directly to the person involved, make very general statements that hint at or imply more specific issues, or disguise statements as questions. Although the supervisor may assume that any idiot with common sense would recognize what she is so obviously leading up to, this style of interaction is very dependent on the other person's attentiveness and willingness to search for underlying meanings. An employee who is distracted by her own concerns or unwilling to pay attention to innuendos is left relatively untouched by this type of nonassertive behavior. Most people have probably experienced an example of this kind of nonassertive behavior—a lengthy phone call from someone that left them wondering why the person had called.

> Francisco, a state police communications supervisor, had become really concerned about an employee's use of state time to conduct personal business. He confronted the employee by making some general remarks about the need for all employees to put in a full effort at work. The employee never realized that he was being confronted about his behavior and, as a consequence, made no effort to change.

◆

In an effort to be tactful, do you disguise your opinions so well that others have to guess what you really mean?

Can you think of someone who states her views indirectly or apologetically? How effective is this person?

◆

Complaints made to the wrong person
Since the nonassertive choice is to avoid direct confrontation, feelings of frustration, disappointment, or anger often are not expressed to the person whose behavior is causing them. This does not necessarily mean that the nonassertive supervisor truly suffers in silence. Often colleagues, superiors, or employees hear in great detail about what someone is doing to create problems. When they suggest talking to the person involved, the nonassertive supervisor generally backs down with a comment like "Oh, I don't want to cause problems. It's not that important."

David, director of hospital supplies in a large hospital, spent hours complaining to his co-workers about his manager's arbitrary changes in policy; however, when the issue came up, he refused to discuss the problem with the manager.

Frequent complaining may be an indication that some assertive action is required. One of the problems with complaining to the wrong person is that generally the person who can do something to change the situation doesn't hear about the problem at all. This situation insures that both the problem and the complaints will continue.

———◆———

Do you find that you often complain about situations to someone who can't do anything to change the situation?

Can you think of someone who often complains to the wrong person? What is it like to interact with this person?

———◆———

Problems not confronted soon enough
Another typical nonassertive behavior is to allow a problem to continue until it has either caused a serious crisis or until so much frustration has built up that the supervisor finally blows up over a relatively minor issue. There is some legitimate basis for giving problems an opportunity to sort themselves out, but problems are a great deal easier to solve when they are small. Situations that lead to severe consequences, that affect department morale, that develop bad work habits, or that become increasingly more irritating need to be confronted at once. By confronting a problem before it becomes a crisis, supervisors can uncover underlying employee behaviors that may lead to other problems and thus prevent future trouble.

If an employee is not doing an adequate job, the nonassertive supervisor is much more inclined to hope that the problem will resolve itself than to actively face and solve the performance problem. She is reluctant to draw attention to problems for fear of risking conflict or confrontation. In a situation where there are no real problems and where all of the employees are highly motivated, nonassertiveness may not hurt productivity at all; however, when problems occur and strong forceful action is required, the nonassertive person finds it difficult to take the kind of action that is needed.

In one office, the secretary chronically misfiled materials. The supervisor would search the files but would avoid mentioning the problem to the secretary because she knew that each time the misfiling occurred, the secretary had been unusually busy. Finally a critical grant proposal was misfiled and was not submitted by deadline. The angry confrontation at this point could not prevent the serious problems that had resulted from continued misfiling.

"Gunnysacking" is a common symptom of not confronting problems soon enough. This term means that the supervisor collects a lot of small angers and frustrations in her psychological "gunnysack." When the gunnysack is full, she dumps all of the collected anger on either a person who has just angered her or who is a continual irritant or on a relatively innocent bystander. The other person is left wondering how she could possibly be so angry and upset about something so trivial. The explosion of built-up anger makes it difficult to handle the situation appropriately and frequently provides the nonassertive supervisor with further justification for trying to hold back all of her feelings until the next time the gunnysack is full.

———————————◆———————————

Do you put off raising issues that you know you should confront? Do you find that you often let things go until you are really angry?

Can you think of someone who doesn't confront problems soon enough? What is it like to interact with this person?

———————————◆———————————

No persistence
The nonassertive supervisor may be able to make a clear, direct statement once, but if she runs into strong resistance, she will either give in or ignore the issue. This behavior can result in confronting a problem and then failing to follow through when the problem continues. It can also mean that the supervisor can be talked into something if someone is persistent enough. This failure to persist will be experienced by others as a sign that the issues were not that important. It also creates an image of uncertainty that invites others to argue about every issue. Often the real difficulty in being assertive is persevering on an issue until it is resolved or continuously saying no until the other person clearly understands that the decision is final.

Ali had made a policy that no employees in his bank would be able to take personal time on Fridays without a week's notice. His first reaction to an employee making an unacceptable request would be a firm no; however, a persistent employee who could give a few plausible reasons for needing a day could usually talk him into making an exception. Soon he had all exceptions and no policy.

Do you find that you often end up giving in when you start out being assertive?

Can you think of someone who is assertive up to a point but gives in under pressure? How effective is this person?

Unclear negotiation and compromise

A nonassertive supervisor is willing to negotiate and compromise but doesn't say what she wants from the negotiations. She expects trade-offs, but never lets the other person know what they are. When the other person doesn't do what she wants, she feels cheated. The nonassertive supervisor may also agree to a compromise in which she gets less than the minimum of what she needs.

Sheena needed to meet with her supervisor to discuss the details of a departmental budget request. She asked for a meeting with him this week but agreed to postpone the meeting until next week. She assumed he would be willing to meet on Monday or Tuesday of the next week. When the manager did not meet with her until late in the next week, Sheena felt cheated. She had not made clear what she was expecting in return for her compromise.

Do you find yourself not stating what you want when you are negotiating and compromising? Do you settle for compromises that give you below the minimum of what you need?

Can you think of someone who does not say what she wants when negotiating and compromising? What is it like to interact with this person?

SELF-TEST

Pick the nonassertive response in the following situations and specify what cues you used.

1. Cora has an employee who comes to her several times an hour for help on problems she could solve herself.
   a. Cora complains to her supervisor almost daily about the worker.
   b. Cora tells the employee she needs to attempt to solve problems herself before asking for help.
2. Don is convinced that the new reporting procedure is slowing productivity and has some data to prove it.
   a. He schedules a meeting with his supervisor to discuss the data and talk about possible ways to modify the procedure.
   b. He hopes management will see and correct the obvious problem.
3. Laura needs her manager's backing when she confronts an employee.
   a. She has a conversation with her supervisor about problem employees in general and the need for management support.
   b. She has a conversation with the supervisor in which she describes the situation with that employee and asks whether the supervisor will support her in reprimanding that employee.
4. Danielle has been taking on extra work from another unit.
   a. She will say something as soon as she begins to feel this is a problem.
   b. She lets the situation go until she is fuming about the unfair and unreasonable demands of the other department and then has an angry confrontation.
5. Dominica has confronted Sandra about making personal phone calls on company time, but there has been no change.
   a. She lets it go for 6 months or so figuring that Sandra will change eventually.
   b. She meets with Sandra again within a week or so to let her know that the behavior is still a problem and they need to develop a plan for modifying it.

6. Hector wants Susan to complete a project by herself. When she outlines her other responsibilities, he decides compromise is called for.
   a. He agrees to assign another worker to help Susan but does not establish a specific agreement about what part of the project he expects Susan to do.
   b. He agrees to assign someone to help Susan if she will do all of the data collection and only use the other person to pull together the final report.

ANSWERS

1. *a* is the nonassertive response because she complains to the wrong person. *b* is assertive because she makes her comments to the person involved.
2. *b* is the nonassertive response because he does not express his expectations and feelings but just waits for the situation to change. *a* is assertive because he takes an active role.
3. *a* is the nonassertive response because she is too indirect in expressing what she wants. *b* is assertive because she clearly describes what she wants.
4. *b* is the nonassertive response because she waits too long to confront the problem. *a* is assertive because she expresses her feelings when the problem begins.
5. *a* is the nonassertive response because she fails to persist and follow up the confrontation. *b* is assertive because she follows up when the behavior continues.
6. *a* is the nonassertive response because he doesn't let Susan know what he expects. *b* is assertive because the other end of the bargain is specified.

Nonassertive Word Choices

Certain kinds of language are obvious cues that reveal a nonassertive supervisory style. One way that someone can learn to identify his own style and the style of others is to listen to the words that are used.

Minimizing words

Phrases and words like *kind of, a little, sort of, maybe* and *perhaps* inadvertently tell others that particular communications are not to be taken too seriously. One way that someone appears nonassertive and dilutes his impact on others is by using minimizing words. People are less likely to pay attention to statements that are delivered in a minimized way (Eisen, 1984).

EXERCISE

Say the following sentences out loud. Which ones would you take more seriously?

I'm upset that you haven't completed this project.
I'm a little upset that you haven't completed this project.

I would like you to be at the staff meeting next week.
I would kind of like you to be at the staff meeting next week.

Apologetic statements

Nonassertive responses are often preceded or followed by phrases that reduce their impact. Sometimes a nonassertive communication is a clear, direct, assertive statement buried in a sentence that blunts or discounts its importance. Sentences like "I know that this will be a bother and you probably won't want to do it, but could you possibly help me with this project?" and "I'd really like some help with this project if you don't mind too much and can fit it into your schedule with no hassle" are examples of this.

Some assertiveness training books recommend never apologizing (Smith, 1975), but there are times when an apology is entirely appropriate. Apologies are appropriate when someone has inconvenienced or caused problems for another. Apologies are only inappropriate and nonassertive when they refer to requests that there is really no need to apologize for. For example, "I'm sorry to have to bring this to your attention, but this is the third time this week you have been late" is an inappropriate apology. Apologizing for confrontations or for requests sends a message that the supervisor is not sure he has a right to make them. The hostile or manipulative employee may see apologies as an open invitation to play on the supervisor's uncertainty.

EXERCISE

Say the following sentences out loud. Which one would you take more seriously?

I don't want you to spend so much time on personal phone calls.

I know you have a lot of calls to make and I really don't want to bother you, but I don't want you to spend so much time on personal phone calls.

Statements made about people in general
instead of to a specific person

Nonassertive supervisors will sometimes confront a problem with a particular employee by announcing in a meeting that "Some people around here have been taking too long a lunch hour lately." Often the employee who picks up the general remark is the one who is not really creating a serious problem; the more difficult employee can be insensitive when it comes to picking up hints. Other supervisors, even in a discussion with a single employee, will talk about "problem employees" in general, "some people," or "one" rather than talking to that specific employee about his specific performance problems. For example, a common supervisory remark might be "You know, David, it's been awfully hard for me to get some of my employees to put in maximum effort here." This type of approach really depends on the employee's self-critical abilities and motivation. A motivated, cooperative employee might very well take the hint, examine his performance, and make necessary changes without any more specific intervention from the supervisor; but the less motivated, less self-aware employee could easily fail to see the message as relevant to him.

EXERCISE

Say the following sentences out loud. Which is likely to have the most impact?

Employees should really make an effort to proofread their work carefully before they submit it.

Helen, I'd like you to proofread your material more carefully before you submit it.

General instead of specific
behavioral descriptions

As presented more fully in Chapter Seven, employees need to know exactly what they are doing to create a problem if they are to be effectively motivated to change. One common nonassertive word choice is to use general, inclusive descriptions of problems rather than pinpointing specific performance problems. Comments like "Your performance could be better" or "Your performance is inadequate" or "You should work harder (be more considerate, make more of an effort, etc.)" might serve as effective introductions to a clearer, more specific description of a problem, but some supervisors never go beyond these general descriptions. The problem with this kind of confrontation is that these general descriptions have many different meanings for different people. If a supervisor tells an employee to "work harder," he may mean that he wants the employee to take shorter lunch hours, not to make personal phone calls, to increase the pace of his work, not to make so many trips to the water cooler, or any number of other specific behaviors. An employee could, with all good intentions, change behavior to conform to his own definition of working harder, and still fail to take care of the supervisor's major concern.

<hr>

EXERCISE

Say the following sentences out loud. Which is likely to convey your concerns more clearly?

> I would really like you to work more carefully.
> I would really like you to proofread all of your letters before they come to me, because I have been finding errors that require me to send many letters back to you.

<hr>

Statements disguised as questions

Another common nonassertive word choice is to ask a question that is really a disguised request or statement of opinion. "You wouldn't want to use that procedure with this problem, would you?" or "Don't you think that Mr. Jones is being unfair?" are questions that allow the questioner to express a point of view without having to take responsibility for it. If someone disagrees, it is always possible for the supervisor to claim that he really doesn't have an opinion but was just asking for information. One result of this kind of statement is that the other person has to guess what the questioner's real opinion is. There are also many stubborn people who respond to this type of rhetorical question by treating it as a pure question. For example, some employees will answer a question like

"Don't you want to clean up your lab area a little?" with, "Not really. I don't mind the mess." At this point the supervisor either has to be more straightforward and say, "Well, the messy lab bothers me; I'd like you to clean it up" or he has to give up.

EXERCISE

Say the following sentences out loud. Which statement sounds stronger?

Wouldn't you like to join this new committee on departmental policy?

I would like you to serve on this new committee on departmental policy.

SELF-TEST

Pick the nonassertive statements and specify what cues you used.

1. "I'm sort of a little concerned about getting this new project done sooner."
2. "We've really been having trouble lately because some of our people haven't been doing their share."
3. "I'd like you to rewrite the last section of the report giving more attention to the statistics."
4. "I don't want to inconvenience you, but could you possibly try to get back to me sooner next time I call."
5. "I'd like you to be more committed to your job."
6. "Please let me know by Monday if you won't be at the meeting."
7. "Don't you think it's a good idea to do the budget section first?"

ANSWERS

1. Nonassertive—This statement is nonassertive because it uses minimizing words.
2. Nonassertive—People in general instead of a specific person are addressed in this statement.
3. Assertive—This statement gives a specific description of the desired behavior.
4. Nonassertive—This request is inappropriately apologetic.
5. Nonassertive—This statement makes a general rather than a specific description of behavior.

6. Assertive—A specific description of desired behavior is given in this statement.
7. Nonassertive—This is a statement of opinion disguised as a question.

Nonassertive Voice Characteristics and Body Language

The impact of an interaction is determined not only by the words used, but also by voice characteristics and by body language. Nonverbal cues are often far more important determinants of others' reaction than verbal cues (Henley, 1977). Becoming aware of nonverbal cues requires careful observation of self and others.

Pleading or questioning voice tone

Nonassertive statements are often delivered with a pleading or questioning voice tone. The speaker's voice may be raised at the end of the sentence as if the statement were a question and may be quiet and not project well. Enunciation may be poor so that messages are mumbled or trail off into inaudibility. The pitch may be high and the tone breathy so that the voice lacks strength and energy. The end result of these voice characteristics is a statement that does not command attention. Since it may be even more vital to sound confident than to feel confident, it is important to develop a strong self-assured tone through practice.

EXERCISE

Say the following sentences out loud as if you are unsure of yourself or afraid of the other person's reaction. Then try the same sentences as if you feel very confident and sure of yourself.

I'd rather do it this way.
No, I can't meet with you this week.

Observe others' voice tone. What do people who sound forceful and confident sound like? What makes people sound uncertain, pleading, or wishy-washy? Tape record your own voice making a request. How do you sound? Have friends listen to you and tell you if your voice projects enough.

Hesitation

Nonassertive speakers sound as if they are not sure of what they are saying. One thing that communicates weakness is hesitation or a lot of "ums" and "ahs." The speaker who wants to sound confident plans and perhaps even practices what she is going to say so that it can come out smoothly and without undue hesitation. A strong, even flow of speech sounds much more assertive than a halting, hesitant statement.

EXERCISE

Say the following sentences out loud. Which sounds stronger?

I, uh, really think, uh, that you should, uh, plan your work before you carry it out.

I really think that you should plan your work before you carry it out.

Lack of eye contact

One of the most critical nonverbal cues for nonassertiveness is lack of eye contact. Looking at someone while talking communicates directness and self-confidence, while downcast eyes communicate uncertainty or hesitation. It is much easier for someone to ignore a message when she never has to look the speaker in the eyes. Eye contact tells the other person, "I am talking *particularly* to you, and what I am saying is important to me."

EXERCISE

Ask someone to say the following sentences with and without eye contact. Which is stronger?

This project is very important to me.

Please do the last part of this report over.

Observe others you interact with. How do you feel when someone doesn't make eye contact with you? Notice whether you make eye contact when you interact with others, and if you do not, try making eye contact for several days and see if it makes any difference.

Slumping, downtrodden posture
Confidence or lack of assurance are clearly communicated even before a person speaks. Nonassertive people move in a jerky, hesitant way—as if they are not sure of their direction. They may slump their shoulders, put their hands in their pockets or hold them tightly at their sides, and look down or away. They often sit tensely on the edge of their chairs with arms crossed or slump down in the chair, shrinking away from the other person.

In a study of "muggability," researchers found that muggers agreed on which people on videotape they would mug because they would not be likely to give the mugger too much trouble ("To Muggers, Some Folks," 1980). Although muggability is not the same as nonassertiveness, this study does highlight the vital importance of posture and movement in determining others' reactions.

EXERCISE

Think of a time that you felt very nonassertive or imagine what it would be like to feel nonassertive. Move around the room nonassertively and see how it feels. How do you stand and move?

Observe others over the next several weeks. Who seems confident, sure of herself? How does this person move and stand? Who seems uneasy and uncertain? How does she move and stand?

Words and nonverbal messages that don't match
When what is said conflicts with the nonverbal part of a message, people tend to believe the nonverbal communication. If someone says, "I'm really angry" with a big smile, people may not take her anger very seriously. Saying "This is a serious issue" and following it with a nervous laugh takes away the impact of the statement. Smiling and nodding too frequently also communicate nonassertiveness. Strong, forceful statements must be supported by consistent, forceful body language, because mixed messages reduce the speaker's impact on others.

EXERCISE

Listen to and observe yourself in stressful situations to see if you tend to have a nervous laugh or other inconsistent gestures. Note whether you tend to smile when you want to be serious. Observe others. Have you seen situations in which gestures such as smiling too much have reduced someone's impact?

Effects of Nonassertiveness on You

A number of verbal and nonverbal cues for nonassertive behavior have been presented. As you observe yourself, you will begin to realize when you are using minimizing words, using a pleading voice tone, and making statements that are too general. You will start to recognize nonassertive behavior patterns; for example, you may catch yourself complaining to someone about a situation you should be confronting or giving up on an issue when you should be persistent. You can also recognize when you are being nonassertive from the way you feel during and after the interaction. Choosing to be nonassertive costs you in some very specific ways, and learning to recognize when you are suffering from your nonassertiveness will help you to choose other ways to act.

Physical tension

One powerful signal that you are being nonassertive is physical tension. If you walk out of a meeting with your shoulders hugging your earlobes or your stomach in knots, there is a possibility that you needed to assert yourself and didn't. It's almost as if your body waves a red flag or flashes red signal lights at you and says, "Hey you! Do something, will you?" Chronically arousing feelings without allowing some outlet for that energy puts a great deal of stress on the body. Although there is no research that proves a link between nonassertiveness and psychosomatic problems, a research study in progress certainly indicates that people who are in psychological treatment for stress-related physical disorders have many difficulties taking a stand with others (Hohlt, 1983). One of the costs of nonassertiveness is the physical strain that the constant tension of holding in your opinions and feelings creates. In addition, since the nonassertive stance is to hope that difficult situations will change rather than to take an active role in changing them, nonassertiveness means that you allow your body to stay in stress-producing situations.

An "unfinished" feeling

Walking away from situations feeling as if you should have said more or going over and over an interaction in your mind thinking about what you could have said may be cues that you needed to assert yourself. One way to keep a situation or a feeling alive for a long time is not to do or say anything about it. For example, if you are angry at someone, you may stay angry unless you do something with that anger. Have you ever had the experience of being angry at someone, talking to him about it, and then not feeling angry anymore? This would be an example of feeling "finished." Feeling finished and being able to let go of a situation in your own mind is one reason that it is often useful to express your point of view even if the other person does not comply with your wishes. You can at least feel as if you have done or said what you needed to do or say to finish the situation for yourself.

> Gloria, supervisor of a shipping department, had gone to a great deal of trouble to fill a special order for a company. After receiving it, the company sent the special order back saying that they had decided to order the material at a later date. Although there seemed to be no real business advantage in confronting them since the company was unlikely to make other orders, Gloria found herself fuming every time she thought about the situation. To "finish" for herself she needed to write a cordial but firm letter letting the other company know that she was happy to fill special orders for them, but that it was very important for them to be sure they needed the material before placing such an order.

Resentment

Agreeing to do things you don't want to do may make you feel victimized and resentful. In a work situation, you may think, "Don't they have any consideration at all? Surely they know that I have my own work to do and can't do theirs too." Assuming that others should be responsible for protecting you or your department leaves you open to being taken advantage of. Often others do not know when something will be inconvenient or problematic unless you tell them. It requires cooperation to be victimized. In a situation where you are the victim, you really have all the power. As soon as you refuse to participate, the interaction is over. The basic message of assertiveness training is that you are responsible for taking care of yourself. If you end up feeling put-upon and resentful, you may not be taking care of yourself well enough. Being aware of resentful feelings can also help you to decide when changing your plans for someone else is nonassertive. If someone asks you to shift your plans and you don't feel resentful, you are not being nonassertive.

Being flexible and responsive to others' needs and priorities is not nonassertive. However, flexibility and responsiveness that results in resentfulness is nonassertive.

◆

What kind of body cues or feelings do you get when you are being nonassertive? Where do you feel these cues in your body?

◆

Others' Reactions to Nonassertiveness

As stated in Chapter One, the way a supervisor interacts with others promotes certain responses. The effective supervisor wants to be assertive most of the time because assertiveness promotes respect and cooperation. Nonassertiveness sometimes elicits positive feelings from others, but often it leads to uncertainty, lack of respect, and attack and manipulation.

Positive feelings
Some people like interacting with a person who acts nonassertively because it allows them to get their own way. Since the nonassertive person does not stand up for himself, it is easy to talk him into following their plans. People who are generally nonassertive also are very polite, gentle, and considerate of others. A nonassertive employee may, on the surface, seem to be a real joy. He follows orders, wants to do things the right way, does not question, rarely makes suggestions, and, in general, goes along with his supervisor. A supervisor who acts nonassertively seldom makes demands, allows almost total freedom to determine work priorities, and does not confront an issue unless absolutely pressed. Looked at from this perspective, it would appear that an organization staffed with nonassertive people would be ideal. The problem with this picture is that it leaves out the negative effects of nonassertive behavior.

Uncertainty
No one knows where he stands with someone who acts nonassertively. A nonassertive boss can be nearly ready to fire an employee before the employee finds out that the boss doesn't feel he is doing an adequate job. A nonassertive employee is unlikely to give a straight answer when asked if there are any problems with the way he is being supervised. The supervisor may sense that there is some kind of conflict or tension with the employee, but with a nonassertive individual it is very difficult to find out what the problem

really is. Since nonassertive people do not give straight feedback, it is difficult to improve relations with them or to satisfy their needs. For example, if the employee will not say no to extra work when he is very busy, the supervisor has to protect him from being overloaded by guessing his feelings. If someone wants to devise a mutually satisfactory plan for handling department procedures, he has to guess whether the nonassertive person is really satisfied with the plan. If a nonassertive employee's productivity seems to be dropping, the supervisor has to guess why. Working for a nonassertive supervisor can provoke a lot of anxiety because an employee is never really sure what the limits are. He spends a great deal of energy trying to guess whether his work is acceptable, whether his suggestions are good or bad, or whether it is all right to handle a situation in a particular way. This lack of clarity can be exhausting and in many cases can make an employee less willing to take risks or to express creativity.

People who act nonassertively are also prone to use passive-resistant behavior. Since nonassertive people cannot openly say when they disagree with something, they may agree to things that they are not really willing to do and simply not get around to doing them. A nonassertive employee may be withdrawn and upset for months before his supervisor finds out that he is angry about the way the supervisor answered his question at a staff meeting. Resentments or disagreements that aren't expressed verbally may be expressed in behavior by procrastination or actual sabotage. In this sense, nonassertive employees are the most difficult to confront if there is a problem. If they disagree, they are unlikely to be openly confrontive. Instead their disagreement will be expressed through complaints to other workers, slowdowns, or sulking.

Lack of respect
If you ask employees in an organization who the best supervisors are, there is usually a clear consensus about the people who command respect. People respect someone who is straightforward and clear and who seems to know what he is talking about. Although employees may like nonassertive supervisors, they seldom really respect them. Ironically, seeming knowledgeable is often more critical in establishing credibility than being knowledgeable. There are many very competent, knowledgeable people who are not taken seriously because they present themselves and their ideas in such a nonassertive way. Gaining respect and credibility depends at least partly on appearances, on style characteristics. The nonassertive style simply does not impress people.

Attack and manipulation

Nonassertive people invite attack and manipulation. They often believe that by being nonassertive, they can protect themselves from attack or rejection by others. But nonassertive behavior may have just the opposite effect on aggressive people. An aggressive bully may find the person who cowers and apologizes for himself presents an almost irresistible invitation to push a little harder. The more the other person withdraws and tries to placate, the more aggressive the bully becomes.

> Krystal was a corporation lawyer who worked for a very aggressive boss. He was prone to call her names in front of others, viciously attack her work, and threaten to fire her almost daily. She was constantly terrified and intimidated and practically tiptoed around the office trying to avoid bumping into him. This behavior continued until she finally started to stand up to him. When she did, the attacks became much less frequent.

Nonassertive behavior can have a number of possible negative effects. Self-observation can help you develop a sense of when nonassertion works and when it doesn't, and help you to modify your behavior accordingly.

When you are nonassertive, what do others do?

Think of someone you consider nonassertive. What are your feelings about this person? What is his effect on you?

Situations in Which
Nonassertiveness Is the Best Response

There are clearly some situations in which it is appropriate to be nonassertive or in which any other strategy costs more than it is worth. Some of these situations follow.

Sometimes the risks of assertiveness are simply too great. In the most extreme case, if someone is being robbed at gunpoint, assertiveness probably is not an appropriate strategy. In another example, assertiveness may not always be the best choice in organizations where there are intense power struggles and maneuvers. Weighing the risks of assertiveness is covered in Chapter Five.

Sometimes it is simply not worth the trouble to be assertive. Some issues are not important enough to use the energy that is required to be assertive. It also may be appropriate to ignore an issue, despite strong feelings about it, when overloaded in other areas. Some people who have taken assertiveness training insist on making an issue out of everything as a matter of principle; but this does not create smooth relationships with others. In every situation, it must be decided whether the problems are significant enough to warrant discussion or confrontation. However, deciding that every matter is too insignificant to discuss is a nonassertive trap. This is where paying attention to feelings can be helpful. Body tension, feelings of being unfinished, and resentments are cues that can help determine when it is important to speak up.

There are some people who take any attempt to be assertive as a threat to their authority. With these people a hesitant, apologetic communication may get the idea across without raising their anxiety or causing a fight.

> Juan worked for a boss who wanted everything done his way. Any changes without his direct approval were considered attacks on his position as the boss. For several months, Juan had been having incoming orders filed in a slightly different way. Juan should have tried to clear the change ahead of time, but hadn't. He was about to have a meeting with the boss in which the new procedure would become obvious. Juan approached the boss very apologetically and said, "I know you really like to know about any changes in procedure and I probably should have cleared this change with you, but I hope that it will be all right." This nonassertive approach reduced any threat to the boss and made him more willing to accept the change.

In Chapter Nine, identifying superiors who respond more positively to a nonassertive approach will be discussed.

Sometimes it is simply not the appropriate time to be assertive. Even though it may cause tension not to be assertive right away in some situations, it may be necessary to tolerate this tension until a more appropriate time for assertion occurs. Confronting employees Friday evening when they are on their way out the door may not make sense. Asking a manager for something innovative when he is in the midst of a critical department review does not make sense. For a new supervisor, temporary nonassertiveness may be an appropriate choice. Some old procedures and policies are frustrating; however, it is important to a new supervisor to build relationships with the people already on the job before instituting too many changes.

Self-Test

For each of the following situations, would a nonassertive response be the best response or create problems? Why?

1. Lydia tends to burst into tears whenever anyone confronts her. Lately her performance has been declining rapidly.
2. You would like to change the interview form in your social service agency, but the boss wrote the current form and happens to think it is particularly effective.
3. Your manager has been berating you in front of your employees.
4. Your manager asks you what you think about the new vacation policies that are being considered. You know they will leave you understaffed in July and August.
5. The highly authoritarian, rigid president of your company has called to ask your opinion about his new sales policy.
6. Your employees have been responding to pressure by spending more time joking and teasing than usual.
7. You need to discuss the new absence policy with your superior. His major grant review is this week.

ANSWERS

1. Asserting yourself is important in this instance even if the employee does get upset. Allowing declining performance to go unnoticed may communicate to the employee that it does not matter.
2. This may be a risky situation where it is not worth it to assert yourself. Unless the old form is creating serious productivity problems, it may be more appropriate to leave well enough alone.
3. It is vital that you maintain your credibility and the respect of your employees. In this situation it is critical to be assertive.
4. Again, not asserting yourself here is foolish. The risk of asserting is probably not high and the cost of not asserting is considerable.
5. Appearing nonassertive may make your comments more acceptable to this person.
6. Unless the joking and teasing seriously affects productivity, it may be important to allow this form of tension release and not be worth it for you to confront the employees' behavior.

7. Temporary nonassertiveness is called for because the timing is off.

———————◆———————

Feelings and Beliefs
That Support Nonassertiveness

The basic motto of the nonassertive person is "My needs and wants do not and should not count. If anyone is to be hurt or inconvenienced in any situation, it should always be me." Careful observation of an interaction between a nonassertive person and someone else shows that the nonassertive person cancels himself out.

Nonassertive behavior choices are not accidental. Often a nonassertive person will have a very negative self-image that allows him to put himself last when interacting with others. Everyone has attitudes about himself and the world that form the basis of his behavior patterns. These attitudes are based on molding and modeling from his parents and on his previous experiences in the world. It is possible to change behavior without changing beliefs, but consistent and comprehensive changes may require understanding of the feelings and the beliefs that support nonassertive choices. Sometimes an effective course of action seems perfectly clear, but the accompanying feelings inhibit its performance and so need to be confronted. Chapter Five discusses ways of changing feelings and beliefs to become more assertive.

There are four major inhibitions to assertiveness. The first is guilt. If a person has been brought up to believe that it is terrible to hurt or offend anyone, that he shouldn't interfere, that he should never make mistakes, that he should always respect the views of someone who is older, and that he should help people when they are in trouble no matter how much it inconveniences him, he may avoid asserting himself in order to keep from violating some of these powerful "shoulds." There is nothing wrong with traditional values, but it is important to separate appropriate adherence to a value system from inappropriate application of "shoulds" to situations in which they do not apply. Inappropriate guilt, for example, might keep a supervisor from confronting an employee with a lot of personal problems. Knowing that the employee might be hurt when confronted and at the same time holding a value that he should never hurt anyone could stop the supervisor from being assertive. Or it could create so much guilt after the supervisor is assertive that he is reluctant to be assertive the next time. Inappropriate guilt can be a very powerful force in keeping someone nonassertive.

Fear and anxiety is another powerful inhibition to assertion. The nonassertive person worries a great deal about the problems that will result if he is assertive. He worries about making a mistake, about looking incompetent, about making someone angry, or about not being liked. These temporary discomforts are seen as total catastrophes. Or the supervisor may build on each of these minor problems a fantasy that he will be fired, lose credibility in the organization, or otherwise ruin his career. Some of these unpleasant expectations may be realistic in some situations and can be legitimate reasons for not being assertive. Others are only fantasy fears and need to be confronted by the supervisor in order for him to become free to be assertive.

Doubt is another inhibition to assertiveness. Often nonassertive people are not sure whether they have a legitimate right to confront an issue. They wonder if they are right and often talk themselves out of being assertive before they start. These negative pep talks include only statements that predict failure or deny rights such as "This will never work," "I'm sure I'm going to blow it," or "I probably have no good reason for mentioning it anyhow." It is important to confront these doubts and uncertainties to become assertive.

Another powerful inhibition to assertiveness is the nice-guy image a person wants to maintain. Often nonassertive supervisors want all of their employees to see them as "really nice." They don't want to blow their nice-guy image and feel that asserting themselves with the resultant risk of upsetting someone will completely change others' opinions of them. They can't imagine being a nice person and being assertive.

Summary

This chapter examines the characteristics of a nonassertive supervisory style. The nonassertive supervisor's behavior patterns include: no expression of expectations and feelings, views stated indirectly or apologetically, complaints made to the wrong person, problems not confronted soon enough, no persistence, and unclear negotiation and compromise. His word choices are characterized by: minimizing words, apologetic statements, statements made about people in general instead of to a specific person, general instead of specific behavioral descriptions, and statements disguised as questions. His voice characteristics and body language include: a pleading or questioning voice tone, hesitation, lack of eye contact, slumping, downtrodden posture, and words and nonverbal messages that don't match.

Nonassertive behavior can leave you feeling physical tension, an unfinished feeling, or resentment. Others may react to nonassertiveness with positive feelings, uncertainty, lack of respect, or attack and manipulation.

Nonassertiveness is the best response when the risks of being assertive are too high, when it is not worth the trouble, when the other person is highly threatened, and when the timing is bad.

The basic motto of the nonassertive person is "My needs and wants do not and should not count. If anyone is to be hurt or inconvenienced in any situation, it should always be me." Feelings and beliefs that support nonassertiveness include guilt, fear and anxiety, doubt, and a preoccupation with maintaining a nice-guy image.

Bibliography

Eisen, J. *Power talk*. New York: Simon & Schuster, 1984.

Henley, N. M. *Body politics: Power, sex, and nonverbal communication*. Englewood Cliffs, N.J.: Prentice-Hall, 1977.

Hohlt, W. *Expanding the possible: A look at women's experiences when using psychotherapy as an aspect of primary care medical treatment*. Unpublished doctoral dissertation, Union of Experimenting Colleges and Universities, Cincinnati, 1983.

Smith, M. *When I say no I feel guilty*. New York: Dial Press, 1975.

To muggers, some folks look like easy marks. *Wilmington News Journal*, December 21, 1980, p. F5.

CHAPTER THREE

The Aggressive
Supervisory Style

In this chapter, you will:
- Learn to identify aggressive behavior patterns;
- Become aware of aggressive word choices;
- Become aware of aggressive voice characteristics and body language;
- Learn the effects of aggressiveness on you;
- Learn others' reactions to aggressiveness;
- Discover why aggressiveness is sometimes such a successful approach in business;
- Learn to recognize situations in which aggressiveness is the best response;
- Become aware of feelings and beliefs that support aggressiveness.

As in Chapter Two, Angela has realized that her employee George is late again in turning in his monthly report. This is the third month she has had to ask George for the report. In this dialogue, she takes an aggressive stance with her employee.

Angela: (Stands over George with hands on hips) George, what is the matter with you? You are so disorganized. Can't you do anything right? You never follow through on your promises. Will I have to continually check up on you to see that you do your work?

George: Well, I have been pretty busy you know. I have this . . .

Angela: I don't care what you have to do. If you organized
           your work better, the report would be done on time.
           I want that report today with no excuses and this
           had better not happen again. We don't need people
           working for us who don't care about doing a good
           job. Get busy on it.

George: All right, I'll have the report to you today.

How effective do you think Angela will be in solving the problem?
When will she get this month's report?
Will George turn the report in on time next month?
How would you feel as Angela? How would you feel as George?
What might be the long-range consequences of this style?

In this dialogue, Angela is accusatory and blaming. She uses
words and phrases like "What is the matter with you?" "Can't you
do anything right?" "Disorganized" and "Check up on you." She is
unwilling to listen to George and thereby clearly indicates that she
is not interested in helping him try to solve his problem of establishing priorities. She demands rather than asks for his report.
She implies George doesn't care about his work. She is likely to get
the report that day and probably will get the monthly report on
time next month, but George's resentment and frustration may be
expressed on another project in the form of foot dragging or lack
of involvement. One of the issues that this dialogue highlights is
that aggressiveness may work well in the short run. Generally,
only a particularly rebellious employee will directly fight the kind
of demands that an aggressive supervisor makes. It's fairly obvious
what is wrong with a nonassertive approach. The difficulties associated with an aggressive style are neither so obvious nor so uni-
versal. Situations in which agressiveness does and does not work
will be covered later in this chapter.

Aggressive Behavior Patterns

The following behavior patterns characterize an aggressive supervisory style. All of these patterns have in common the tendency to
make people defensive.

Critical expression of expectations and feelings
Aggressive people express their expectations and feelings by attacking the other person. For example, an aggressive supervisor would say, "That's a dumb idea" rather than "I see the situation differently." Even when the statement does not explicitly attack the other person, there is often an implied "you dummy" in the statement: "It certainly seems clear to everyone but you that we should do it this way." The most common effect of this kind of statement is to put the other person on the defensive. Unfortunately, people tend to stop listening when they feel they are being attacked and thus don't hear the part of the message that may be constructive.

Not only do aggressive people express themselves by attacking others, they also continue to attack and argue even when it is clear that the other person is strongly committed to her own view. This absolute insistence on proving others wrong communicates a lack of respect for alternative points of view. In addition, attack fosters defensive arguments rather than open discussion of the issues.

> One trainee in an assertiveness workshop could not understand why she kept getting feedback on her job that she was too aggressive. As far as she was concerned, she was just being appropriately assertive. When she was asked to give an example of an interaction that others labeled aggressive she said, "All I said was—'In the last place I worked it only took 2 weeks to solve this problem. I don't know why it is taking you so long.'" She didn't say "You dummy," but that message was certainly implied in her statement.

Are you critical of others when you express your expectations and feelings? How does this influence your relationships with others?

Can you think of someone who is critical of you in expressing expectations and feelings? What is it like to interact with this person?

Blaming and judgmental criticisms
When there is a problem, the aggressive supervisor usually will attack the other person rather than describe the situation and discuss strategies for solving the problem. The emphasis is on discovering who is to blame for the problem instead of working together to solve the problem. This focus is reflected in statements

such as "What's the matter with you?" or "If you would get your act together, we wouldn't have a problem." Criticisms about personality rather than behavior are seen as a way to fix blame: "Your incompetency caused the firm to lose this contract," "You are so careless it's no wonder this happened." Making an employee accept blame for problems and see her personality faults is often thought of as a way to motivate the person to change.

> Franklin felt very strongly that employees needed to be set straight about their faults. He was convinced that telling someone what was wrong with her was the most effective way to motivate her to change. He was particularly concerned about one employee and frequently would tell this employee that her incompetence and inefficiency were going to get her fired. His theory was that keeping employees on guard improved productivity. Morale and productivity among Franklin's employees, however, was lower than in other departments.

Do you find yourself blaming and making judgmental criticisms instead of solving problems?

Can you think of someone who is blaming or uses judgmental criticisms? What is it like to interact with this person?

Negative intentions attributed to others
One particularly frustrating kind of blaming or judging behavior is the attribution of negative intentions to someone else. If someone is told that she doesn't care about her job or that she has no interest in cooperating, she will almost automatically become defensive. There are two reasons that this kind of communication tends to provoke a negative reaction. The first, as stated in Chapter One, is that such negative statements tend to become self-fulfilling prophecies. When people are told that they obviously don't care about their jobs, they may decide, "Why bother trying?" or think, "Well, if that's the way you feel, I'll show you." The second reason is that most people deeply resent having others try to read their minds. The most likely response to an attempt to describe someone's intentions is an argument about that interpretation. Attributing negative intentions directs the focus of the conversation away from solving the problem and toward defending motives. For this reason this strategy can interfere with productive solving of problems.

What a person is doing can be seen; what this behavior means cannot be seen.

> Larry was the supervisor of a small vocational rehabilitation agency. One of the counselors would not discuss cases with Larry even though Larry was expected to provide regular case supervision. Larry assumed that the counselor personally disliked him and was trying to undermine his role as a supervisor. Later he discovered that the employee misunderstood the supervisory relationship and felt that discussing cases was a reflection of incompetence.

If the supervisor had approached this employee by saying "Clearly you aren't discussing cases with me because you don't like me and want to undermine my authority," it might have sabotaged any possibility of working with this employee to uncover the real problem. In Chapter Five there is a discussion of ways to separate the facts (or behaviors) in a situation from assumptions about the meaning of those behaviors.

———◆———

Do you find that you often make assumptions about what particular employee actions mean? What do you do with these assumptions when you talk to the employee?

Can you think of someone who attributes negative intentions to you? Does it enhance or inhibit your cooperation with that person?

———◆———

"Muscle level" too high

Muscle level refers to the strength or leverage of someone's interactions with others. There are four levels of muscle (Butler, 1976).

1. Muscle Level I is a polite request: "I'd like you to let us know when you can't come to a steering committee meeting."
2. Muscle Level II is a request that is stronger in word choice, voice characteristics, and body language: "When you don't let us know that you're going to miss a meeting, we sometimes end up meeting without a quorum, which is useless. I need to know when you can't make a meeting."
3. Muscle Level III is a statement of the consequences if the behavior doesn't change: "If you can't let us know when you'll miss a meeting, we will have to ask you to resign from the committee."

    4. Muscle Level IV is the application of the consequences stated in Level III: "Since you have not been keeping us informed about your attendance, I will have to ask you to leave the committee."

Often an aggressive supervisor will start at Muscle Level III. For example, one person's supervisor was inclined to storm in with a handful of letters and say, "You had better catch these errors before I get them, or I will have to ask you to leave." Raising the muscle level to Level III before going through Muscle Levels I and II generally is experienced as very aggressive.

There is another reason for not starting at Muscle Level III. If a supervisor starts with Muscle Level III, she has no way to increase her leverage if that becomes necessary. Also, a supervisor cannot use Muscle Level III unless she has control of some consequence that matters to the employee. For example, if an employee wants time off, it would be ineffective to use suspension at Muscle Level III. It is also very important for a supervisor not to raise the muscle level to Level III unless she is willing to raise it to Level IV if the other person does not respond to Level III. Threatening high-muscle-level responses and not following through ruins credibility.

Aggressive people sometimes start with general threats that would be very difficult to carry out rather than with specific high-power consequences like "I'll have to write you up" or "I'll have to put you on probation." It is a great deal more difficult to fire someone than some aggressive threats would imply. Threats such as "We don't need people like you" can create defensiveness without providing an effective deterrent.

> Greta was a very cooperative employee and wanted to do a good job. A mild warning would have been entirely sufficient to motivate her to correct her behavior. Unfortunately, her supervisor would never provide gentle warnings. When she did something wrong, she would get immediate threats to dismiss her. Although she knew that the threats probably would not be carried out, she was constantly tense and intimidated at work. She was beginning to look for another job because she was so nervous all of the time.

The four muscle levels follow quite closely the proper steps in disciplinary action with an employee: warning about inappropriate behavior, providing a stronger warning, stating the consequences, and carrying out the consequences. A supervisor might actually go through several Muscle Level III interventions with consequences of increasing power such as a counseling session, a disciplinary action in the personnel file, probation, and firing.

Do you find that sometimes you use Muscle Level III responses without using Levels I and II first? If so, what happens?

Can you think of someone who starts at a very high-muscle-level response? How does it affect your interaction with that person?

Problems acted on too quickly

While the nonassertive person waits too long to act, the aggressive person often "shoots from the hip"—acts too quickly without finding out all of the facts. Aggressive people tend to draw very quick conclusions about the causes of a particular problem. This tendency to jump to conclusions, when coupled with a tendency not to listen carefully to others, can lead to impulsive action. Effective problem solving requires some consideration of the possible causes of a problem, the alternative solutions, the advantages and disadvantages of potential solutions, and the potential difficulties in implementing a particular problem-solving plan (Kepner & Tregoe, 1965). Aggressive action can interfere with systematic problem solving.

> Linda worked for a supervisor who viewed herself as very decisive. When Linda would bring her a problem, she would tell Linda what to do to solve the problem before Linda had time to describe the problem in detail. When Linda would try to describe the problem more fully, the supervisor would simply say, "Don't talk about it; just go ahead and do what I told you." Linda found herself very frustrated because the supervisor's suggestions did not consider the complexities of the problem.

Do you find yourself acting on issues quickly without considering all aspects of the situation and potential solutions?

Can you think of someone who acts without thoroughly considering the situation? What is it like to interact with this kind of person?

Unwillingness to listen

If others' ideas are basically seen as irrelevant or wrong, there is no particular reason to listen to them. The aggressive person is much more likely to interrupt someone to finish what she wants to say than to stop and listen to the other person. In a crisis, aggressive people are much more likely to say what they think about the problem over and over than to try to find out how someone else sees the problem. The disadvantage of this is that the aggressive person misses a great deal of potentially useful information by not listening. To solve a problem permanently, it is necessary to uncover what is creating the problem. As mentioned in Chapter One, when an employee's behavior causes problems, there may be reasons for the behavior that are not obvious. Listening provides an opportunity to uncover the obstacles to good performance and take positive action to remove them and permanently solve the problem. If skills, equipment, understanding of the job, organizational abilities, or something else is causing the problem, an aggressive approach simply puts on a Band-Aid for the moment. Unwillingness to listen also stifles creative ideas and information that could prevent problems.

> Herman was the head librarian in a technical library. When an employee would come to him with a problem, he would listen just long enough to find out what was wrong and then would either tell the person what he ought to do about the problem or would berate the employee for causing the problem. As a result, employees were reluctant to discuss problems with him until a real crisis occurred.

Do the people who work with you seem to feel free to talk to you about problems? How much information do you get about creative ideas or potential problems?

The last time that you interacted with an employee, who did the most talking? Were you completely clear on her point of view?

Can you think of someone who does not seem to listen to you? What is it like to interact with this person?

Refusal to negotiate and compromise

The aggressive person wants what she wants when she wants it. Since aggressive people are generally convinced that they are right and that their priorities are most important, they simply are not interested in negotiation and compromise. They often view other people's needs or organizational priorities as attempts to question their authority or sabotage their work. As pointed out in Chapter One, this "do your own thing" approach is aggressive, not assertive. Often this refusal to compromise or negotiate leads to rigidity. At best, it encourages others to fight for their priorities in the same manner. If interactions are structured as win-lose situations, people have to fight not to lose, and cooperation and teamwork are discouraged.

Jose worked for a boss who insisted that there was one right way to do things—his way. New approaches were not well received, and even routine work was often interrupted by the boss's shifts in priorities. Jose had very little control over his time. When he tried to explain why doing a certain project before another would be better, he was ordered to do what he was told. Gradually he lost interest in creative involvement in the organization.

———————◆———————

Do you find yourself insisting that everything be done your way? When others have different priorities than yours, are you willing to compromise?

Can you think of someone who will not negotiate and compromise? What effect does this person's behavior have on you?

———————◆———————

SELF-TEST

Pick the responses that best reflect aggressive behavior patterns and specify what cues you used.
1. "You had better remember to make those phone calls, or I'll take away that responsibility."
2. "When you don't finish your accounts receivable accurately, it throws off the totals and then someone has to stay and reconcile. Please be more careful."
3. "You are the laziest employee I have ever met. The whole problem is that you don't do a darn thing here."
4. "I don't care when you think we should start the new samples. We'll do it Wednesday."
5. "I know that you feel we should meet with the whole committee first, but I disagree. Here's why."

6. "That's a really ridiculous way to approach the situation. You're clearly wrong."
7. "Just fire her. You don't need to ask a lot of questions about why she acted that way."
8. "You obviously aren't serious about your work."

ANSWERS

1. Aggressive—This statement uses Muscle Level III in what sounds like an early intervention.
2. Assertive—The problem and why it is a problem are described nonjudgmentally.
3. Aggressive—The focus of this statement is on blaming and judgmental criticism.
4. Aggressive—This statement reflects a refusal to negotiate and compromise and an unwillingness to listen.
5. Assertive—An opinion is expressed here without putting down the other person and there seems to be a willingness to listen.
6. Aggressive—The opinion in this statement is expressed in a disparaging manner.
7. Aggressive—Action is taken too quickly here without fully considering the situation.
8. Aggressive—This statement attributes negative intentions to the employee.

Aggressive Word Choices

The kind of words used is often a clear reflection of supervisory style. This is particularly true for the aggressive approach because it uses especially negative language and demanding statements.

"Loaded" words

There is a considerable difference between a description of someone's behavior and judgments of the person's character. There are some words that simply cannot be used in a neutral and objective description. Words such as *lazy, incompetent, stupid, unmotivated,* and *worthless* are judgmental in themselves and provoke a negative reaction. Even less clearly judgmental words can be loaded. For example, a supervisor wanted to confront an employee about the employee's practice of coming into his office to ask him questions before he had his coat off in the morning. In his confrontation his first sentence began "When you jump all over me in the morning. . . ." "Jump all over" is not a neutral description. It implies negative intent and a number of other negative qualities. His confrontation would have been more successful if he had said, "When you come in and ask me questions before I get my coat off, I end up not really listening to what you say." The more loaded the language used to describe a problem, the more likely the other person will become defensive and stop listening.

Aggressiveness communicated by loaded words is quite difficult to control because loaded language sometimes slips out without awareness. If a supervisor finds that others often seem defensive when he approaches them, he needs to monitor his language carefully to see if his words are more judgmental than he realizes.

EXERCISE

Say the following sentences out loud. How would you feel hearing these sentences?

You are doing shoddy work.

You need to check your work more carefully.

Don't be so lazy.

I want you to finish your assigned work before you take a break.

"You" statements

A "you" statement is *you* followed by a loaded word. Even *you* followed by a description tends to provoke more defensiveness than a description of the same behavior done without a verbal finger-pointing "you" statement. For example, "You need to proof your work more carefully" is likely to be more loaded than "Your work needs to be proofed more carefully." "You're late too much" tends to provoke more defensiveness than "I need you to be here at 8:00."

Another problem is that such statements are often rather general. Saying "You are very illiterate" gives the employee much less information than saying "I would like you to reread each of your reports for grammatical errors before you submit them." General personal judgments often are substituted for much more specific requests for behavioral change.

―――◆―――

Say the following sentences out loud. How would you feel on hearing these sentences?

You're really inefficient.
I would like you to get more reports finished in a day.

You're so rude.
I wish you would knock before you enter my office.

―――◆―――

"Always" or "never" statements

Another way to put someone on the defensive is to tell him that he "never" does his work on time or that he is "always" late. It is rarely true that a person never does what he is supposed to do. When a supervisor uses "always" or "never" statements, employees will tend to defensively point out the exceptions.

―――◆―――

Say the following sentences out loud. How would you feel on hearing these sentences?

You never get your work in on time.
Your work is often late.

You have been late the last six mornings.
You're always late.

―――◆―――

Demands instead of requests

Although there are times when it is necessary to make an outright "do it now" demand on an employee, requests are generally received much more responsively. As stated in Chapter One, most people strongly resent being told that they have to do something. As soon as something is demanded, they dig in their heels and resist.

Often the difference between a request and a demand is the addition of a phrase like "I want you to . . ." or "Please do . . ." or "I need . . ." to a demand to create a request. There is a considerable difference in effect, for example, between "Clean up your desk right now" and "I'd like you to clean up your desk now," "I need to have your desk clean today," or "Could you please spend some time today cleaning your desk?" Demands communicate what must be done, but they do it in a way that sounds overbearing and obnoxious. There is no attempt to elicit the other person's cooperation in a demand. It is assumed that he must comply. Some situations require supervisors to give orders, but, in general, use of demand statements can create a great deal of resentment.

EXERCISE

Say the following sentences out loud. How would you respond to each of these sentences?

I would like to have your report by Monday.
Get me your report by Monday.

Judgments disguised as questions

Another aggressive approach is to ask a question that really expresses a judgment. For example, an aggressive person might ask, "When *are* you going to get your report done?" when what he really means is "You should have done that report a long time ago, you dummy." The nonassertive person asks a question and hides his feelings. The aggressive person asks a question, but makes his real feelings obvious through word choice, voice tone, and body language.

EXERCISE

Say the following questions out loud as simple requests for information and as attempts to communicate your judgments.

When will you be able to meet with me?
Where is the Jones report?

SELF-TEST

Pick the aggressive statements and specify what cues you used.
1. "Please establish a more uniform procedure for handling the mail."
2. "Do it now! I don't care what else needs to be done."
3. "What don't you like about the new procedure?"
4. "When did you *finally* get that project done?"

5. "You never have been very good at following through on things."
6. "If you weren't so sloppy, we wouldn't have all of these problems."

ANSWERS

1. Assertive—This statement makes a request instead of a demand.
2. Aggressive—This is a demand rather than a request.
3. Assertive—This question simply elicits information.
4. Aggressive—The word *finally* reveals that this is a judgment disguised as a question.
5. Aggressive—The use of *never* in this statement makes it aggressive.
6. Aggressive—*Sloppy* is a loaded word.

Aggressive Voice Characteristics and Body Language

Someone may make a perfectly assertive statement, but say it in a way that creates defensiveness as surely as if she had said "You dummy." The subtlety of some of the nonverbal cues of aggressiveness accounts for surprising reactions from others. Unless a supervisor is aware of her voice characteristics and body language, she may feel as if she is being perfectly assertive and then be surprised to discover that others are acting as if they are being attacked.

Sarcastic, judgmental, overbearing voice tone

Assertively phrased sentences can sound quite aggressive if delivered in an aggressive, overbearing tone of voice. Since people are not often aware of their own voice tone, recognizing this subtle sign of aggressiveness may be very difficult. A loud volume is one indicator of an aggressive tone. Although speaking in a tone that clearly projects is necessary for an assertive style, shouting almost always appears aggressive. Another aggressive voice characteristic is overemphasis on particular words or phrases in the sentence. For example, the positive statement "You did a good job on the Allen case" sounds aggressive if delivered with an emphasis on *Allen* that implies that it's too bad you didn't do well on other cases. Clipped or very deliberately stated messages, or messages forced out through clenched teeth, may also appear aggressive.

Say the following sentences out loud with emphasis on the italicized words. How do they sound?

I'd like *you* to do this part of your report over.
I'd like you to do *this* part of your report over.
I'd like you to do this part of your *report* over.

How would you say this same sentence nonassertively? Listen to people around you. What makes some people sound more aggressive than others?

Interruption

Since the aggressive person is not really interested in listening to other people's points of view, she often does not give them an opportunity to finish what they are saying. She may actually tell a person to shut up or may simply start talking before the other person has finished. (There are legitimate assertive reasons for interrupting someone. These will be discussed in Chapter Seven.) Even when an aggressive person does not actually interrupt, her responses may seem to have little to do with what the other person said. She carries on "shoot-and-reload" conversations. In a shoot-and-reload conversation, one person says her piece (shoots) and then thinks of what she is going to say next while the other person talks (reload). This style of discussion tends to cut off a great deal of potentially valuable information about the other person's position.

Listen to yourself over the next several days. How often do you interrupt? What effect do you think this has on your conversations?

How do you feel when you are interrupted?

"Looking-through-you" eye contact

While the nonassertive person avoids eye contact, the aggressive person may stare at someone without really making eye contact. Interestingly enough, neither one really sees people's reactions to what they are saying. A person can't really observe others without genuine eye contact. Staring at someone is certainly more powerful than not making eye contact at all, but it can be intimidating and minimize access to information about the other person's actions.

Think of a time when you felt very aggressive. What was the person you were interacting with wearing? What kind of facial expression did she have?

Tense, impatient posture

A person can communicate aggressiveness by standing over someone with her hands on her hips, pointing her finger at someone, or moving so close to someone that personal space is invaded. Aggressive postures also can involve clenching fists, tightening jaw muscles, and waving arms. When walking, the aggressive person may push past others or move so forcefully that people feel obligated to step out of the way. The aggressive person may appear tense and as though she can barely contain her impatience long enough to carry on a conversation. Attending to other work or looking around the room while others are talking communicates this unwillingness to sit and listen respectfully to someone else's view.

One of the problems Debbie Jean had with her supervisor was his aggressive posture. Although he gave lip service to a willingness to discuss problems openly, he would stand at the door with his hand on the doorknob or would pace around the office while she was talking. His nonverbal expressions of tension and impatience communicated very clearly that he did not feel as if he should have to sit and listen to her.

EXERCISE

Think of a time when you felt very aggressive. Move around the room as if you were feeling aggressive. How do you stand and move? How does it feel?

Observe people you consider aggressive. How do they stand and move?

Effects of Aggressiveness on You

One of the reasons it can be very difficult to alter an aggressive interaction style is that aggressive behavior doesn't create as many painful internal signals that can motivate you to change. Nonassertiveness generally is accompanied by a great deal of internal tension or a strong sense that somehow you should have said or done something more. This is not usually true of aggressiveness.

There are, however, some internal signals that can sometimes accompany aggressiveness. When people are being aggressive rather than assertive, they are often strongly emotionally aroused. The most common emotion is anger, or its less controlled form, rage. Sometimes an aggressive interaction style is born of a tendency to lose your temper easily. Thus, even when you intend to handle a situation in an assertive way, you may find yourself furiously attacking the other person. When more controlled, this anger may take the form of a sense of your "rightness" or of everyone else's "wrongness." Although a negative attitude may at times seem quite justified, it fosters an aggressive approach and tends to put others on the defensive. Focusing on and searching for mistakes and errors instead of looking for successes and good behavior can be a manifestation of an aggressive approach.

Ronetta was a supervisor in the water purification department of the state Environmental Protection Agency. She learned to recognize the times she was likely to be aggressive by noting her attitude toward her employees. When she felt irritated, found herself constantly checking her employee's work and saying to herself "No one around here can do anything right but me" she knew that she was being aggressive.

Although the physical tension of aggressiveness may feel different from the tension of nonassertiveness, aggressiveness is certainly not a relaxed interaction style. Even when anger isn't present, there is generally a sense of drivenness in the "I'm going to get mine no matter what" position that brings with it physical stress.

Sometimes, particularly if you are only aggressive occasionally, aggressiveness can be accompanied by a sense of guilt for losing your cool or for not handling the situation the way you planned. Therefore, if you are fairly self-aware, aggressiveness can result in an unfinished feeling.

What kind of body cues or feelings do you get when you are being aggressive? Where do you feel these cues in your body?

Others' Reactions to Aggressiveness

The real cue for aggressive interaction is what it does to others. The strongest signals of aggressiveness are external.

Defensiveness
One way to know if someone is being aggressive is to notice when other people respond as if they are being attacked. There are a number of defensive signals that can mean someone feels he is being attacked:
1. Physical withdrawal
2. Monosyllabic answers or less verbal interaction
3. Increase in explanations, excuses, or justifications
4. Nonverbal agitation such as fidgeting, breaking eye contact
5. Anger or frustration, which may emerge as sullenness
6. Avoidance of contact altogether

The problem with these cues is that people sometimes become defensive even when others are not being aggressive because of the nature of the material being discussed. If, for example, a supervisor is discussing serious performance problems with a very sensitive and defensive employee, there may be no way to interact with that person that will not provoke a defensive response. Therefore, a defensive reaction from an employee does not necessarily mean that a supervisor is being aggressive. It does mean that it may be worthwhile for the supervisor to listen to and observe himself to see if he is doing something to provoke that response. This is particularly true if he often finds many people responding defensively or finds people responding defensively at certain times.

> One supervisor reported in an assertiveness training group that she had always seen herself as very assertive until she began to observe closely one particular employee. She noticed that sometimes this employee's eyes would "get very big." She began to learn that this employee's eyes were a very good clue to her aggressiveness.

Asking for feedback is another way for someone to tell if he is being aggressive. If he has some employees or a supervisor he can trust, he can say something like "Hey Joe! I know that sometimes I come on too strong. Would you let me know when I'm doing that?" Having several people give feedback is even better. When an employee becomes defensive, a supervisor can also check out his response by asking him for feedback: "I had a feeling maybe I was too aggressive a few minutes ago. Is that true?"

Lack of involvement and teamwork
There are several important ways in which the aggressive supervisory style discourages involvement and teamwork. First, because

the supervisor focuses on blame and attack, this style fosters a climate of defensiveness rather than open communication. When employees feel that they will not be listened to and will be attacked if they make a mistake, they are reluctant to discuss problems; open communication is not safe. Not only does this cut down on the flow of information between the supervisor and the employees, but it also encourages employees to be defensive with each other as well. When honest communication within a work unit is discouraged, it is extremely difficult to build a sense of teamwork. Second, the frequent emphasis on negative feedback in an aggressive style and the lack of encouragement for alternative points of view stifles creativity and risk taking. Employees who feel that their ways of looking at situations are not valued are not as likely to really become involved in the organization. This style encourages careful, but not very committed or creative, work. Third, aggressiveness can provoke underlying resentment within employees that may be expressed in passive-resistant ways. For example, an employee who has been aggressively criticized may do an adequate job on that particular task but then may do only the minimum on other tasks that are not so closely monitored.

There is no question that aggressive supervision can often get the job done efficiently in the short run. Some supervisors believe that keeping employees off balance and on the defensive with an aggressive approach is an effective way to increase their motivation. This approach does increase their motivation to avoid punishment, but this is not the same thing as increasing full and energetic involvement in the organization. Although aggressiveness may be an effective short-term strategy, it is not the best strategy for producing long-term commitment and productivity.

When you are aggressive, what do others do?

Think of someone you consider aggressive. What are your feelings about this person? What is his effect on you?

Successful Aggressiveness in Business

There are many top company executives who are clearly aggressive and yet have been very successful. There is absolutely no question that aggressiveness gets results. It is probably also true that erring on the aggressive side will work better in many organizations than erring on the nonassertive side. People listen to the aggressive person and take her seriously because she will not back down. Since aggressive people are not concerned about the priorities of others, they will single-mindedly stick with something and fight for it against all kinds of obstacles. In addition, because they have no need to be seen as "nice guys," they are free to take difficult steps to increase productivity. Not paying attention to others' reactions allows the aggressive person to do what is necessary for the company even if it greatly inconveniences or distresses others. Aggressive people also generally make themselves quite visible in the organization, so if they are competent and knowledgeable, they don't fail to be noticed and appropriately rewarded. As another advantage, employees and managers may give in to an aggressive person in order to avoid the conflict that they know will result if they don't go along with her. If a person is aggressive enough, she can intimidate many people into at least minimal cooperation. The aggressive person also will confront problems quickly rather than just allowing them to fester. And finally, bullying her way into certain situations can give the aggressive person power and information that she can later use to advance herself. There are obviously some advantages to an aggressive style.

Some organizations support an aggressive management philosophy. A supervisor who is not aggressive in these organizations may simply be pushed aside. Organizational philosophies that focus on excellence through intense intraorganizational competition may reward aggressive styles (Peters & Waterman, 1982). Also, the style of top managers is reflected at all levels of the organization. Aggressive top managers may seek to promote those who share their approach to management.

People who have built very successful business careers on being aggressive are very careful and very politically astute. Successful supervisors and managers are generally not aggressive toward someone above them who would be upset or offended by their style. Their style is under their control and is used when appropriate and curbed when inappropriate. It is also essential to be extremely competent to be successfully aggressive. This is because others are looking for mistakes by the aggressive person so that they can use these to "win" in future confrontations and make up for their past losses.

Successful aggressive supervisors provide support as well as punishment. Although they can be harsh and demanding, they utilize their aggressiveness to get rewards for employees who are performing well. The classic image of this kind of boss is the old ward boss who was very intimidating to enemies but provided plenty of rewards for those who proved loyal.

Roy was known as a very aggressive supervisor. He was demanding, rigid, and uncompromising, tending to make snap decisions and really chew people out whenever they did anything wrong. His employees and co-workers were afraid to cross him. However, he worked hard to get resources for his unit, took every opportunity to promote himself and his unit, and made some powerful friends in management. He also was competent and knowledgeable in his field. Roy was able to be aggressive and still be successful because he balanced his aggressiveness with support, built a power base with management, and had good judgment in his field.

Under certain circumstances, less careful aggressiveness does not harm a person's career. The owner of a business may be able to act any way she pleases and still succeed. Or, if someone is not in any one position for too long, an aggressive posture may work well; many times the company hatchet man is aggressive and this aggressiveness is of value because the person moves on after a short time. When the aggressiveness is balanced by a willingness to be assertive and listen to others, it can be nondestructive. For example, a supervisor who loses her temper and rants and raves in a very aggressive fashion whenever there are problems may be effective if she can sit down after she has been angry and say, "Now, let's take a look at how we can solve the problem. What do you think about it?"

This book does not recommend aggressiveness as an overall approach for supervisors because it is a high-risk strategy and because it can have long-range detrimental effects on cooperation and teamwork. The social climate has changed from an authoritarian one in which people automatically followed orders to a more democratic one in which people expect to be treated with respect. Aggressiveness probably does not work nearly as well with the current group of new workers as it once would have (Yankelovich, 1981). The current trend in organizations is toward interaction and teamwork. The more oriented toward teamwork and cooperation an organization is, the less likely it is that an aggressive approach will be valued.

Situations in Which
Aggressiveness Is the Best Response

In several situations, aggressiveness may be very useful. Aggressiveness may be a very effective way to get a person's attention and impress upon him that the issue being confronted is an important one. There is an old story about someone who hired a man to train his mule. The first thing the mule trainer asked for was a two-by-four. When asked why he would possibly want a two-by-four, the man said, "First, I've got to get the mule's attention." If a person has been asserting himself with someone, has raised the muscle level, and in other ways has maximized his assertive influence and still is not getting a response, he can use his aggressiveness as a two-by-four to get the other person's attention. Aggressiveness can communicate to a distracted or inattentive employee that the supervisor means business—that he has reached a limit. However, aggressiveness loses its attention-getting value if used too often.

> Clara, a head surgical nurse, had been working with an aide for several weeks to get the aide to be more careful in cleaning up the operating room. Her assertive action was having no effect. Finally she became very angry and said, "You are driving me crazy. I have confronted you about the materials left on trays and the failure to replenish supplies and you just aren't listening. From now on I want you to clean up all of the leftover supplies and replenish the stock and I'd better not have to talk to you about it again." The aide looked genuinely startled, as if she had not heard about the problem before, and from then on her behavior did improve.

Becoming aggressive can also be a way to clear the air when a great deal of tension has built up in a relationship. There are times when most people need to just "blow off steam" (Bach & Goldberg, 1974). Attempting to mask or bury these aggressive feelings results in continued tension. However, when a person is too angry to be assertive, he can deal with his feelings in ways other than an angry outburst. Some people work out their anger by physical activity such as jogging or sanding a board. Others discharge anger by writing an aggressive letter or memo that is never sent. Another way to express anger is to have an imaginary aggressive conversation with someone. Sometimes, however, there is really a need to tell the other person off. It is important to be aware that getting aggressively angry with an employee may be a way to discharge tension and get some feelings out in the open, but by itself, it is a poor way to do rational problem solving. The focus on personal attack prevents objective discussion of the problem. Aggressive interactions need to be followed by assertive problem solving in order to make permanent changes.

Some people will escalate conflict in an interaction until they provoke an aggressive response. They see assertiveness as a sign of weakness. With this kind of person, an aggressive approach may be necessary in order for him to recognize that a limit has been set. There are other kinds of power confrontations in which aggressive responses may be necessary in order to intimidate the opponent and thereby enhance personal power. This book will not address in detail the use of aggressiveness as a power maneuver, as there are other books that describe this positive use of aggressiveness in considerable detail (Korda, 1975; Ringer, 1977). Experience and observation of others helps in recognizing those situations in which aggressiveness may be a desirable approach.

————◆————

Self-Test

For each of the following situations, would an aggressive response be the best response or create problems? Why?

1. You are really angry at Joe because he has just repeated a mistake that cost the company nearly $10,000. You have confronted him about the same problem several other times and were convinced you had the problem solved.
2. Your staff nurses have a tendency to be careless about the times at which they take vital signs and you need to talk to them about it.
3. Your head machinist is widely known as a bully. He argues with you and with everyone else in authority. You have noticed that he will back off when he senses you have reached your limit.
4. You are upset because your manager has been making arbitrary decisions about issues that affect your department and has not even been informing you.

ANSWERS

1. You are sufficiently angry that you probably couldn't be assertive. It might help to let Joe know how angry you are. It could also be an effective way to get his attention.

2. In this situation, aggressiveness is probably uncalled for and can create potential tension and resentment.

3. This machinist may need to make you really angry to realize that you are at your limit. Aggressiveness may be appropriate.

4. In this case, aggressiveness is probably not appropriate and may be quite risky. It is particularly important not to be aggressive to those higher up in the organization because it often seems like an attack on their authority.

Feelings and Beliefs
That Support Aggressiveness

The basic motto of the aggressive person is "I want what I want when I want it; your needs are irrelevant." In an interaction between an aggressive person and someone else, the aggressive person cancels out the other person. It's as if the other person doesn't matter.

There are a number of underlying feelings or beliefs that may be associated with this aggressive motto. The most prominent one is anger. When someone is really very angry, especially when the anger is based on judgments about the other person's intentions or personality, this anger is very likely to be expressed in aggressive, attacking communications. To describe it another way, aggressiveness is based on Theory X assumptions about others (McGregor, 1960). This belief that others are inherently lazy and unmotivated, coupled with assumptions that a good employee would naturally do things the way they ought to be done, often leads to a very aggressive approach whenever there is a problem.

> Mary believed that her employees wanted to do as little work as they could and that without her constant vigilance they would do nothing. She resented the time she spent confronting problems and invariably came across as very aggressive in interactions with employees. She simply could not understand how any reasonable person could not do things the way they should be done without being told.

It is possible to be assertively angry when the anger is not too strong. However, if someone finds herself getting angry and outraged very easily, it may be difficult for her to be assertive rather than aggressive. Therefore, she may need to find ways to control anger in order to free herself to be assertive.

For the aggressive person, there is a feeling that constant vigilance is necessary to protect herself from others and that any compromise or negotiation will make her appear weak. There is also often an underlying concern that others will "win," "get the better of me," or "put something over on me." In this sense, the aggressive position is based on fear and insecurity. The behavior represents an attempt to "get the other person so she won't get me." The assertive supervisor has more faith in others and also more faith in herself. The person who is sure she can handle whatever happens doesn't need to attack first to protect herself.

Judgments of others are associated with this vigilance. The feeling is "if everyone around here weren't so lazy (incompetent, stupid, etc.), things would work right." Others are not to be trusted because basically they are out to do as little as possible and get as much as they can. In other words, the aggressive person doesn't trust herself or other people. In order to become assertive, the aggressive supervisor may need to confront and alter her suspicion and negative assumptions about others and herself.

Summary

This chapter examines the characteristics of an aggressive supervisory style. The aggressive supervisor's behavior patterns include: critical expression of expectations and feelings, blaming and judgmental criticisms, negative intentions attributed to others, muscle level too high, problems acted on too quickly, unwillingness to listen, and refusal to negotiate and compromise. Her word choices are characterized by: loaded words, "you" statements, "always" or "never" statements, demands instead of requests, and judgments disguised as questions. Her voice characteristics and body language include: a sarcastic, judgmental, overbearing voice tone, interruption, looking-through-you eye contact, and tense, impatient posture.

Aggressive behavior can be difficult to change because it does not always create the painful internal signals that nonassertive behavior does. The best way to recognize aggressive behavior is through self-observation and observing others' reactions. People often react to aggressive behavior with defensiveness or lack of involvement and teamwork.

There are many aggressive people who are successful in the business world. They are generally aggressive only when it is not likely to get them into trouble. Aggressiveness is not recommended to supervisors though, because it is a high-risk strategy and the long-term effects on working relationships can be detrimental.

Aggressiveness may be the best way to get someone's attention, to clear the air, and to establish limits.

The basic motto of the aggressive person is "I want what I want when I want it; your needs are irrelevant." The feelings and beliefs that support aggressiveness include anger, fear and insecurity, and a lack of trust of self and others.

Bibliography

Bach, G. R., & Goldberg, H. *Creative aggression.* New York: Avon, 1974.

Butler, P. *Self-assertion for women: A guide to becoming androgynous.* New York: Harper & Row, 1976.

Kepner, C. H., & Tregoe, B. B. *The rational manager: A systematic approach to problem solving and decision making.* Princeton, N.J.: Kepner-Tregoe, 1965.

Korda, M. *Power.* New York: Random House, 1975.

McGregor, D. M. *The human side of enterprise.* New York: McGraw-Hill, 1960.

Peters, T. J., & Waterman, R. H. *In search of excellence: Lessons from America's best run companies.* New York: Harper & Row, 1982.

Ringer, R. *Looking out for #1.* Beverly Hills, Calif.: The Los Angeles Book Corporation, 1977.

Yankelovich, D. *New rules: Searching for fulfillment in a world turned upside down.* New York: Random House, 1981.

CHAPTER FOUR

The Assertive
Supervisory Style

In this chapter, you will:
- Learn to identify assertive behavior patterns;
- Become aware of assertive word choices;
- Become aware of assertive voice characteristics and body language;
- Learn the effects of assertiveness on you;
- Learn others' reactions to assertiveness;
- Become aware of feelings and beliefs that support assertiveness.

Once again in this example, Angela needs to confront George about his failure to get his monthly report to her on time. In this dialogue, she uses an assertive supervisory style.

Angela: (Pulls up a chair and sits down next to George's desk) George, I need to talk to you about two things. One is that I need this month's report today so I can submit the summary tomorrow. Second, this is the third time the monthly report has been late. The late reports create problems. Our department looks really rotten when our reports are delayed, and I end up having to come talk to you a lot, which doesn't improve our relationship. I would like to find a way for the report to be on my desk on the first without my reminding you. Are you willing to do that?

George: Well, I'm willing, but there are a lot of other high priority tasks that come up.

71

Angela: This report is a real priority for me. When would you have to start the report to make sure some other high priority task doesn't interfere, and how long does it take to do the report?

George: It only takes 2 hours. I suppose 2 days would give me enough extra time for crises.

Angela: Would you be willing to save 2 hours in your schedule 2 days ahead of time and then let me know if other tasks are interfering so I can help to clear time?

George: Yes, I can do that.

Angela: I need this month's report this afternoon. Can I expect it by 4:00?

George: I have some other work, but I'll put it aside until I get you the report.

Angela: So this month's report will be on my desk by 4:00. Next month, you'll start 2 days ahead and let me know before the first if there is a conflict in priorities so that the report can be in by the first. Do you agree?

George: Yes.

How effective do you think Angela will be in solving the problem?

When will she get this month's report?

Will George turn the report in on time next month?

How would you feel as Angela? How would you feel as George?

What might be the long-range consequences of this style?

In this dialogue, Angela tells George exactly what she wants, why she wants it, and when she wants it without personally attacking him. She removes the obstacles interfering with getting the job done once and for all by asking questions to establish a specific plan for solving the problem and asking George to commit himself to the plan. Before leaving the situation, she summarizes their agreement. This dialogue is longer than the nonassertive and aggressive dialogues. Assertive interactions are frequently somewhat longer because they involve sitting down and solving problems. If there were severe time pressure, the assertive interaction could have been shortened to Angela's first statement and a persistent request for George to commit himself to a plan. However, the extra minutes may be worth it when the problem is solved and stays solved.

Assertive Behavior Patterns

As with the nonassertive and the aggressive ways of acting, the assertive style is characterized by certain behavior patterns. Assertive supervisors can be easily recognized by these effective patterns.

Clear, direct, nonapologetic expression of expectations and feelings

An assertive person usually states in the first few minutes of an interaction exactly what he wants. People do not have to guess what he wants or listen to several minutes of hinting. Statements are specific and are directly addressed to the person for whom they are meant. This directness occurs in assigning tasks, in criticizing others, in responding to criticism, in giving praise, and in other interactions. The assertive person is willing to let others know clearly and directly where he stands. Since he is clear about his right to express his opinion to others, an assertive supervisor does not need to apologize for his requests. His assertive statements are not buried by apologetic or indirect introductions or followed by rambling comments that blunt their impact.

> Vito was the supervisor of an auto leasing firm. He was noted for his straightforward interactions with others. When he assigned responsibilities for maintaining vehicles or for staffing the office, he always made it clear what he expected and why a particular job was important. When employees made mistakes, Vito would let them know clearly and immediately what they were doing that was a problem and what he wanted them to do.

The direct, assertive supervisor takes responsibility for taking care of himself in the world. Others do not have to try to take care of him, nor is he dependent on the willingness and ability of others to guess what is needed. How many times, for example, do people say, "They should have known better than that. . . . I never would have done it that way."

Do you let others know where you stand on issues? Are you direct about your expectations, your disagreements, and your positive feelings? How much do others have to guess to know how you really feel about something?

Can you think of someone who is always clear, direct, and non-apologetic about where he stands? What is it like to interact with this person?

Descriptive instead of judgmental criticisms

Assertive criticism describes behavior that is creating problems without attacking the person involved. The purpose of assertive criticism is to solve the problem, not to punish the other person for his behavior. As a consequence, the language is "nonloaded," and the criticism process involves mutually exploring what is preventing things from working and generating a concrete plan for removing obstacles and solving the problem. Assertive criticism at its best creates a sense that the supervisor and the person being criticized are a team working together to solve a problem. This sense of objectivity and teamwork comes from the language used to describe the problem and from the voice characteristics and body language used to deliver the criticism.

> Jason had recently inherited a new secretary from another office. Although she had come with a good performance record, she made many errors in her typing, had trouble locating materials she filed, and sometimes answered the phone in a way that customers thought was rude. After giving her some time to adjust, Jason sat down with her to talk about how both of them thought things were going. He let her know that he understood that she was new on the job, but that there were several problems he was concerned about. He wanted to see what could be done to improve her typing accuracy and the filing system. He wanted to know about problems that might be interfering with clean, accurate letters and a good filing system. He also let her know that he had been getting some feedback from customers who were upset by her phone style and discussed with her why this might be the case. Together they came up with some specific plans for improving these areas of performance and established a 2-week follow-up date.

Do you give your employees feedback when their performance isn't up to standard? The last time you did give criticism, what was the effect of your criticism? Do you think you were able to make the criticism descriptive rather than judgmental?

Can you think of someone who has given you particularly helpful criticism? What did he do or say?

Persistence

The assertive person will continue to follow through on an issue until it is resolved. This is true even when the initial response to his assertion is not positive. He understands that although some people almost automatically resist change or the views of others, that initial resistance does not always last and being assertive may work in the long run. He also looks for other ways to solve a problem when one way is blocked.

> Graham very much wanted to get a computer for his chemical lab. Although there was a computer group in the company, they had not been able to provide all of the computer resources he felt he needed. The management rejected his first request with a comment that the computer group in the company ought to be adequate. He told management exactly what computer work he needed and arranged for a 3-month trial to see if the in-house equipment could do the job. In 3 months, he returned with a report and made an even stronger case for the lab computer. It took nearly a year, but his lab now has its own computer, and the computer group is also making more effort to provide other kinds of computer resources as they are needed.

Persistence also implies a certain amount of patience. Persistence does not mean that the assertive person insists on an immediate response on all issues. That kind of persistence is an aggressive denial of the needs and priorities of others. If something is important to a person's part of the organization, he should continue to press for it at appropriate times. It may also be important to acknowledge other organizational constraints that may delay or interfere. Pushing too hard on an issue can be as self-defeating as giving up too soon. In order to survive in any organization, it is important to know when to accept the reality of the "givens" in the situation.

The Alcoholics Anonymous prayer offers a reasonable motto for assertiveness in business as well:

> God give me the courage to change what I can change, the serenity to accept what I cannot change, and the wisdom to know the difference.

The assertive stance involves the courage to change what can be changed through persistent, effective action and the serenity to gracefully accept what cannot be changed.

Persistence also involves a willingness to raise the muscle level when necessary. Failing to use more muscle when it is necessary is nonassertive. For example, if a supervisor has an employee with a serious performance problem and has confronted the employee about the problem once, confronting him again with much stronger verbal and nonverbal behavior is to be expected. Willingness to use the leverage of whatever disciplinary actions are available is required if the behavior continues. A supervisor must confront problems with appropriate muscle. If other employees see an employee failing to do his job and not experiencing any consequences, a norm (or unspoken rule) may begin to develop within the unit that not doing the job is acceptable.

Are there times when you do not follow through persistently? What has happened as a result? Do you use increasingly powerful consequences when necessary?

Can you think of someone who is persistent and uses increasingly powerful consequences when necessary? How effective is this person?

Willingness to listen

One very important characteristic of an assertive style of interaction is the willingness to listen to others. In a meeting, the assertive person may disagree with others, but he always makes them feel that they have been listened to. One of the results of this careful listening is the communication of respect for the other person. The other prime benefit to the assertive person is his access to concrete information about the cause of problems. As seen in the example with Angela and George, the assertive style often takes a little longer initially because it generates a dialogue with the employee;

however, problems are more likely to be solved because the assertive supervisor finds the source of the problem rather than settling on a quick or arbitrary solution. He also encourages his employees to be creative and involved by listening attentively to their suggestions and their points of view.

It is important not only to be able to listen to what others say, but also to be able to communicate to them that they have been heard and understood. Effective listeners are not passive when they listen. One of the techniques they use effectively is to summarize or paraphrase what they are understanding to make sure they are hearing accurately. This feedback process also helps others to know whether they are being accurately understood. Chapter Six will cover listening effectively and using paraphrasing and questioning to help clarify what people are saying and to draw them out.

In the model of assertive supervision presented in this book, assertiveness is a style of interaction that is characterized both by taking a personal stand and being responsive to another's needs and priorities. Listening skills are central to this subtle balancing of priorities.

> Antonio was an engineering supervisor in a large chemical company. He was respected and valued by management and by the men he supervised. In part, people respected Antonio because they all knew where they stood with him; but the most striking characteristic of his supervisory style was his ability to listen. When one of his men had a problem, Antonio would concentrate fully on what the employee had to say. He would talk with and question his employee until he was certain that he fully understood the problem and how the employee viewed the problem. At times, Antonio found that simply listening and repeating what he understood the employee to be saying helped the employee to solve the problem himself. When he did give advice or make suggestions, the suggestions were appropriate for the problem and for the employee because he had taken time to explore and understand before offering advice. When he rejected a suggestion, employees felt certain that he understood their point of view.

When a problem occurs, what do you do with an employee? Do you understand his point of view? Who talks the most? How do you communicate your understanding of the employee's view?

Can you think of someone in your organization who seems especially good at listening to others? What effect does this have on others? What does this person do to communicate that he is listening?

Negotiation and compromise

The assertive person is concerned with finding a way that both people in an interaction can win. He knows that anytime he wins at someone else's expense, the other person is then motivated to find a way to win the next time. He persists in meeting his needs and priorities, but not at the expense of the organization or other people. He will not settle for solutions that disregard issues that he thinks are important, but neither will he continue to demand that others give up their legitimate priorities. As stated in Chapter One, being assertive does not mean that a person will always get what he wants. It does mean that he will strongly and forcefully state his views and that he will be willing to fight for what he believes to be right. This is a difficult balancing act. There is no secret formula that determines when persistence becomes aggression or when persistence is useless. Judgment, sensitivity, and awareness of self and others are the only guides for effectively balancing personal needs and views with those of other people.

> Mabel, nursing supervisor for a large hospital, believed that nursing notes should be written in chronological order. Some of the nurses on the unit had been trained to write a different type of nursing note. Although she would have preferred to have all of the nurses do it her way, she recognized that the style of nursing notes would not really affect patient care and that there were many alternative views about how appropriate notes should be written. She told nurses that they could choose the form of their notes as long as they included certain specified information.

There is a difference between an assertive and a nonassertive compromise. An assertive compromise involves trade-offs: "I'll grant you this, and I expect this in return" is the basic form of an assertive compromise. In an assertive compromise, a supervisor might say something like "All right, I'd be willing to postpone the meeting this week if we can meet at the beginning of next week." To assertively compromise, a person must decide what he is willing to trade and make the conditions explicit for the other person. The assertive supervisor would make every effort to let the other person know what minimum he is willing to settle for in a given situation and to make a case for why compromise is necessary. He would confront the other person on that person's unwillingness to compromise if necessary.

There are times when compromise is not possible nor acceptable. The manager has the authority to make final decisions about how some functions of a unit are performed, overriding supervisors' positions on issues. In an effective organization, the manager will not always override the supervisors' decisions. The effective manager will consult and work with supervisors as team members, just as they try to work with their employees as team members whenever possible. There are times when supervisors have to make decisions that overrule or disregard their employees' views— situations in which no compromise is possible. There are also times when supervisors may need to leave positions or companies because of management's unwillingness to negotiate or compromise on vital issues. The assertiveness model does not say that compromise is always possible. It only says that when possible, compromise and negotiation are likely to lead to more productive teamwork.

Under what circumstances are you willing to negotiate and compromise? How do you make that decision?

Can you think of someone who is willing to negotiate and compromise with you? What is it like to interact with this person?

SELF-TEST

Pick the assertive response in the following situations and specify what cues you used.

1. Myra has an employee who has not been attending staff training sessions. She feels that this staff member needs training.
    a. She does nothing and hopes the staff member will realize what he is missing.
    b. She lets him know that she feels he could use the training and that she wants him to attend. She also explores why he is not attending.
2. Myra's employee still fails to attend the training.

    a. She confronts him again and lets him know that failure to attend the training will have to be documented in his next performance review.

    b. She calls the employee in and tells him that she is going to fire him if he fails to attend one more training session.

3. Patrick's manager has suggested a change in reporting procedure for his department. Patrick much prefers the old way.

    a. He explores why the manager sees a change as necessary and suggests some alternative processes that might meet his and the manager's needs.

    b. He insists that the new method is no good and that it ought to be done his way. When ordered to do it the new way, he continues to complain.

4. Kelly's employee comes in to explain to her why some important reports are late.

    a. She lets the employee know in no uncertain terms that she doesn't want to listen to any excuses.

    b. She listens carefully to uncover problems that need to be taken care of in order for the work to be done. At the same time she continues to reiterate the importance of completing reports on time.

5. One of the veterinarian medical students that Bert supervises at the zoo has been careless in giving the animals scheduled inoculations.

    a. Bert tells her that she's endangering the animals' lives because of her irresponsible and careless behavior.

    b. Bert tells her that she is endangering the animals' lives when inoculations are missed and asks her to be more careful from now on.

ANSWERS

1. *b* is the assertive response because it involves stating expectations and feelings clearly and listening to the other person. *a* is nonassertive because no action is taken when needed.

2. *a* is the assertive response. The muscle level is raised appropriately and persistently. *b* is aggressive because the consequence of not changing behavior is too high at this time.

3. *a* is the assertive response because he uses compromise and negotiation. *b* is aggressive because of his unwillingness

to compromise and acknowledge the superior's legitimate authority.

4. *b* is the assertive response because she uses listening to uncover the reasons for the problem and specifies what she wants. *a* is aggressive because of the unwillingness to listen.

5. *b* is the assertive response because he simply describes the problem and asks the other person to correct it. *a* is aggressive because of the use of the loaded words *irresponsible* and *careless*.

Assertive Word Choices

Assertive word choices, unlike nonassertive or aggressive choices, are neither apologetic, angry, nor judgmental. They tend to be neutral and focused on solving problems.

Neutral language

Chapters Two and Three described in some detail how messages sound nonassertive or aggressive when certain kinds of language are used. Assertive statements command serious attention without arousing defensiveness. For example, saying "It is very important that the results be reported carefully" is much more assertive and will have better results than saying "It's kind of important that the results be reported a little more carefully." The statement "I'd like you to think of the possible negative consequences before you decide to refuse a particular set of samples" arouses much less defensiveness than the aggressive statement "Don't make such stupid decisions about which samples to refuse."

EXERCISE

Say the following sentences out loud. Which would command serious attention without arousing defensiveness?

You are incredibly rude and inconsiderate to interrupt me when I'm talking on the phone.

I would like you to wait to speak to me until I'm free.

I would sort of prefer if you could be a little more careful about talking to me when I'm talking to someone else.

Concise statements

Assertive statements get right to the point. It's not necessary to wade through a lot of words to find out what the assertive person wants. For example, the assertive supervisor would be likely to say, "I'd like to talk to you about the number of typing errors that have been showing up lately" rather than, "You know, we've been having more and more problems getting work done properly around here lately. Only last week, Helen Jones was telling me what a problem she was having with one of her typists. . . ."

◆

EXERCISE

Say the following sentences out loud. Which statement would have the most impact?

> There have been a number of problems around this department. For example, some people are talking on the phone or taking long lunches, or leaving early. I wish people would work harder. For example, I would like you to limit your lunch time to one hour.
>
> I would like you to limit your lunches to one hour.

Listen to yourself. Are you getting to the point quickly or losing your point in too many words?

◆

Personalized statements of concern

The old supervisory adage used to be that the most effective way to supervise is never to use the word *I*. However, in reality, part of the influence a supervisor has with an employee is through personal contact between herself and the other person. It is a great deal easier for someone to ignore the needs of the organization or the company than it is for her to ignore the needs of a person she faces every day in the office. Using the organization as the person with the problem may inadvertently communicate to the employee that the supervisor doesn't really care about the problem. As described earlier, addressing concerns to "some people" who are not doing their jobs can reduce the impact. This does not mean that it is not important to inform employees about company policy; however, saying "Company policy is that breaks are to be limited to 15 minutes. I would like your breaks to be limited to 15 minutes" is likely to be more effective than "According to company policy, you should only take 15 minute breaks."

Say the following sentences out loud. Which would have the most impact?

Our company expects employees to say where they are when they sign out for the field.

I would like you to let the secretary know where you will be when you sign out for the field.

Specific behavioral descriptions

The assertive person not only directs her remarks to a specific person, but also describes specific behavior. One of the most common communication problems is the assumption that others know exactly what is meant by a general remark. For example, if a supervisor says to an employee, "I would like you to show more concern for the patients," the employee may think that the supervisor wants her to be quieter when she comes into the room when what the supervisor had in mind was to encourage her to speak to the patient by name. The more general the supervisor is when describing behavior, the more danger there is that the other person will misunderstand what she wants.

Think of the first five behaviors that come to you when someone says, "I want you to be more cooperative." If you were being confronted about your cooperativeness, would you know which of these behaviors was meant?

Pay attention to peoples' levels of specificity. What seems to happen when people are very general in their comments? What happens when someone confronts you in a general way?

Cooperative words

The assertive person would be likely to say things such as "How can we resolve this?" or "Let's work on shortening turnaround time for these new programs." One of the purposes of an assertive supervisory style is to develop a sense of team effort. It therefore becomes important to make requests and comments that provide a sense that the supervisor and the employee are working together to solve the problem. One way of doing this is to state that "we" need to work on the problem. This means determining what the employee will do to take care of the problem and what the supervisor needs to do to help.

Say the following sentences out loud. Which statement would best develop teamwork?

What can we do to improve communications in our department?

What are you going to do to improve communications in our department?

Let's see if there's a better way to handle this situation.

You ought to find a better way to handle this situation.

Think of someone in your organization who is particularly good at eliciting teamwork. What kinds of things does she say?

Requests instead of demands

As mentioned in Chapter Three, demands tend to appear much more aggressive than requests. Although there are certainly times in emergencies when a demand might be appropriate, in most cases, people will be more cooperative when they are asked to do something rather than ordered to do something. Requests can be made forcefully as in "I need that material by Monday" or not quite so forcefully as in "I'd like to have that material by Monday." Both of these statements are less aggressive than saying "Get me that material by Monday." Avoiding demands except in emergencies not only elicits more cooperation, it also insures that when orders are given they will be taken seriously. Too much use of demands dilutes the forcefulness implied in such statements.

Say the following sentences out loud. Which would be likely to elicit more cooperation?

Finish all of the vital signs before you clean up!

I'd like you to finish all of the vital signs before you clean up.

No statements disguised as questions
As mentioned in Chapters Two and Three, both nonassertive and aggressive supervisors tend to use questions when they really have some underlying statement to make. No one needs to guess the assertive person's view nor feel trapped in rhetorical questions that are really sarcastic ways of criticizing. For example, an assertive person would be likely to say "I don't agree with the new procedure" rather than "You don't really agree with that new procedure, do you?"

◆

EXERCISE

Say the following sentences out loud. Which would have the most impact?

You don't want to meet this week, do you?
I would rather not meet this week.

Don't you think that this new staff member will be a real addition to our unit?
I think that this staff member will be a real addition to our unit.

◆

SELF-TEST

Pick the assertive statement from each pair of statements and specify what cues you used.

1. a. "You are always 10 minutes late."
   b. "The last several weeks you have been 10 minutes or more late on three occasions."
2. a. "Let's see if we can find a way to reduce accounting errors enough so that we don't have to repeat the weekly summaries."
   b. "You'd better figure out a way to reduce accounting errors if you want to work here."
3. a. "I'm upset that you have been complaining about me to others."
   b. "I wish that people in this company wouldn't complain about others behind their backs."
4. a. "I get angry when you promise to finish a report by a certain time and don't get it done."
   b. "I can't see how you can be so inefficient about getting things done when you promise."

5. a. "You wouldn't want to do it that way, would you?"
   b. "I'd rather you do it this way."
6. a. "Get the conference room cleaned up now!"
   b. "Please clean the conference room by 3:00 today."

ANSWERS

1. *b* is the assertive statement because it is specific and uses neutral language. *a* is aggressive because of the word *always*.
2. *a* is the assertive statement because it uses cooperative words. *b* is aggressive because it is threatening and the muscle level seems to be too high.
3. *a* is the assertive statement because it is direct and personalized. *b* is nonassertive because it is indirect and focuses on people in general.
4. *a* is the assertive statement because it uses a specific behavioral description. *b* is aggressive because it uses the loaded word *inefficient.*
5. *b* is the assertive statement because it is a direct, clear statement of what is wanted. *a* is nonassertive because it is a statement disguised as a question.
6. *b* is assertive because it is a request. *a* is aggressive unless this is an emergency situation.

Assertive Voice Characteristics and Body Language

Assertive voice characteristics and body language are firm and straightforward. They convey a sense of purpose and assurance.

Even, powerful voice tone

An assertive voice is loud enough to command attention without being overbearing. The voice is low pitched, words are clearly enunciated, and there is adequate breath to give the voice power and strength. The most important quality of an assertive voice is neutrality; words are not emphasized in a sarcastic or loaded way. Statements sound like statements rather than questions or buried accusations. There is a calm, matter-of-fact quality to assertive communication that is not characteristic of either nonassertive or aggressive approaches. An assertive voice sounds solid, firm, and commanding.

◆

EXERCISE

Say the following statements out loud as if you are feeling strong, confident, and self-assured.

I'd rather do this my way.
No, I won't be able to help you with that project.
I'd like you to do this part of your report over.

Listen to your co-workers. Who sounds confident, firm, assertive? What is the tone of his voice like? How do you sound?

◆

Eye contact

Probably the most important nonverbal cue for an assertive interaction style is eye contact. Looking at someone while speaking to him acknowledges his presence and communicates the seriousness of what is being said. The key word here is contact. To have an assertive interaction, the supervisor must be in contact with the other person. Making eye contact brings the supervisor to the other person's attention and makes what he says more powerful. It also says to the other person "I see and recognize you. You matter to me." Making eye contact allows the supervisor to pay much closer attention to the person's reactions. When the supervisor is not making eye contact or is glaring at someone, he is so caught up in himself that he simply does not really see the other person. Since assertiveness involves balancing two people's needs and priorities, the assertive person must be able to pay attention to himself and to the other person at the same time. Eye contact can help him to accomplish that task.

◆

EXERCISE

Talk to a friend with your back to him. How does that feel?

Now turn toward him but look away. How does the interaction feel?

What is it like for you when someone makes good eye contact with you?

◆

Erect, relaxed posture

The assertive person does not stand over someone, point a finger, or threaten; neither does he slump, shuffle his feet, or look apologetic. Assertive posture is relaxed, balanced, and erect. An assertive supervisor walks through the building in a confident and relaxed manner. He moves as if he has a clear direction but at the same time can acknowledge others by a smile or a nod. When sitting, an assertive person neither sprawls nor is poised on the edge of his chair. He faces the person he is interacting with squarely with an open posture. His arms are relaxed rather than tightly crossed, and he either leans forward slightly or sits back in a relaxed but attentive manner.

EXERCISE

Think of a time that you were feeling very assertive. Move around the room as if you were feeling assertive. How do you stand and move? How does it feel?

Observe others in your organization. How do the assertive people move, sit, and stand?

Words and nonverbal messages that match

As stated in Chapter Two, communication is confused when a person says one thing verbally and another nonverbally. A common contradiction is to smile a lot when talking about something serious. An assertive person uses voice characteristics and body language that are serious when the message is serious and playful when the message is playful. Nervous gestures of various kinds detract from an assertive message and need to be controlled in order for the speaker to appear really assertive.

EXERCISE

Stand in front of a mirror and make the following statement. One time say the statement with a smile. The next time say it without a smile. Which would you take most seriously?

It's very important that we solve this problem.

Effects of Assertiveness on You

When you have been assertive, you have a "finished" feeling, a sense that you have done or said what needed to be done. You can probably remember times when you were upset, said or did something about it, and then felt relieved. If you are consistently assertive, you do not gather a lot of unfinished business to be obsessed about nor do you feel constantly tense. Although someone may be tense while being assertive and immediately afterwards, the assertive person does not build chronic body tensions as the nonassertive person does. Often there is a sense of relief that accompanies assertive action. In other words, the presence or absence of chronic physical tension and resentment can be a way to tell if you are being nonassertive or assertive.

> Carl had come to recognize over time that tension in his back and a clenched jaw were signs that he needed to directly confront a problem. He found that when he did directly confront someone about a problem he would feel a sense of relief followed by a sense of self-respect and a feeling of being able to let go of the situation because he had done everything he could. Once he began to identify the negative feelings associated with nonassertiveness and the positive feelings associated with responding assertively, he found that he was much more motivated to be assertive when a problem did occur.

One theory behind assertiveness training is that you don't have to be self-confident to act self-confident. Acting as if you have self-confidence can help to build your self-respect and confidence and make assertive action easier each time you do it. Also, since being assertive often results in correcting a problem that is a source of stress and tension, being assertive can lead to a feeling of being more in control of your life. The assertive person does not have to feel as much like a victim of circumstances. It is very difficult to feel good about yourself if you feel out of control.

Of course, good feelings do not always follow assertive action. If assertiveness is a new behavior, it may feel very uncomfortable. After an assertive interaction, you may find yourself with shaking knees and sweaty palms even when you have acted appropriately. This is especially true when you are asserting yourself in a crisis situation. If you have a great many beliefs that work against assertiveness, you may find yourself feeling extremely guilty when you act. This anxiety and guilt is an unavoidable part of the process of learning.

It is also true that even if you are assertive you may not feel finished or relaxed because of unchangeable circumstances that will continue to irritate you.

> Lynn was a social services supervisor. Through funding cuts, she had lost 25 percent of her staff and yet the agency was making the same demands. Two staff members were threatening to resign and one was getting an ulcer. She knew that the demands on her staff were unreasonable, and she also knew that no matter how she asserted herself she could do very little to change the situation. This left her with a sense of anger and helplessness, although gradually she was learning to accept the funding situation of her organization as unchangeable.

Coping with frustrating and demoralizing organizational realities requires more than assertiveness. It requires an ability to accept *what is* without driving yourself crazy. The section in Chapter Five on dealing with anger can help you adapt to difficult situations.

———◆———

What kind of body cues or feelings do you get when you are being assertive? Where do you feel these cues in your body?

———◆———

Others' Reactions to Assertiveness

Assertive supervision generally encourages others to take the supervisor seriously without threatening them or making them feel defensive. This can help supervisors and employees work together effectively.

Trust and teamwork
Employees are more likely to cooperate with their supervisor to finish a job when they feel that the supervisor is serious about the work and respects their contribution. What makes the assertive style so effective is the balance between respect for others and a firm and fair approach to solving problems. The assertive supervisory style promotes trust because the supervisor is clear about where she stands and is willing to listen, negotiate, and compromise. This clear, firm, and fair stand helps to create a personal

commitment within employees to the achievement of organizational priorities and goals.

Arun was best known for the creativity of his sales development team. His encouragement of open communication and his modeling of respectful treatment of others had created a climate of spirited interaction between the workers in his group. At meetings, people were not afraid to make suggestions or to disagree with one another, because they knew that Arun and their co-workers would be honest and respectful in return. Others in the organization were surprised to find such a strong sense of teamwork and creative cooperation.

Resistance

Some people will experience any assertive action as a threat. Even when a person is very careful not to be aggressive, some people will be angry and upset when they do not get their own way. If a person has been used to getting her own way, there is no reason why she should be delighted to have to begin to compromise and negotiate. Initial attempts to be assertive may also activate intense efforts to maintain the status quo. In a recently completed research study on assertiveness and marital interaction, many women reported that initially their husbands did not like their increased assertiveness. However, the increased ability to communicate was paying off in better marriages 2 or 3 years later (Drury, 1981). This same initial resistance may occur in work situations. If a supervisor has been very nonassertive, it is important for her to realize that it may take others a while to adjust to an assertive approach. Sometimes it helps to be assertive first in areas that are not highly emotional for the other person. For example, it does not make sense for a person to start asserting herself by criticizing her superior's pet project.

There are still circumstances in which women or members of minority groups who assert themselves in any way are considered "uppity" or aggressive. In an organization with a rigid white male power structure, they may find that even mild assertiveness provokes a great deal of resistance. They will need to build a power base to support their assertiveness. Generally, the first several women and members of minority groups in an organization pave the way so that those who follow will find it easier to be assertive. More about sexual and racial barriers to assertiveness is found in Chapter Five.

◆

When you are assertive, what do others do?

Think of someone you consider asssertive. What are your feelings about this person? What is her effect on you?

◆

Feelings and Beliefs
That Support Assertiveness

The basic motto of the assertive person is "I want to find a way for both of us to win. I don't want to ignore my priorities to pay attention to yours. Neither do I want to ignore your priorities." In an interaction between an assertive supervisor and another person, both people count. The need for negotiation, compromise, and the balancing of priorities does require self-awareness and a willingness to be sensitive to others, but the effort that is required pays off in a climate of teamwork and mutual support.

The most basic support for an assertive approach is a positive self-image. The assertive supervisor trusts himself. He believes that he is worthwhile and competent even if he sometimes makes mistakes. This sense of self-esteem enables him to live with criticism or anger from others. Since people will sometimes initially respond negatively to assertiveness, it is impossible to be assertive and to always be liked or appreciated. The assertive supervisor also trusts that he will be able to handle problems if they occur. In other words, he doesn't always anticipate failure.

The assertive supervisor also trusts others. Although he knows that some employees will not be motivated to do a good job, he tends to assume good intentions and look for the obstacles to productive work. When problems do occur, they are treated as problems to be solved rather than as indications that the employee is worthless or is out to undermine the supervisor. This basic trust allows the supervisor to take a more relaxed position with his employees. He is alert to problems and is willing to confront people when necessary, but he does not have to be constantly vigilant for fear that an employee will "get away with something." Nor does he feel it necessary to attack the employee out of fear that he will be attacked.

Ralph was the supervisor of the delivery men for a large beverage distributor. One of his drivers had been late in making his deliveries for the past week. This employee did consistently good work, but occasionally would fall behind for a few days. Ralph knew that whenever this employee fell behind, there had been a valid reason such as construction along his delivery route or delays in receiving the goods he distributed. Ralph trusted this employee to do his best and was not afraid that he was trying to get away with something. He did not discipline him for being late, but instead he asked him if there were any problems with his route that needed resolving.

A feeling of entitlement also supports assertiveness. Entitlement means that the supervisor feels that he has a *right* to expect certain kinds of behavior from others. For example, a supervisor has a right to ask employees to be at work when they have agreed to be there; to ask employees to do the job they are paid to do; to ask them to stop doing something that is interfering with the accomplishment of organizational goals; to say no when a request will interfere with the work; to ask that employees comply with company rules, and so on. The notion of entitlement or rights is important because if a supervisor does not feel entitled to make certain requests or to take certain positions, he will present these positions hesitantly and apologetically. Chapter Five outlines supervisory rights and responsibilities in more detail and discusses how supervisors can use knowledge about rights to give themselves permission to be assertive even when the other person does not like it.

Objectivity is a third feeling that supports assertiveness. The assertive supervisor exhibits objectivity in several ways. He does not make minor irritations into major catastrophes. For example, if he has to confront an angry employee, he does not imagine that the employee's anger means that he has permanently ruined his relationship with that employee. He does not take events or interactions personally. It is easy to assume that difficulties with a particular employee or co-worker are a personal affront. This is particularly true when others are criticizing some aspect of the supervisor's behavior. Most people are not very good at giving criticism, and therefore may phrase their criticism in very aggressive, attacking ways. The assertive supervisor is able, through objective listening and questioning, to help others to describe the situation that is creating problems rather than respond to the criticism as a personal attack. The assertive supervisor bases his behavior on the facts in the situation, not on his assumptions about what a particular behavior means. For example, if an employee who had been recently transferred to a new job was not doing well, the supervisor would talk to the employee about the problem rather than assuming he couldn't do the new job and transferring him back. Chapter Five has a discussion of ways to separate facts from assumptions to check out assumptions and to perform other strategies for enhancing objectivity.

Summary

This chapter examines the characteristics of an assertive supervisory style. The assertive supervisor's behavior patterns include: clear, direct, nonapologetic expression of expectations and feelings, descriptive instead of judgmental criticisms, persistence, willingness to listen, and negotiation and compromise. His word choices are characterized by: neutral language, concise statements, personalized statements of concern, specific behavioral descriptions, cooperative words, requests instead of demands, and no statements disguised as questions. His voice characteristics and body language include: an even, powerful voice tone; eye contact; erect, relaxed posture; and words and nonverbal messages that match.

When you are assertive, you may have a finished feeling and a feeling of relaxation unless the assertive behavior is new. Being assertive does not insure that you will be able to avoid the frustration of unchangeable situations.

Assertiveness encourages others to take the supervisor seriously while at the same time encouraging trust and teamwork. However, some people will initially resist and be angry at attempts to be assertive. Women and members of minority groups are particularly vulnerable to accusations that they are being aggressive when they assert themselves.

The assertive motto is "I want to find a way for both of us to win." Assertiveness is supported by self-esteem and by trusting others. It is also based on a sense of entitlement and on objectivity.

Bibliography

Drury, S. *Assertive supervision: Successful management of people.* Unpublished training manual, 1981. (Available from 1613 Orchard Lane, Arden, Delaware 19810).

CHAPTER FIVE

Overcoming Difficulties in Being Assertive

In this chapter, you will:
- Come to understand how your beliefs and thoughts, not the situation, cause your feelings;
- Learn how you create guilt that can interfere with your assertiveness;
- Learn how you create fear and anxiety;
- Learn how you create doubt;
- Learn how you create anger;
- Learn how your feelings create an inflexible or negative self-image;
- Acquire some specific techniques for overcoming these destructive emotions and freeing yourself to be assertive;
- Learn about sexual and racial blocks to assertiveness and how you can overcome them;
- Learn about using support for overcoming difficulties in being assertive.

Maintaining consistency in performing assertively as a supervisor is difficult. You will have times when you know what you should be doing, but find yourself being nonassertive or aggressive instead of assertive. For example, a supervisor may know that she needs to confront an employee. She may be aware of the need to maintain eye contact, speak in an assertive tone of voice, and let the other person know clearly and directly what she wants. Yet even with this knowledge she may hesitate to confront or confront in a weak, ineffective way. She may also find herself becoming aggressive when she has carefully planned an assertive intervention. What keeps her from being as assertive as she wants to be? In this case, the problem is neither lack of information about the appropriate assertive response nor a lack of assertive techniques, but probably habit and inhibiting feelings and beliefs.

As stated in Chapter One, the most natural and comfortable way to respond to a supervisory problem is the one that you are accustomed to. This is true even when that way of responding regularly fails to produce the desired results. Changing a habitual way of responding requires conscious effort and a willingness to endure the unnatural, awkward process of learning to respond some other way. Someone who is habitually nonassertive will have to initially force herself to act more assertively. A nonassertive response will occur almost automatically if she does not. Change will also be uncomfortable and anxiety provoking to the aggressive person. Someone who is habitually aggressive will find it uncomfortable to listen to others and to negotiate and compromise. Therefore, the first step in overcoming difficulties in being assertive is to become aware of your habitual response and make a conscious decision to change.

Your feelings and beliefs can also stop you from being assertive. Reacting with strong feelings makes it difficult to take a firm and objective view of problems. Strong feelings also affect your voice characteristics and body language. For example, when you are angry, you will come across as aggressive and when you feel guilty, you will seem nonassertive. To control how you appear to others, you must control your emotions. In order to be assertive, you will need to learn to act rather than simply react emotionally to your supervisory problems. This does not mean that you must deaden yourself emotionally. Deadening all negative emotions can lead to deadening of positive feelings. Everyone will sometimes become so angry or fearful or doubtful that she cannot respond in the best way. However, regaining objectivity requires that you be able to examine, understand, and control your emotional reactions. This chapter explores several feelings that make it difficult to be assertive, how they interfere with assertiveness, and how they can be overcome, as well as sexual and racial blocks to assertiveness and support for overcoming difficulties in being assertive.

Think of a situation in which you wanted to be assertive but were nonassertive or aggressive instead. How did you prevent yourself from being assertive? What were your feelings in this situation?

<hr>

Beliefs Cause Feelings
That Make It Difficult to Be Assertive

In order to talk about changing feelings, certain basic assumptions must be examined. Most people assume that feelings are caused by situations. Even their language reflects this assumption: "She made me angry," "He makes me feel guilty," "She scares me." These statements present feelings as inevitable products of other people's actions and therefore totally out of personal control. The belief that feelings are caused by events in the world does not leave much room for controlling or changing them.

> Betty was a supervisor in a beauty shop in a large department store. One of her major problems was the failure of her operators to clean up general areas of the shop. She was very reluctant to be assertive in asking them to clean up because in the past some of the operators had become very upset and cried when she confronted them. She assumed that if a person cried that meant that the person was devastated and that she was to blame for that person's unhappiness. Betty thought, "I can't confront my operators because they make me feel too guilty." However, examination of her assumptions about crying made it clear that the guilt did not come from the employees. Rather, she was making herself feel guilty when she caused someone to cry.

This book's approach to assertiveness is based on the assumption that other people do not make you feel anything. Other people offer you invitations to feel guilty, to get angry, to be afraid; you create your feelings by what you say to yourself or by what you believe about the situation. This model of feelings, developed by Albert Ellis (Ellis & Harper, 1975) and expressed in a number of books about feelings and attitudes (Burns, 1980; Dyer, 1976; Lazarus & Fay, 1975), assumes that you can change feelings about a situation if you change your understanding of the situation. For example, Betty could change her guilty feelings about being assertive by questioning the assumption that crying always indicates that the person is irreparably hurt by the criticism. Many people cry as a tension release. Even if someone is crying because she is hurt by a criticism, it is unlikely that she will suffer permanent psychological damage from that experience with hurt feelings. Most people are not so fragile that they need to be protected from ever being hurt or angry. If you believe that someone can be very upset and can recover from those upset feelings, you can stop creating guilty feelings when you upset or hurt someone. Therefore, Betty needs to learn to say to herself something like "My criticism may upset this operator, but I am not doing her any permanent damage. She can cope with being upset. I am not a bad person for upsetting her." If Betty could believe this, she would feel less guilty and would be more able to be assertive in asking her operators to clean up the shop.

Ellis, in his ABC Theory of Emotion (Ellis & Harper, 1975), says that it is not the situation (A), but the belief about the situation (B) that causes the emotion (C). For example, it is not your employee's anger at you (A) that makes you feel guilty (C). Your guilt is caused by your irrational belief (B) that if everyone does not like you at all times, it is a catastrophe. Freeing yourself from destructive emotions requires that you first become aware of your beliefs about events and situations and that you then dispute irrational beliefs.

Ellis describes 11 common irrational beliefs.

1. Everyone must like and approve of me at all times.
2. I must be perfect, totally competent, and productive in order to consider myself worthwhile.
3. It is a catastrophe when things are not the way I want them to be.
4. If something is dangerous or frightening, I should worry about the possibility of its happening.
5. Past events control my present behavior.
6. It is easier to avoid than to face certain difficulties in life.
7. Other people should act as I want, and I can and should control the behavior of those around me.
8. There is always a correct and perfect solution to a problem, and it is a catastrophe if I don't find it.
9. When people do something bad, they should be blamed and punished.
10. My happiness is externally caused and controlled.
11. I should have someone stronger than myself on whom to depend.

It is clear that we can have many other irrational beliefs, but Ellis believes that these 11 cause most human emotional disturbance and misery. These beliefs are irrational because not one of them is realistically possible in all situations. For example, there is no way to be effective as a supervisor and still be liked and approved of by everyone all of the time. An effective supervisor will inevitably upset her employees and be disapproved of at times.

The disturbing emotional reactions that irrational beliefs create can lead to nonassertive or aggressive responses. This example shows how that can happen.

A An employee points out to his supervisor that the supervisor gives very unclear directions.

B The supervisor believes that he must be perfect in order to be worthwhile. Since he realizes that he does give unclear directions sometimes, he feels he is being told he is worthless.

C The supervisor becomes very hurt and angry. Instead of assertively asking the employee to describe situations in which his directions are unclear and then working with the person to solve the problem, he becomes very defensive and apologizes profusely for his inadequacy. This leaves the employee doubting the supervisor's competence and effectiveness.

According to Ellis, the supervisor could change his feelings of distress by developing antidote rational beliefs that will not cause such negative reactions. The more rational belief he might hold would be something such as "I would like to give clear directions all of the time, but the fact that I don't does not mean I'm no good. What can I learn from this experience so that I can give better directions?"

David Burns (1980) uses a similar concept. He believes that problematic feelings are created by distorted beliefs, attitudes, and perceptions of the world. He calls these "cognitive distortions." Some common cognitive distortions include:

1. Labeling others or yourself as totally bad on the basis of one or a group of traits you dislike,

2. Magnifying the consequences of events or your power to control events or people out of proportion,

3. Personalizing other's behavior by assuming their actions are a reflection on you,

4. Mind-reading by believing you know why others act in certain ways,

5. Believing in rigid "shoulds" and "shouldn'ts" for your own and other's behavior.

When you have feelings that make you act in nonassertive or aggressive ways, examining these feelings can uncover the cognitive distortions that create them. You can learn to substitute more rational thoughts for the problematic ones and thereby free yourself for assertive behavior. Cognitive distortions and irrational thoughts have an almost automatic quality. You may feel very upset about something without even being aware that you are making damaging assumptions about the situation. Becoming aware of these beliefs is the important first step to developing a new, more objective view of the situation.

> Sun Li had a very poor working relationship with her assistant. The assistant sometimes complained about Sun Li and about her job to other workers. Sun Li magnified these complaints out of proportion until she believed the assistant hated her. She then became defensive and withdrawn and her assistant, who felt rejected, complained more and became quite sullen. Sun Li was eventually able to recognize that all workers have some complaints about their jobs and supervisors and that her assistant probably did not hate her. She was able to change her behavior towards her assistant and improve their relationship.

This chapter examines in detail some of the beliefs that create feelings that block assertion. To reiterate the basic principle: no one causes you to feel anything. Your feelings are caused by the way you look at the situation, not by the situation itself. To change your feelings, you need to change your beliefs about the situation.

◆

SELF-TEST

For each of the following situations, what are some of the irrational beliefs and cognitive distortions that might be involved?

1. Helen is very afraid to be assertive with her employees. She worries that she will not handle the situation exactly correctly and that any mistake on her part will permanently ruin her supervisory relationship.

2. Kwan is very angry because his head computer systems man is not as committed to his job as Kwan is. He works the required number of hours but is unwilling to put in large amounts of overtime because he feels his family is very important.

3. Jack feels very guilty when he confronts the three older people in his department.
4. Chris responds very aggressively to her employees. She is convinced that she cannot and should not change because she has always been this way.
5. Sean tends to stutter when he becomes nervous. He feels that this problem makes him a terrible supervisor. He also thinks that his manager, who is quite reserved with everyone, must dislike him because of it and wants to fire him.
6. Roberta is miserable in her job because she does not get the recognition and positive feedback she feels she deserves.
7. Carol anxiously asks her supervisor for advice on every decision. When she does make a mistake, she guiltily tells her supervisor what she has done, how sorry she is, and how hard she will work to make things right.
8. Caleb often avoids or postpones confrontations because confronting people seems to cause a lot of trouble. He doesn't like to make other people feel bad.

ANSWERS

1. Helen probably believes that she should be totally competent and that there is a correct and perfect solution to every situation that she must find. She is also magnifying the consequences of her action out of proportion.
2. Kwan believes in rigid "shoulds" for others' behavior. He is angry because he thinks that others should behave as he wants them to and that it is a catastrophe when things don't go his way.
3. Jack is probably operating from a belief that everyone should like him and should never be upset by what he does. There may also be a belief that he should be kind to his elders under all circumstances.
4. Chris seems to believe that the past totally determines the present and that change is impossible.
5. Sean is labeling himself as a terrible supervisor on the basis of one problem. He is also trying to read his manager's mind.
6. Roberta operates on the belief that the outside world determines her happiness. She also seems to believe it is a catastrophe when things are not as she wants them.
7. Carol probably believes that she should find someone wiser to lean on. She also seems to think that people who make mistakes should be punished.

8. Caleb seems to believe that it is easier to avoid than to face life's difficulties. He may also be personalizing others' upset feelings as a reflection on him.

Guilt

Guilt is a feeling that afflicts many supervisors. Since supervisors who are otherwise very assertive can find themselves becoming very nonassertive when they begin to feel guilty, it is important to explore the ways in which guilt is created and some techniques for confronting guilt-producing beliefs.

Not all guilt is bad. People who experience no guilt are called psychopaths and are very dangerous to themselves and to others. Guilt is a necessary and helpful feeling when it highlights violations of your own value system. For example, it is not inappropriate to feel somewhat guilty when you have been genuinely inconsiderate of a friend. This twinge of guilt can remind you that you do not value inconsiderate behavior in yourself or others. However, guilt is inappropriate when it is disabling or paralyzing. If you were to anguish for days over your inconsiderateness to your friend, the guilt would be inappropriate. Guilt feelings can also be inappropriate when they are the result of an irrational belief, cognitive distortion, or an old childhood message that is being employed in an adult situation to which it does not apply.

Sources of guilt

When you feel guilt, the feeling is not coming from the other person; it is coming from your own inner critic.

> Corinthia was assertive with almost all of her telephone operators; however, with one employee she was nonassertive. When she examined her feelings about this employee, she realized that the employee was a single parent like Corinthia herself and was having a very difficult time managing her child and her job. When Corinthia did confront the employee, the employee would become quite upset and would tell Corinthia all of her troubles managing as a single parent. Corinthia felt sorry for the employee and would usually feel guilty when she did confront her. When she further examined her beliefs, she realized that she was saying to herself, "This poor woman is hardly making it. Correcting her will push her over the edge. You are a hard-hearted person if you continue to confront her."

Corinthia is not feeling guilty because her employee says, "How can you pick on me? I can barely manage to hold my life together as it is." Her guilt comes from her distorted belief that she is totally responsible for her employee's survival. She believes that the employee is too fragile to survive being upset and that not upsetting the employee is more important than getting the work done. In addition, she may be operating from some old messages from her parents that say, "Don't hurt anyone's feelings. Nothing is worth really upsetting someone."

Several irrational beliefs can generate guilt feelings that may interfere with assertive action. If you feel that everyone should like and approve of you at all times, you may feel very guilty when someone reacts badly to an assertion. Her negative reaction will mean that you were "bad" and, therefore, should feel guilty. Or, if you believe you must be perfect all of the time, you can make yourself feel guilty. For example, if you believe that you should be kind and softspoken at all times, you may feel very guilty when, in a moment of frustration, you are assertive in a very loud voice. You may even hesitate to be assertive at all for fear you will not sound kind or softspoken. Both anticipation of guilty feelings and the feelings themselves inhibit assertive action. The belief that when people do not do what they should they ought to be blamed and punished may also lead you to blame and punish yourself when you fail to live up to your own rigid expectations.

Viewing situations in inaccurate or distorted ways can also create guilt feelings. For example, Corinthia, the supervisor described previously, has greatly overestimated her power to "make or break" her employee's life. This distorted view of the situation generates inappropriate guilt. Several of Burns's (1980) cognitive distortions can create guilt. For example, a supervisor may see that an employee is upset after an assertive interaction and magnify this upset into a feeling that she has permanently harmed the person. Or a supervisor might be demanding with an employee on one occasion and label herself as an overly demanding person. This labeling may discourage her from being assertive in other situations. A supervisor may also create guilt by personalizing, for example, by assuming that an employee's sulking after a confrontation is her fault. When she takes responsibility for the employee's choice of responses to her confrontation, she may make herself feel guilty. Inappropriate "shoulds" also cause guilt: a supervisor may secretly believe that she should be perfect, all-knowing, or all-powerful. This supervisor might then react to a very difficult employee by saying to herself "If only I were more effective as a supervisor, I could make this person change." This attitude can also create a great deal of anger because the employee's failure to change is seen as a direct indictment of the supervisor's effectiveness—the employee's actions are then taken very personally by the supervisor.

Another source of guilt feelings is outgrown "parent messages." Most people are exposed to a number of "shoulds" and "should nots" when growing up that, if taken literally, inhibit assertiveness. Think back to your own childhood. You probably heard people say, "If you can't say anything nice, don't say anything at all," "Don't rock the boat," "Be a lady or a gentleman," or "Don't upset your aunt. You never know what will happen." You may not even remember these messages now, but when you violate the "shoulds" and "should nots" you may feel a twinge of guilt. This guilt occurs even though the parent message either no longer applies or does not apply in the current situation.

> Peggy was the director of the guidance office in a high school. She was the youngest of the six people in the office. In her family, she had received very strong messages about respecting her elders. Although she did not realize it, her early programming persisted and made her very reluctant to confront her "elders" in the guidance department. She felt that she was being disrespectful by confronting them. Only after she realized that this early message was still present was she able to tell herself "Peggy, you are not being disrespectful when you ask your employees to do their jobs."

Parent messages are likely to be present when a supervisor comes from a family in which open and honest communication was strongly discouraged. If your parental programming was strong enough, you may have to learn to tolerate the discomfort of your own guilt and must gradually desensitize yourself to it in order to be assertive. After a few assertive confrontations, this guilt will probably subside enough to be bearable. If guilt over assertiveness is very strong because of early childhood programming, it may be necessary to get some counseling in order to be free enough from guilt to be assertive.

What parent messages did you hear that discourage assertion?

What are some of your irrational beliefs and cognitive distortions that might lead to guilt?

Guilt triggers

Guilt triggers are environmental stimuli that people are likely to respond to with guilt. They come from previous life experiences and personal value systems, differ for everyone, and may not be consciously associated with guilt. It is the automatic quality of these guilt triggers that makes them so detrimental. You may find yourself feeling vaguely guilty or uncomfortable; you may then become less assertive without really knowing why you are backing off. For example, one person may find that people with emotional problems almost always trigger guilt in her and therefore lead her to be less assertive. It is not inappropriate to make allowances for an employee with emotional problems, but deciding not to push that person should be a considered choice rather than an automatic response to a guilt trigger. Recognition of your guilt triggers can reduce their potency. When faced with a situation that triggers guilt in you, it may help to imagine yourself "nailing your feet to the floor." For example, if you always felt guilty confronting an employee with emotional problems, you might say to yourself, "I am a sucker for depressed people. I need to be especially careful not to be less assertive if she is feeling bad."

Are there particular situations that often leave you feeling uncomfortable or vaguely guilty? What are some of these guilt triggers?

Overcoming guilt

The first step in overcoming guilt is to become aware of your guilt feelings. Guilt can be particularly difficult to recognize because it occurs so quickly and automatically. This is especially true in the case of guilt triggers.

The second step in overcoming guilt is to uncover the parent messages, irrational beliefs, or cognitive distortions that might be creating guilt. Ask yourself "What am I saying to myself that makes me feel guilty?" You can almost imagine a nagging judge sitting inside of your head saying something like "You are really a rotten person. That poor employee is already depressed and you are going to make more demands on her. That's awful." To be able to distinguish inappropriate and damaging guilt from appropriate guilt, you must really hear what your inner critic is saying.

The third step in overcoming guilt is to develop antidote statements to dispute the damaging messages of your inner critic. You must examine these judgmental statements and substitute more rational ones. This is not unlike disputing a real critic who is unfairly criticizing you: "Wait a minute, inner critic. I am concerned about my depressed employee. That does not mean that I never should make any demands of her. I am not being a rotten person by doing my job as a supervisor." Sometimes it is helpful to chant an abbreviated statement about what is appropriate to yourself when confronting a situation that makes you feel guilty: "It is appropriate for me to ask my employee to do her job even if she is upset."

> Bud is managing the accounting department of a large hospital. He has been a supervisor for 15 years, but all of his experience prior to the last year has been with male accountants in an accounting firm. He feels very comfortable assertively supervising the men in this department but terribly uncomfortable being assertive with his female employees. He recognizes that he feels vaguely guilty being confrontive with a woman. When he explores his feelings, he realizes that he has come from a family where men were expected to treat women very protectively. He had been saying to himself "I'm responsible for protecting and taking care of women. It is terribly important that I not treat women roughly. Confronting a woman about a problem is being rough." Now when he needs to confront a female employee, he says to himself, "My role isn't to take care of and protect women here. My role is to get the work done. I am not doing anything wrong by confronting or upsetting a woman in this context."

Changing any feeling that makes assertiveness difficult takes time. Some backsliding, as well as overlooking of triggers, is inevitable. Initially, you may only become aware of inhibiting guilt feelings after the fact. It may take a great deal of work with yourself to overcome guilt messages that have been with you for a long time.

In summary, you can learn to overcome guilt by:
1. Becoming aware of guilt feelings and guilt triggers.
2. Uncovering irrational beliefs, cognitive distortions, and parent messages and deciding if the guilt is appropriate.
3. Developing an antidote statement.

Are there particular situations that often leave you feeling uncomfortable or vaguely guilty? What are some of these guilt triggers?

Have you ever been less assertive than you wanted to be because of guilt feelings? What were you saying to yourself to make yourself feel guilty? What would have been a rational antidote statement?

SELF-TEST

For each of the following situations, what would be a good antidote statement for guilt?

1. Jorge feels very guilty when he needs to be assertive with his superiors about something they are doing. In his family and in the strict Catholic school he went to, the most powerful message was "Be respectful and don't talk back to authority figures."

2. Francie has great difficulty confronting her secretary because the secretary will withdraw and sulk for a week after any confrontation. Francie then ends up feeling terribly guilty because she feels that if she isn't liked she is being mean or cruel.

3. Susan was very reluctant to ask for help from anyone because she believed that she should always know how to handle everything or she was completely inadequate as a supervisor. Her rigid "shoulds" made her feel guilty when she assertively sought information.

ANSWERS

1. Jorge might say something to himself such as "I'm not being disrespectful when I let my superiors know about problems that need to be solved to improve my effectiveness. I'm doing a good job."

2. Francie could say something to herself such as "I don't have to be liked by everyone to be a worthwhile person. Sometimes being disliked is a part of my job as a supervisor."

3. Susan could say something to herself such as "I don't always have to know the answers to be competent and effective. It's O.K. to ask for help."

Fear and Anxiety

Fear and anxiety are powerful emotions that can make being assertive difficult. Supervisors who are afraid or anxious may wait too long before being assertive about a problem, avoid being assertive altogether, or confront an issue but at the same time express fear or anxiety in their voice characteristics and body language. In these cases, the fear or anxiety has reduced the supervisor's freedom to be effectively assertive. Fear can also lead to aggressive behavior. Aggressiveness is often based on a fearful mistrust of others' intentions—a belief that it is necessary to attack first or to fight to protect yourself. Thus, a strong set of fearful assumptions about others can lead you to be aggressive when you may intend to be assertive. As with guilt, it is very important to be aware of fearful and anxious feelings so that they do not cause you to automatically react nonassertively or aggressively.

Fear can be a useful feeling. The person without any fear may act in the world with reckless disregard for possible problems. A reasonable amount of fear may help a person to consider the risks of a particular course of action. Sometimes, the consequences of an assertive action could be disastrous, and the action is not worth the risk. Fear is useful when it signals the need to realistically evaluate possible risks. It is not useful when based on vague, catastrophic fantasies nor when it is so strong that it paralyzes the ability to take action.

> Juanita was very afraid to discuss with her manager the problems that the general assistance workers in her department were having in completing the new assistance application forms. She knew that further training time was absolutely essential, but she could not bring herself to let the manager know about the need for training. When she explored her fear of asserting herself, she realized that she was assuming that the manager would believe that the problems were all her fault. Since the manager was inclined to be aggressive and to blame others for problems, her fear was not entirely unrealistic. However, she realized as she thought about the situation that the manager's initial response to any assertion was always aggressive but that he had not to Juanita's knowledge ever held assertiveness against someone in evaluating performance. In fact, later he often congratulated supervisors who called his attention to problems. Juanita decided that asserting herself was worth the risk.

Anxiety can also be useful when it is not overwhelming. When mild, it can energize you for action. For example, many performers feel as if stage fright makes them more alert.

Sources of fear and anxiety

One type of fear is the fear of the consequences of an action. Anytime someone is afraid of or anxious about consequences, there is an underlying "what if . . ." fantasy. Many times people are not aware of exactly why they are afraid. They keep their fears in an amorphous, monster-under-the-bed form and, like children frightened at night, they huddle under the covers and worry, but don't look under the bed. Since people often do not closely examine exactly what is frightening about a situation, they don't have the opportunity to see whether the fears are realistic or are catastrophic fantasies.

One major difficulty in assessing "real" risks in a situation is the tendency to distort reality through irrational beliefs or cognitive distortions. All of the irrational ideas and distortions explored earlier can interfere with a realistic assessment of the risks in a situation.

> Frank had recently been promoted within a large library system. He was unfamiliar with aspects of his new job and found himself unsure of what to do in some situations. He was afraid to ask his manager for help because he felt that he should be perfectly competent and effective at all times. He assumed that if his manager knew that he was unsure of himself, he would be demoted or fired. His irrational fear caused him to take much longer to learn his new job than if he would have asked for help.

Another type of fear is an underlying mistrust or fear that others will get the better of you if you are not constantly defensive and vigilant. One origin of this type of fear is messages about others transmitted in the family. A child might hear, for example, "You have to be tough in this world and fight for everything you get. Don't let anyone push you around!" These beliefs may be confirmed by experiences in the family or neighborhood. For example, a child who attends a school dominated by gangs of bullies might come to believe that you must constantly be on guard with others. Experiences in the work world may also confirm this mistrust of others. If a supervisor is aggressive because he fears that his employees will try to do as little work as possible, he may provoke the very behavior he is afraid of and, thus, confirm his assumptions. Employees who are treated aggressively will be less involved and less motivated and will tend to act in passive-resistant ways. This fear of being taken advantage of may also be supported by irrational beliefs and cognitive distortions. For example, the supervisor may believe that others should understand the job without being told, may take every employee behavior personally, and may label people as totally untrustworthy on the basis of mistakes. The same type of assumptions that lead to mistrust and defensiveness can also lead to anger.

Paulo was the head of a pharmacy in a hospital. He had always had to battle to be recognized and successful and as a result he had a tendency to be defensive and mistrustful. Whenever a critical order that required formulation came in, Paulo would assign it very defensively. He would say, "Make sure that you do this right. Any mistakes mean trouble." His employees, who were all quite experienced, resented his attitude.

Overcoming fear
The first step in overcoming fear of negative consequences is to ask "What exactly is the worst possible thing that could happen in this situation?" It is often useful to exaggerate the worst possible outcome. If you are going to scare yourself, do an extra good job; carry the catastrophic fantasy to absolutely ridiculous extremes. Once you have exaggerated the fantasy, it is then appropriate to ask "What's really likely to happen?" For some reason, taking the fantasy to its most ridiculous extreme makes it easier to rationally examine the real risks in the situation.

Christine knew she needed to confront a very aggressive employee about failure to complete paperwork that was essential to that person's job, but she was afraid to. When she examined her thoughts, she uncovered a catastrophic fantasy of being fired by her boss that she exaggerated by saying to herself "If I confront this employee, he will go to the boss and tell him I am totally incompetent as a supervisor. The boss will believe him and will then give me a very negative rating and put me on probation. I will probably be unable to perform under those conditions and will therefore be fired. Since I am being fired for incompetence, I will not be able to get another good job. I'll probably be working in a low-paying, low-status job for the rest of my life." After exaggerating her fantasy Christine was able to say to herself: "It is true that my boss might wonder if I am doing something wrong as a supervisor if this employee comes to him to complain. It is highly unlikely that he will fire me as a result of any questions that this interaction may raise. I am effective in many areas of my job and will not be seen as totally incompetent because of one situation."

Asking "What is really likely to happen?" and receiving a realistic answer will be very difficult for someone bound by overly rigid expectations of himself and of the world. Thus, you need to examine your assessment of risks to see if you are magnifying the risks out of proportion through distorted beliefs. For example, if you believe everyone must always like you, an angry employee may seem like a catastrophe. If you know that you have a tendency to operate on irrational beliefs, you will need to ask yourself both "What's really likely to happen?" and "What's really so awful about that?" Tipoffs to possible irrationality are extreme statements like "He'll never trust me again" and "This will ruin our relationship forever."

There may be times when the real risks involved in being assertive are greater than the potential benefits. For example, someone working for a manager who has fired the last six people who have in any way questioned any of his suggestions is being realistic to assume that assertiveness carries a high risk of being fired. In two cases of this nature in assertiveness workshops, one person decided that the stakes were high enough that she had to be assertive and was fired; another person decided being assertive was not worth the risk.

It is important in deciding whether to be assertive to weigh both the short-term and the long-term costs of not being assertive. In many cases, being assertive may carry with it short-term risks or problems, but the long-range consequences of not being assertive may make it worth the risk. For example, an employee may be prone to get very hostile when confronted about a problem. This hostility creates tension in the office now; however, not being assertive and allowing problems to continue may create a precedent with other employees in the long run that may make the short-term risks worth confronting. It is also useful when considering the risks of being assertive to ask yourself how likely it is that each consequence will occur and how serious it would be. Some consequences may be likely to occur but not very serious if they do occur. For example, an employee may be quite likely to sulk when confronted, but this would not cause too many problems. Other consequences may be unlikely but potentially much more serious. An employee could, for example, file a lawsuit. In examining the risks, ask yourself, "Can I live with the negative consequences that might occur when I assert myself?" If you can't, ask yourself if there is anything you can do to prevent negative consequences. In other words, decide what you can do to cover yourself.

> Simon wanted to ask his manager to give him responsibility for job assignments within his unit, but he was afraid to ask. When he examined his fear, he discovered that he imagined that his manager would feel as if Simon was questioning his competence and would be very insulted. He also imagined that if he were given the job, he would make some serious errors in assignments that would cause everyone to question his judgment. He exaggerated these fears by imagining that the manager would be so insulted that he would never trust Simon again and would ultimately have him transferred or fired. He also imagined that he would misassign an employee and everyone would say, "I knew you were incompetent." As he examined these fears, he realized that the worst that was really likely was that the manager could feel threatened if he was not very careful in how he presented the proposal. He also realized that responsibility did carry risks, but that he generally did not make bad judgments and would be unlikely to make a serious error in job assignments. Not asking for this change meant that his employees were being placed in jobs in which they could not do their best work and productivity was reduced. Simon decided that he could protect himself by carefully assuring the manager that he was not questioning his authority, and that he could live with the risk of making a mistake. Therefore, he decided to be assertive.

A fear of being taken advantage of is more difficult to overcome than fear of consequences because this kind of fear is often a deeply ingrained aspect of a person's approach to the world. The first step in overcoming this kind of fear is to recognize the feeling and the negative assumptions that are a part of it. Then, it is necessary to consciously dispute these beliefs: "It isn't necessarily true that everyone is out to do as little as possible," "Others won't get the better of me," "When others make mistakes that doesn't mean that they are trying to take advantage of me." More about uncovering these types of assumptions is found in this chapter in the section on anger.

In summary, you can learn to overcome fear of the consequences of an action by:
1. Uncovering your catastrophic fantasy and exaggerating it.
2. Asking yourself "What's really likely to happen?" and being alert for irrational beliefs and cognitive distortions.
3. Weighing the risks of being assertive and the costs of not being assertive.
4. Assessing what you need to do to protect yourself from negative consequences.

You can learn to overcome fear of being taken advantage of by:
1. Recognizing your fear and the assumptions behind it.
2. Disputing your assumptions.

Have you ever been less assertive than you wanted to be because of fear? What did you imagine would happen if you were assertive? Blow it up! What is the worst possible thing that could have happened? How likely to happen and how serious were the consequences? What were the costs of not being assertive? How could you have protected yourself?

Are you afraid that others will take advantage of you? How do you act? What could you say to dispute this feeling?

Overcoming anxiety
Sometimes assertiveness is blocked not by a focused fear but rather by a generalized nonverbal anxiousness or nervousness that makes it difficult to appear confident and relaxed. For example, a supervisor who blushes, stammers, uses anxious mannerisms, speaks tensely or in a squeaky voice, sits very stiffly, holds his breath, or hyperventilates will have a difficult time appearing assertive. Confronting catastrophic fantasies and irrational beliefs will help reduce the overall anxiety level in a given situation; however, it may also be necessary to use nonverbal relaxation techniques to control the physical anxiety symptoms that reduce effectiveness.

Anxiety can also inhibit assertiveness because a supervisor can become afraid of being anxious. In this anxiety spiral, any situation that might arouse anxiety triggers fear of an anxious reaction. Recognizing that she is already anxious, the supervisor becomes even more afraid of being anxious, which makes her more anxious and more afraid of being anxious, and so on. She avoids assertiveness because she believes that if she becomes anxious she will completely fall apart.

Barbara was generally a rather nervous person. She was startled by loud conversation. When she did have to discuss something with an employee or with a manager, she would find herself stammering, blushing, losing her train of thought, and otherwise becoming so nervous that she felt very ineffective. Not only did her nervous mannerisms make her appear hesitant and nonassertive, but she was also so uncomfortable with experiencing that anxious feeling that she had a tendency to avoid situations in which she might feel it.

To break the anxiety spiral, it is important to use techniques that can help to control anxious reactions, but also to accept that you can become anxious and uncertain and still function. Anxiety will not necessarily cause you to be unable to act rationally. Although nonanxious voice characteristics and body language certainly contribute to assertive impact, it is probably still better to act in certain situations with blushing or hesitation than not to act in the situation at all.

In addition to the quick techniques for reducing nervousness and anxiety to be described here, there are many excellent stress management books that provide useful activities for reducing your overall anxiety level (Tubesing, 1981; Woolfolk & Richardson, 1978). If you are generally anxious, it may be very important to find some deep relaxation methods that you can practice on a regular basis over many weeks. These techniques require finding a quiet place and perhaps lying down in a comfortable position. A sample relaxation script using tensing and relaxing of muscles follows.

Make yourself as comfortable as possible, loosen any tight clothing that you can, and get relaxed in your chair. Just focus on your body and feel the tension flow out as you relax more and more. Now, stretch out your legs, lift them slightly off the floor, point your feet back toward your face as much as you can. Tighten your toes, your ankles, your calves, and your thighs—tighten and tighten, as tense as you can. Now relax . . . feel the warmth of relaxation in your legs and feet as you relax. Feel how pleasant it is to feel that warmth as it flows through your legs even to your toes.

Now tighten your buttocks and stomach as hard as you can. Tighten and tighten. Hold it a bit more. Now, relax . . . buttocks and stomach. Notice the pleasant contrast between the relaxed feeling you experience now and the tightness you experienced a moment ago. Take a deep breath now. As you slowly let it out, also let out the remaining tension in your feet, legs, buttocks, and stomach.

Now tighten your back muscles, your chest, and the muscles just under your armpits. Harder. Hold it a little bit longer. Now relax. Let yourself feel the tranquil flow of relaxation as it moves up your body into your back and chest. Imagine the word *calm* or the word *relax* and think that word to yourself slowly about ten times. Take a deep breath and let it out slowly as the tension drains away.

Extend your arms and make two fists. Tighten your triceps, your forearms, and your fists. Hard. Really hard. Then let your arms fall to your lap with the pull of gravity. Relax. Notice the tingling sensation of relaxation in your fingers and hands. Feel the warmth in your arms. Enjoy this beautiful relaxation. Imagine a peaceful, tranquil scene that is really relaxing. Picture that scene and how warm and comfortable that image is for you.

Now, hunch up your shoulders as though you are trying to touch them to your ears. Tighten your neck, too. Tighter and tighter. Hold it just a bit more so that your neck actually shakes. Now, relax. Feel the heaviness in your shoulders and the warm feeling of relaxation. Take a deep breath and slowly let it out. Imagine saying to yourself, "I am calm and relaxed." Enjoy the comforting feeling of being tension free.

Now, open your mouth as wide as you can. Wider. Hold it. Now, relax. Feel the warm, tingling sense in your face. Let your mouth hang open as it relaxes. Breathe deeply. Now, furrow your brow and tighten your cheek and face muscles into a tight grimace. Tighter. Hold it. Now, relax. Feel the flow of warm relaxation enter your face and eyes. Enjoy the wonderful feeling of relaxation through your entire body.

Now take a deep breath and hold it. As you let it out fully, let any tension drain from your whole body. Imagine that your body is being immersed in a warm fluid which absorbs any remaining tension. Feel your body sink into this pleasant fluid little by little and the tension seep from your body. First your feet and legs, then your torso, your arms, your neck, and your head. Breathe deeply and enjoy this relaxed feeling.*

Learning to tense and relax muscles of the body, learning to relax the mind through guided imagery, or increasing concentration and calm through meditation will enable you to handle any

---

*Adapted from P. Jakubowski & A. J. Lange. *The assertive option: Your rights and responsibilities.* Champaign, Ill.: Research Press, 1978.

stressful situation more effectively. However, most of these techniques are not useful for calming yourself down in the midst of a
tense confrontation. Rarely do you have the luxury of saying to an
employee "I need to confront you about what you just did, but first
I need to go into my office and relax for half an hour." Fortunately
there are several relaxation "quickies" that can be used just before
confronting an employee to help maintain your calm throughout
the confrontation.

The most important quick stress management technique is deep
breathing. One reason this is so important is that most people have
a tendency to hold their breath when they are under stress. Holding your breath increases the physiological stress response and increases the anxiousness. Anxiety can be thought of as "excitement
without oxygen."

> Inhale deeply and exhale as if you are blowing out a candle.
> Repeat this deep breathing 5 or 10 times, gradually deepening
> the breaths. It is sometimes helpful to inhale for a count of
> 4 and exhale for a count of 4. As you inhale and exhale, try
> to let your shoulders drop and relax. This activity may be
> done in your office, in the hall, or even in the room with
> an employee.

Another technique that can be used to produce a sense of calm is a
short meditation.

> Close your eyes, take a few deep breaths, and let your shoul-
> ders drop. Now imagine that as you breathe in you are inhal-
> ing warm, golden light. Feel this warm, golden light filling
> your lungs and then washing through your whole body, bath-
> ing each cell in warmth and light. Feel this light washing
> anxiety and tension out of your body and filling each part of
> you. Now imagine the word *calm* written in large letters in
> front of you. As you see these letters, let yourself experience
> calm feelings filling your whole body. Now, imagine that you
> are surrounding yourself with a strong, clear plastic shield.
> This plastic shield will seal in the calm feelings, and anything
> negative from the outside world will bounce off the shield.
> Feel the calm and the warm light filling you within your
> shield and then come back to your ordinary world.

Each person develops his own techniques for calming down. For
some people, physical activity is calming, so a walk through the
halls before a stressful conversation might be helpful. For someone
else, talking to a colleague about a problem might help to reduce

tension. Whatever techniques work for you, it is vital that you develop some repertoire of relaxation strategies to help you to be able to be calmly assertive.

In summary, you can learn to overcome anxiety by:

1. Realizing you can still act rationally when you're anxious.
2. Practicing relaxation techniques.
3. Using deep breathing or a short meditation before confrontations.

Have you ever been less assertive than you wanted to be because of anxiety? What happened when you were anxious? What did you do to manage the anxiety? What could you have done?

SELF-TEST

For the following situations, substitute more rational thoughts that would minimize fear and anxiety.

1. "If I don't do this project exactly as my supervisor wants, he surely will be very disappointed in me. He'll think I'm worthless and do terrible work if I make any mistakes. I have to be perfect, or he'll never trust me again."
2. "I just can't trust my workers to do anything if I don't watch them constantly. I know that they resent me for having power over them and would do anything they could to irritate me or make me look bad—all workers are like that."
3. "I'm so anxious that I can't confront my employee. I'm sure that my voice will crack and my hands will shake. I'm really going to seem so weak and make a huge mess of this confrontation."

ANSWERS

1. "My supervisor may be disappointed in me if I make many mistakes on this project, but he won't think I'm worthless, untrustworthy, or do terrible work. He's not perfect, so why would he expect me to be?"
2. "Some workers may resent their superiors and try to irritate them or make them look bad but that is not true in most cases. If I don't hover over my workers, they may feel that I trust them and do better work. I need to give them the benefit of the doubt."
3. "It doesn't matter if I'm anxious when I confront my employee; the point is to confront him. I can be anxious and

still do my job. If I take some deep breaths and relax my body, I'll calm down."

◆

Doubt

Another emotion that makes it difficult to be assertive is doubt. It is difficult to be assertive when you are uncertain about your right to be assertive, or when you have convinced yourself that your assertiveness will fail. However, doubt and uncertainty can be very useful in stimulating you to examine your choice of action and to prepare a well-thought-out case for a particular stand.

Doubt and uncertainty can be particularly useful in a situation new to a supervisor. A supervisor who has just been promoted or has been transferred to a new department should feel somewhat tentative about her actions until she has had time to assess the situation. Aggressive supervisors are not doubtful even when they have very little clear data about a situation and should be feeling some hesitation. One characteristic of an aggressive approach is to confront before there has been an analysis of the situation. This "shoot-from-the-hip" approach can create some hard feelings and contribute to a tense and uncooperative climate. Acting on the basis of extremely limited data may be as destructive as failing to take a stand when the facts are clear. Any action should follow a thorough assessment of the situation. The assertive supervisor is not afraid to take a stand but does so on the basis of considered analysis.

Doubt is not useful when a supervisor has researched the situation, has a right to be assertive, and still feels uncertain and hesitant. Excessive doubt can lead a supervisor to back down on issues when she should stand firm. Also, since uncertainty is expressed in voice characteristics and body language, doubt can encourage the other person in an interaction to become more demanding. A classic example of this situation is a parent who says in a doubtful tone, "Johnny, you probably should go to bed." Johnny hears the uncertainty and says, "Ah, Dad, I really want to see this program. Let me stay up just another hour."

Sources of doubt
One source of doubt and hesitation is negative pep talks. Imagine a coach giving his team the following pep talk before the big game: "You know that there is no chance that you can win. Clearly the

other team is much better than you are. The best you can possibly hope for is not to get massacred too badly. Just try not to lose by too many points in this game." How well do you think that the team would play? Yet many supervisors chronically give themselves negative pep talks about their assertive interventions.

> Katrina had promoted an employee who also happened to be a friend to a position as director of a project in her department. After several months and extended discussions with the employee, it became apparent that the promotion was not working out. She was very hesitant to talk to the person about being demoted because she knew that the person would be upset and because she was saying to herself "This is going to be a disaster. I'll never be able to handle her reaction. I'm sure that I'll handle this in a way that will ruin our working relationship and friendship forever."

Our images of how things will go exert a powerful influence on actual events (Maltz, 1969). Picturing yourself failing in your assertive action makes it much less likely that you will succeed. This kind of discouraging self-talk creates doubt and erodes confidence.

A second source of doubt is lack of clarity about your legitimate rights as a supervisor. Being assertive requires a clear sense of entitlement, the belief that you have the right to act assertively. When a supervisor is not sure of her rights, it is very easy for employees to play on this uncertainty and to sidetrack her in a confrontation. At the other end of the spectrum is the supervisor who is not clear about the rights of her employees and can aggressively infringe on their legitimate rights and create frustration and friction. Both supervisors and employees have rights and responsibilities to each other in the work environment. You must be clear about your legitimate rights as a supervisor and your responsibilities to your employees. As Jakubowski and Lange (1978) have pointed out, each right carries with it the responsibility to respect the other person's rights.

Overcoming doubt

The best protection from doubt is to do a good job of thinking through the situation before asserting yourself. The supervisor who asserts herself without doing adequate homework—who has not decided what she wants to accomplish by being assertive and has not checked out the facts of the situation—is very vulnerable to doubt and likely to be ineffective.

Glenda was the new curriculum supervisor for special education for a large school district. On her initial visits to schools,
she recognized that some special education teachers were not
following district guidelines. She knew that if she confronted
these teachers without more information, she would be somewhat uncertain of her position. She asked the teachers many
questions about past practice, about their understanding of
district guidelines, and about their principal's position on the
special education curriculum. She was then prepared to confront the problem with a sense of clarity and certainty that
made her much more effective in her confrontation.

If you have done your homework and still have doubts, you
may need to confront this inappropriate doubt by stopping negative pep talks and substituting positive pep talks or positive
images. When you begin to erode your confidence with negative
self-statements, it is important to immediately think, "What can
I say to myself or what can I picture that would support success
and confidence?"

Katrina, faced with confronting a friend about demotion, prepared herself by thinking the following: "It will be hard to let
my friend know I am giving that responsibility to someone
else, but I can handle it. Even if she's upset, I can be firm and
clear." She also pictured herself remaining firm even though
her friend argued and pleaded with her.

In order to be confidently assertive, it is also important for supervisors to be very clear about their rights as a supervisor. (For
more general assertive rights see Alberti and Emmons [1975] or
Bloom, Coburn, and Pearlman [1975].)

Supervisors have the right to:

1. Say directly what they want or expect from others,
2. Ask employees to do the job they were hired to do,
3. Say no when it is in the company's best interest even if
    others don't like it,
4. Insist that employees be at work for the time they are paid
    to work,
5. Require that employees keep the commitments they have
    made,
6. Confront failure to perform even if it upsets employees,
7. Ask employees to stop engaging in behaviors that keep
    others from doing their work,
8. Set appropriate limits on how employees express disagree-
    ments,

9. Insist that employees follow fair and reasonable direct orders,
10. Ask employees to follow company rules and policies,
11. Be confronted directly when someone is upset about the supervisor's work,
12. Have a major say in establishing goals, priorities, and job assignments for their employees,
13. Ask management to support their authority as supervisors,
14. Ask management for the resources to do the job,
15. Be kept informed about data relevant to their jobs,
16. Be listened to with respect even if others disagree with them,
17. Decide whether they will accept responsibility for solving other people's problems,
18. State their disagreement with others or with company policy.

This list of supervisory rights is not meant to be exhaustive, but it includes some of the most basic of supervisory rights. These rights can be used effectively to support supervisory confidence in a confrontation.

> Rosetta found that one employee's reaction *really* stopped her in a confrontation. The employee asked, "Well, what should I do about all of my responsibilities at home? How can you expect me to be at work on time?" She felt an obligation to solve the employee's problem and spent a great deal of time suggesting ways for the employee to improve her situation at home. If she had been clear about her right to decide whether to solve other people's problems, she could have said, "I don't really know, but I want you to work it out so that you can be here on time."

Sometimes it is helpful to chant a supervisory right to yourself on the way to an assertive interaction. For example, on the way to a conference with a manager about the manager's tendency to undercut the supervisor's authority, the supervisor might say to herself, "I have the right to ask management to support my authority as a supervisor. I have the right to ask management to support my authority as a supervisor. . . ." However, not only do supervisors have rights; they also have responsibilities. For example, supervisors have the responsibility to:

1. Listen to others with respect even if they disagree with what the others say,
2. Let others know clearly what is expected from them,

3. Communicate employees' concerns to management,
4. Give others clear feedback on how they are doing,
5. Let others know directly when they are dissatisfied with their work,
6. Support company rules and policies,
7. Keep others informed about data relevant to their jobs,
8. Give employees a fair hearing before making judgments about them,
9. Allow employees leeway in the accomplishment of a job instead of insisting that everything be done their way,
10. Acknowledge and reward excellence,
11. Take action to correct conditions that endanger employees or prevent them from doing their jobs.

The nonassertive supervisor may take her responsibilities seriously but not her rights, and the aggressive supervisor might emphasize her rights but fail to respect and acknowledge others' rights. Assertive supervision requires a balanced awareness of both the rights and the responsibilities of the supervisory role.

In summary, you can learn to overcome doubt by:
1. Doing your homework—knowing what you want to accomplish and the facts of the situation.
2. Substituting positive pep talks for negative pep talks.
3. Focusing on supervisory rights and responsibilities.

———————◆———————

Have you ever been less assertive than you wanted to be because of doubt? Did you give yourself a negative pep talk in that situation? How did it influence your confidence? What kind of positive images could you have substituted for the negative ones? What were your supervisory rights in that situation?

Think of a situation in which you wanted to be assertive but did not know all of the facts in the situation. What information did you need to know before acting? How did you find out this information?

———————◆———————

SELF-TEST

For each of the following situations, specify what supervisory right could be used as an antidote to doubt.
1. Several of your workers smoke in the warehouse during their breaks. Smoking is forbidden in the warehouse, but your company does not have a lounge or lunchroom where employees can smoke.

2. You have told one of your employees to complete a task that she is having great difficulty with. She does not want to do it.
3. The few typewriters in your company are always in heavy demand. You need one for 2 weeks to complete a project.
4. One of your employees has a lot of family problems and talks to his co-workers as an outlet. This interferes with others getting their work done.

ANSWERS

1. It is your right to ask employees to follow company rules even if they become upset. You may want to try to establish a lounge where employees can smoke.
2. You have the right to require that employees keep the commitments they have made.
3. You have the right to ask management for the resources to do the job.
4. You have the right to ask employees to stop engaging in behaviors that keep others from doing their work.

Anger

One of the primary feelings that promotes an aggressive reaction is anger. As is the case with other feelings, anger can be very useful. Anger tells you when you are being infringed upon. Angry feelings often signal the need to be assertive. Someone who is out of touch with his own anger is like someone without physical pain. A person who does not experience physical pain is very vulnerable to hurting himself and not knowing it; someone who cannot feel anger can be damaged by others without knowing it. Anger, therefore, serves a very important function. However, rage, or extreme anger, does not promote effective action. Extremely angry feelings are expressed nonverbally and these nonverbal signals may appear to be very aggressive. There is also a tendency to be blaming and judgmental when very angry instead of objective and this generates defensiveness. Anger is also not useful when it is based on distorted perceptions or irrational beliefs. Although it is useful to be aware of angry feelings, it is not useful to be constantly angry and frustrated. Learning to control anger is a very important part of learning to be assertive.

Keith very much wanted to be more assertive. He frequently got feedback from his manager and from his employees that his approach to many supervisory tasks was aggressive. He realized that one problem was his rage at his employees. He felt very strongly that he should not have to explain any tasks to them. He was convinced that they were deliberately doing as little as possible to see what they could get away with. Whenever a problem did arise, he immediately became very angry and would aggressively berate the employee. Later he would realize that he might have been unreasonable, but rarely did this realization come soon enough to prevent damage to his relationship with the employee. When he examined his expectations for his employees, he began to realize that he was making very unrealistic demands. His employees were doing poorly, not as a way to do as little as possible, but because they were inexperienced and lacked his understanding of the job.

Sources of anger

Assumptions about what particular behaviors mean constitute one of the main sources of anger. For example, an employee may come in and ask questions while a supervisor is on the phone and this may infuriate the supervisor. Although this behavior is irritating, if the supervisor is really furious, he is making some anger-producing assumptions. He might be assuming that the employee has no respect for him as a supervisor, or is interrupting him to annoy him. He may believe that such behavior means the employee is generally rude and inconsiderate and will not behave in appropriate ways in any other situations. Any of these assumptions would be likely to generate anger. It is often not the behavior that is infuriating but the assumptions about what that behavior means.

Once a person develops an assumption about a behavior, he tends to operate as if that understanding were the only possible explanation, that is, as if that assumption is the truth. There are usually many possible explanations for a set of facts. For example, if your best friend walked by you on the street without saying hello, she might have been angry, preoccupied, or upset, she might not have seen you, or she might not want to be your friend. Everyone has a desire to try to understand what others' behavior means, and the explanations we adopt will strongly influence how we feel and act. If you believed that your friend was snubbing you, your reactions would certainly be different than if you believed that she didn't see you. Therefore, there are two important things to remember. One is that assumptions are guesses about what something means. Until they are checked out, they should be treated as hunches, not as the truth. The other is that there are many possible explanations of the same facts. A person who is frustrated often leaps to the most negative of all the possible alternatives.

Martin was supervising the engineering department of a small production company. One engineer in this department was very bright and very knowledgeable, but for the last several months had been involving herself in little but busywork. Martin assumed that the engineer was uninterested in the job and was unmotivated; however, as he reflected on the situation, he remembered that the employee had made a serious mistake on her first project. He further realized that the employee did not fully understand what had gone wrong. When he realized that the employee could be afraid to invest herself in another project, he talked to the employee openly about what had happened and was able to remotivate her.

Although in some cases certain behaviors may really mean that the employee doesn't want to do a good job, operating as if this is the case when you don't know what the behavior means creates unnecessary anger and makes it more difficult to be objective. Giving the other person the benefit of the doubt and seeking the most benign explanation of the problems can help to reduce anger.

Negative assumptions are sometimes based on anger-producing irrational beliefs and cognitive distortions that need to be examined and disputed. One irrational belief that can lead to anger is the belief that if you try hard enough, you can control anyone's behavior and get him to change. Sometimes you may feel that if you give up your anger, the employee will have no motivation to change. You do not have to be enraged in order to work for change. You can accept others as they are and still do what is realistic to bring about change. Another irrational belief that leads to anger is the notion that if things don't go the way they should, it must be someone's fault. This way of looking at the world leads you to blame people when things don't go as you want rather than taking an objective problem-solving approach. Not focusing on blame enables you to be more objective and less angry.

One of the cognitive distortions (Burns, 1980) that causes anger is labeling. For example, an employee who talks too loud at times may be labeled as a crude and raucous person. More anger is then directed at this person than talking too loudly would merit. Labeling emphasizes the negative and overlooks any of the person's positive qualities. Mind-reading can also be responsible for negative assumptions that cause anger: "He doesn't care about me" or "He doesn't like the job." Magnifying events out of proportion can also cause anger. For example, someone who tends to magnify things might respond to an employee's failure to answer one phone call on the required three rings as if that were a total disaster and react with rage. Personalization is another common distortion that can cause anger. Supervisors often see employee's problem behaviors as a personal affront. They assume that lack of performance means employees don't value them. Rigid "shoulds" and "shouldn'ts" are another prime source of anger. A supervisor may genuinely believe that employees should have the same work motivations as he does. He may believe that all employees should be self-motivated and that providing extensive supervision is a violation of the proper supervisory role. With these beliefs, a normal supervisory job—in which some employees share the supervisor's values and some do not and in which there are unmotivated employees—becomes a constant source of rage. Regardless of what should be, the world is as it is. People differ in values and life-style. Tenaciously hanging on to a belief that the world ought to live up to your expectations is guaranteed to generate a lot of frustration.

Anger can be a useful feeling when it alerts you to the need for change. Anger that is based on irrational beliefs and cognitive distortions is often out of proportion to the event and mainly serves to interfere with handling the situation objectively.

Think of a situation in which someone was doing something that you didn't like. What specifically (behaviors that you can see or hear) was the person doing? What did you assume that the behaviors meant? What other assumptions would explain the same behaviors?

Anger triggers
Most people have anger triggers as well as guilt triggers. Employees sometimes use these anger triggers to sidetrack supervisors from confrontations. Once the supervisor is very angry and defensive, he is less able to keep the conversation focused on the problems, so the employee may get out of the situation.

Perry, a supervisor of a janitorial service, was extremely sensitive to any suggestion that he might not have carefully considered the alternatives before making a decision. Since he prided himself on his rationality, questioning of this kind was an insult. He found that he could maintain a calm objective approach with an employee unless that person questioned his judgment. One employee, Carla, knew Perry's anger trigger and used it to her advantage. When he confronted her about taking too long on a job, she questioned his ability to estimate how long a job should take, saying he always forgot something that needed to be done. At that point his resolve to be objective broke down and he found himself angrily defending his ability to schedule jobs. He became so angry that he ended the confrontation without resolving the issue.

A special kind of anger trigger is a "red-flag" person; there are some people toward whom you feel angry before they even say or do anything. Although you may develop some reasons to be angry with them after the fact, in reality the anger preceded the reasons. In this situation, the person often is either a reminder of some person from the past or a reminder of some part of yourself that is rejected.

Don found himself constantly angry at one of his employees. Her performance was good and the other employees liked her, yet Don found himself irritated when she entered the room. As he examined his feelings, he realized that she reminded him of his somewhat bossy older sister. He was reacting to this employee with the same feelings he had experienced with his sister. Once he identified the source of his anger, he was able to see the ways that this employee and his sister differed and was less angry.

Combating anger triggers requires enough awareness of your sensitive areas to be able to interrupt the automatic anger process. For example, Perry could interrupt the anger process by saying to himself "I don't have to be defensive about my ability to schedule jobs. By defending myself I just get sidetracked from the issue." Awareness can deactivate these anger triggers.

What are some of your anger triggers? Do you know any red-flag people? What are they like? Why might you feel anger toward these people?

Overcoming anger

When working to overcome your anger, examine your negative assumptions about the other person's behavior and come up with an explanation that is less anger producing. Uncover the irrational beliefs and cognitive distortions that lead you to anger. Being aware of your anger triggers, such as red-flag people, can also help you to overcome anger.

Another very important antidote to anger is empathy (Tavris, 1983). One useful assumption is that even though others' behavior may look stupid or self-defeating to you, they would not be doing it if it didn't make some sense to them. A powerful way to reduce anger is to put yourself in the other person's shoes, to try to understand the situation from his perspective.

> Sylvia was the nursing supervisor on a psychiatric unit. One employee would often approach patients in a way that Sylvia felt was very destructive. The nurse lectured the patients about all of the reasons they should not feel the way they did. Sylvia knew that this kind of intervention was not only unhelpful, but sometimes could actually make the patient feel worse. This nurse's approach infuriated her. When she talked to her, she discovered that the woman had come from a family in which people helped each other by lecturing. Since the nurse had had no real psychiatric training, she felt that what she was doing was the most helpful thing that she could do. By understanding her employee's perspective, Sylvia could be more understanding in working to correct the problem.

Understanding the other person's perspective may not make the behavior acceptable; however, it will often reduce the rage that can occur when you see someone behaving in a destructive way. The question to ask is "Why might this person be doing what he is doing? How could this make sense to him?"

In summary, you can learn to overcome anger by:

1. Examining negative assumptions and looking for more benign alternatives.
2. Looking for and disputing irrational beliefs and cognitive distortions.
3. Watching for anger triggers, especially red-flag people.
4. Empathizing—putting yourself in the other person's shoes.

Have you ever been less assertive than you wanted to be because of anger? What were your beliefs or assumptions in the situation? What could you have said to yourself that would have been less anger-provoking? How could you have empathized with the other person?

SELF-TEST

For each of the following situations, substitute a more positive assumption for the negative anger-producing one.

1. Frank's new salesman is slow in turning in his paperwork. Frank thinks he's lazy or doesn't want to do it.
2. One of Jenny's employees is generally very friendly but lately will hardly say hello to Jenny. Jenny assumes the employee dislikes her.
3. One of Athena's employees in customer service has been failing to return calls that come in while she is gone. Athena assumes she is avoiding returning the calls.
4. Dondi's new cashier has been a little short every day for her first week. Dondi assumes she is incompetent.

ANSWERS

1. Frank could assume that he doesn't know how to do it and instruct him.
2. Jenny could think that something is troubling the employee and ask her what's wrong.
3. Athena could assume the employee never got the message about the calls.
4. Dondi could think that she may be having a hard time learning to run the cash register and could reinstruct her.

Self-Image

Most people invest a great many feelings in defining and maintaining a particular image of themselves. Some people become so concerned with how they appear to others that their behavior is governed more by this concern than by a considered decision about the appropriate supervisory response. It is healthy to develop a sense of who you are and how you want to present yourself; however, when your self-image becomes too inflexible it can paralyze action.

Marsha strongly values interpersonal relationships and wants others to see her as a warm, supportive person. When she needs to be tough and confront problems, she worries about what others will think and fears ruining her image. This concern for her image leads her to be less forceful than she might need to be in order to be effective.

An aggressive supervisor may worry that sympathetic concern for an employee's problem will ruin his "tough" image, or he may fear that consideration will make him appear to be a pushover. A nonassertive supervisor may be afraid that he will appear mean or selfish or that he will lose his nice-guy image. This overconcern with image is based on two irrational beliefs. One is the belief that the overall image others have of you will be built or destroyed on the basis of one or a few actions. Magnification of the impact of a particular interaction makes it difficult to develop a flexible approach. Your behavior does not have to be consistent at all times in order to maintain an image. The other belief involved in a rigid self-image is the belief that others must approve of you at all times. Employees may be convinced that you are being mean and inconsiderate when you insist that they perform in certain ways. This does not mean that you actually are mean or inconsiderate. Others' images of you are not necessarily accurate descriptions of your character.

A fundamentally negative image of yourself also interferes with assertiveness. Someone who believes that he is basically worthless, incompetent, or unlikable will be much more likely to approach others in a hesitant (nonassertive) or defensive (aggressive) way. Without the protection of basically positive feelings about yourself, it can be very difficult to tolerate the inevitable negative interactions supervisors face. Each negative experience then becomes one more indication of your fundamental inadequacy.

Your basic evaluation of yourself developed from the way that others interacted with you when you were growing up. You maintain a negative self-image through self-putdowns ("I'm really a dope. How could I have been so stupid?"); unrealistic expectations of yourself ("I should have been able to do that right the first time"); destructive comparisons with others ("I'll never be as good at supervising as John"); dismissals of your strengths ("Oh, anybody could have done that. It's nothing"); magnifications of faults ("I knew I'd never be able to be a good supervisor. Helen is really angry at me"); overreactions to criticism ("He said I made a mistake on the report. He must think I'm totally incompetent"); and self-blame for events that are out of your control ("I should have known that they were going to reorganize this division").

Wendell had been promoted to a very visible supervisory position, but he maintained an inner conviction that he was inadequate and that any minute others would find him out. This self-doubt sometimes made him hesitant to speak up at all; at other times, he would approach people with a chip on his shoulder because he anticipated criticism and punishment. He worried about being fired even though it would have been apparent to anyone but Wendell that his work was valued by the organization.

Overcoming an inflexible or negative self-image

One way to overcome an inflexible image is to help yourself to see that one interaction will not make or break your image. You need to put other's reactions in perspective by asking yourself "What's the worst that can happen? Can I live with her having a negative image of me?" You may also need to remind yourself that it is possible to act in opposing ways and still maintain your image: "I can be tough and still be caring"; "I can be supportive and still confront problems"; "I can take care of my wants and needs and still be considerate of others."

To change a negative self-image, it is important to uncover and dispute the ways in which you undermine yourself. For example, you can begin to listen for self-putdowns, unrealistic expectations, destructive comparisons, dismissals of your strengths, magnifications of your faults, overreactions to criticism, and self-blame for events that are out of your control. You can begin to consciously acknowledge and give yourself credit for your strengths. Accepting the fact that you will have faults and inadequacies and forgiving yourself for your flaws can also help you to develop a more positive image of yourself. If you find yourself with a persistent feeling of inadequacy and worthlessness, or if you find yourself unable to give up self-punishing ways of treating yourself, it may be very useful to seek counseling. For further information on overcoming a negative self-image see Maltz (1973) and Rubin (1975).

In summary, you can develop a more flexible self-image by:
1. Realizing that one or a few interactions will not make or break your image.
2. Reminding yourself that you can act in opposing ways and still maintain your image.

You can develop a more positive self-image by:
1. Identifying and disputing ways that you undermine yourself.
2. Giving yourself credit for your strengths.
3. Forgiving yourself for your flaws.

Do you worry about ruining your image by acting in certain ways? Does this interfere with assertive action? How could you make your image more flexible? What kind of basic feelings do you have about yourself? How do you think this self-image influences your approach to the supervisory job?

SELF-TEST

Pick the statements that reflect a damaging self-image and specify why.

1. "I never do anything right. I'm sure they're calling me in to chew me out."
2. "Just because she accuses me of being selfish when I insist that she take our department's needs into account doesn't mean that I am selfish."
3. "I don't always do things perfectly but that doesn't mean I'm not O.K."
4. "I don't want people to think that I am unconcerned about their views, so I'd better not say anything."
5. "If I'm not tough in every situation, my employees will think I'm weak."

ANSWERS

1. Damaging—This statement is a self-putdown.
2. Not damaging—This statement reflects an appropriate way to deal with others' reactions.
3. Not damaging—This statement describes a positive forgiving attitude towards yourself.
4. Damaging—The first half of the statement represents an appropriate concern for others but the second half reflects the damaging view that you can't express yourself and still show concern for others.
5. Damaging—This statement represents the belief that you cannot be flexible because one or a few interactions will ruin your image.

Sexual and Racial Blocks to Assertiveness

Women and members of racial and ethnic minorities may find special blocks to being assertive in the white male dominated world of many organizations. These blocks involve both how others see them and how they perceive themselves.

Sources of sexual
and racial blocks to assertiveness

Assertiveness is accepted from those who have traditionally had power, while it may not be accepted from those who have not had power. The classic joke describes a male who is assertive as forceful but a female who is assertive as pushy. Behavior that would be seen as appropriate and necessary in a white male supervisor might be perceived as aggressive, threatening, and inappropriate in a female or a member of a minority group. Gaining power and recognition within an organization requires assertive behavior. Female and minority supervisors can easily find themselves working twice as hard as white male supervisors and having much less influence unless they assert themselves. Thus, the first several women and members of minority groups in management must brace themselves for resistance to their appropriate assertiveness.

A second block to assertiveness has to do with the inner effects of being discriminated against or of being a member of a group that has been denied power. Both members of minority groups and women (who are minorities in management) have learned to avoid trouble by being inconspicuous, pleasing others, and not speaking their minds. Changing deeply ingrained habits of nonassertive behavior is very difficult to do. Although the women's movement and minority groups' movements for power have certainly led to or encouraged some visibly aggressive behavior, these movements have been a response to the passivity and powerlessness that have dominated the self-concept and behavior of these groups. The outward lack of rights has pervaded the consciousness of these groups so much that even when external barriers to participation in management are removed, internal barriers may prevent this participation. This is one reason that assertiveness training was initially focused on women; women have been systematically discouraged from taking an assertive role. Both men and women in supervisory positions can have difficulties with aggressive and nonassertive supervisory styles; however, women seem to be more likely to be nonassertive, while men are more likely to be aggressive.

Overcoming sexual and racial blocks to assertiveness

Supervisors who are women or members of minority groups will often have to struggle with internal programming that says, "Don't speak up," "Don't make yourself visible," "Don't ask questions or they will assume you're dumb," "Be a lady," "Don't rock the boat." Stating rights, formulating antidote statements to feelings, and disputing irrational beliefs and cognitive distortions may be especially important for people who have been strongly programmed to be nonassertive because of sexual or racial identification. Members of minority groups may have as many or more problems than women in being assertive because of learned patterns of response that are nonassertive or aggressive (Cheek, 1976).

Another difficulty with assertiveness that many members of minority groups have is that they overgeneralize from the intolerance and bias of some members of the organization to everyone in the organization. There will be some people who will never accept assertiveness from members of minority groups. Recognizing those individuals and finding ways to avoid or work around them when assertiveness is not worth the trouble may be helpful. It is also important, however, not to let negative experiences with some people inhibit all assertiveness.

> Leann was a young black woman who had been promoted to a supervisory position in the financial department of a large business because of her excellent skills in the area of finance. The manager of the department was concerned because her performance so far had been disappointing. She did not speak up in meetings where her input was important. When asked for an opinion she was often agreeable and noncommittal. Her learned pattern of staying as invisible as possible was damaging her performance.

These supervisors may need to say things to themselves like "I don't have to be liked or approved of by everyone in order to do my job," "I have a right to let people know what I expect even if they don't like it," and "I will meet some resistance to my assertiveness, but that does not mean that I am doing the wrong thing." Clearly defining negative reactions as inevitable responses to changes in the traditional distribution of power may help female and minority supervisors to withstand pressures to become less assertive.

Women and members of minority groups may also need to build a power base to support their assertiveness. Building a strong mentor relationship with someone who does have power can protect women and members of minority groups in situations where their assertiveness may be resisted. There are power dynamics involved in women and members of minority groups asserting themselves in an organization with a rigid white male power structure that are beyond the scope of an assertive supervision text. There are many books that deal with the special problems of women in business, including those by Cannie (1979), Hennig and Jardin (1977), Trahey (1977), and Williams (1977). For more information on the problems of members of minority groups in business see Almquist (1979) and Fernandez (1981).

It is also important to acknowledge that sometimes women and members of minority groups who do achieve powerful positions begin to behave in aggressive rather than assertive ways. Refusing to listen to or to value others' opinions, putting others down, and ascribing negative intentions to others can inhibit involved teamwork no matter who behaves in that way. However, it is clear that members of the traditional power groups can get away with such behavior more easily than women or members of minority groups.

In summary, you can learn to overcome sexual and racial blocks to assertiveness by:

1. Disputing internal programming that keeps you from being assertive.
2. Defining negative reactions as inevitable responses to changes in the traditional distribution of power.
3. Building a power base to support your assertiveness.

Support for Overcoming Difficulties in Being Assertive

One of the most valuable resources in learning to overcome difficulties in being assertive is a support network of colleagues and friends. When you are in the middle of a tense situation, it is often difficult to step back from your feelings long enough to see how your irrational ideas or cognitive distortions might be interfering with your objectivity. At this point, someone who can serve as a sounding board and can give you an outsider's view can be invaluable. If you are not sure how you appear to others, it may be helpful to ask for feedback directly by saying something such as "I know that I come on too strong sometimes. Would you let me know when that is happening?" Roleplaying an interaction allows you to get feedback from the person you roleplay with about your approach in a confrontation: "Let me try this with you. Do I come across as if I really mean what I'm saying?" Discussing supervisory problems with others and actively soliciting their feedback can sharpen and refine your assertive skills.

An unanticipated benefit of one in-house assertiveness training workshop was the development of better communication between supervisors in that organization. Before the workshop, everyone assumed that he was the only one with supervisory problems. Discussing problems with other supervisors seemed like an admission of incompetence. During the training, everyone came to realize that all supervisors have supervisory problems. They began to see how someone else's perspective could help them to handle problems more effectively. After the workshop, when supervisors needed to tackle difficult situations, they would often go to a colleague and say something like "Let me run this by you. I want to make sure I'm being objective before I confront the employee."

The goal of all of your self-exploration is to be able to *act* rather than to *react*. Awareness and control of your feelings through self-examination and through discussion with your support network can free you to be thoughtfully and effectively assertive. You will find as you practice disputing irrational beliefs, revising distorted perceptions, evaluating risks, learning your supervisory rights, examining your negative assumptions, and developing empathy that you are building a positive self-image, trust of others, a sense of entitlement, and objectivity that will support your assertiveness.

◆

SELF-TEST

Specify the feelings that each of the following statements reflect and if they would support or undermine assertiveness.

1. "How dare he behave that way! Obviously he is not committed to the organization. He should know better."
2. "I know that she is having a hard time right now; however, I clearly need to let her know how her work problems are affecting the rest of the unit. And I'm not being an ogre in doing that."
3. "I just don't know whether I'm being fair or not. After all, she has been doing most of her work. I don't think that I have the right to harass her until her work is really bad."
4. "I know that if I do confront him, he will raise a huge stink. It will probably ruin morale in the unit from now on. He could turn the whole staff against me."
5. "Even though confronting this problem may cause some immediate anger and sulking, I have a right to ask her to

do the work she is paid to do. I also have a responsibility to give her feedback about her work."

6. "I can see that he is not doing his share of work on that project. I wonder what this means; however, since I don't know for sure, I have to just stick to confronting the behavior."

7. "I shouldn't upset her or hurt her feelings. The poor thing has so many troubles I can't add to them."

8. "I can see that confronting the staff about very long lunches when the other supervisors in the division allow lunches to drag on for 1½ hours is going to create some tension and stress. I think that I need to see if I can get my manager's support in enforcing division policy before I confront my staff."

9. "Even though I'm new here, it's clear that this place needs some change. I don't care how things have been done. From now on, things are going to be different around here."

10. "I don't dare speak up. Black people have to walk on eggshells around here."

11. "I'm anxious about this meeting, but I know that if I take some deep breaths while I'm in the meeting I can relax."

ANSWERS

1. This statement includes anger-producing assumptions that would make assertion difficult.

2. This understanding yet firm attitude would support assertive action.

3. This doubt-producing approach undermines assertiveness, especially since it uses the word *harass*.

4. This statement sounds like a fearful catastrophic fantasy, especially the words *ruin from now on*, that could undermine assertiveness.

5. The feeling of entitlement and the clear understanding of rights and responsibilities in this statement will support assertiveness.

6. The open-minded approach of this statement and the carefulness not to make negative assumptions about what the behavior means prevents anger and aids assertiveness.

7. This statement reflects guilt that can inhibit assertiveness.

8. The calm assessment of real risks in this statement and the attempt to get protection from them will support assertiveness.

9. The lack of caution and failure to do homework reflected in this statement lead to aggression.
10. This statement reflects a fear that may come from over-generalizing about how assertiveness will be accepted in the organization or from past conditioning. It will inhibit assertiveness.
11. This statement supports assertiveness because it reflects the realistic feeling that you can be anxious and still be assertive.

Summary

In this chapter some of the difficulties in being assertive and ways to overcome them are examined. Changing feelings that stop you from being assertive can be uncomfortable and anxiety-provoking and requires a conscious decision and effort.

Your feelings about a situation are the result of your beliefs and are not an inevitable result of the situation. You can change your feelings if you change your understanding of situations. Ellis has called this idea the ABC Theory of Emotions—situations (A) are interpreted by beliefs (B) that create emotions (C)—and described 11 common irrational beliefs that cause disturbing emotions. Burns uses a similar concept called cognitive distortions. Some of the common distortions include labeling, magnifying, personalizing, mind-reading, and believing in rigid "shoulds" and "shouldn'ts."

Guilt is one feeling that interferes with assertiveness. Inappropriate guilt feelings are created through irrational beliefs, cognitive distortions, or outmoded parent messages. Everyone has guilt triggers—environmental stimuli they are likely to respond to with guilt. You can learn to overcome guilt by becoming aware of guilt feelings and guilt triggers, uncovering irrational beliefs, cognitive distortions, and parent messages and deciding if the guilt is appropriate, and developing an antidote statement.

Fear and anxiety can also interfere with assertiveness. One fear is fear of the consequences of an action, which interferes when it is based on unrealistic catastrophic fantasies or is so strong that it paralyzes action. There also is fear that others will take advantage of you. You can learn to overcome fear of the consequences of an action by: uncovering your catastrophic fantasy and exaggerating it, asking yourself "What's really likely to happen?" and being alert for irrational beliefs and cognitive distortions, weighing the risks of being assertive and the costs of not being assertive, and assessing what you need to do to protect yourself from negative consequences. You can learn to overcome fear of being taken advantage of by: recognizing your fear and the assumptions behind it, and disputing your assumptions.

Sometimes generalized anxiety or nervousness can interfere with assertiveness, especially when there is a fear of losing control because of anxiety. You can learn to overcome anxiety by: realizing you can still act rationally when you're anxious, practicing relaxation techniques, and using deep breathing or a short meditation before confrontations.

Doubt is another feeling that causes difficulty in being assertive. Negative pep talks and lack of clarity about rights can make you doubtful. You can learn to overcome doubt by doing your homework —knowing what you want to accomplish and the facts of the situation, substituting positive pep talks for negative pep talks, and focusing on supervisory rights and responsibilities.

Anger is another emotion that can inhibit assertiveness. Anger can come from negative assumptions about what behavior means and from irrational beliefs and cognitive distortions. Anger triggers, such as red-flag people, can make you respond with anger automatically. You can learn to overcome anger by: examining negative assumptions and looking for more benign alternatives, looking for and disputing irrational beliefs and cognitive distortions, watching for anger triggers, especially red-flag people, and empathizing— putting yourself in the other person's shoes.

An inflexible or negative self-image can also interfere with assertiveness. An inflexible self-image is based on too much concern for how others see you. A negative self-image is based on unrealistic assessments and expectations of yourself. You can develop a more flexible image by: realizing that one or a few interactions will not make or break your image, and reminding yourself that you can act in opposing ways and still maintain your image. You can develop a more positive self-image by: identifying and disputing ways that you undermine yourself, giving yourself credit for your strengths, and forgiving yourself for your flaws.

Women and members of racial and ethnic minorities may find special blocks to being assertive. Assertiveness may not be accepted from these groups. Members of these groups may also have developed deeply ingrained habits of nonassertive behavior that may be difficult to overcome. You can learn to overcome sexual and racial blocks to assertiveness by disputing internal programming that keeps you from being assertive, defining negative reactions as inevitable responses to changes in the traditional distribution of power, and building a power base to support your assertiveness.

One of the most valuable resources in helping you overcome difficulties in being assertive is a support network of colleagues and friends who can serve as a sounding board for your feelings and perspectives. Your goal is to be able to act rather than react and be effectively assertive.

Bibliography

Alberti, R. E., & Emmons, M. L. *Stand up, speak out, talk back.* New York: Pocket Books, 1975.

Almquist, E. M. *Minorities, gender, and work.* Lexington, Mass.: Lexington Books, 1979.

Bloom, L., Coburn, K., & Pearlman, J. *The new assertive woman.* New York: Delacorte Press, 1975.

Burns, D. *Feeling good: The new mood therapy.* New York: William Morrow, 1980.

Cannie, J. K. *The woman's guide to management success: How to win power in the real world.* Englewood Cliffs, N.J.: Prentice-Hall, 1979.

Cheek, D. *Assertive black . . . puzzled white.* San Luis Obispo, Calif.: Impact Publishers, 1976.

Dyer, W. W. *Your erroneous zones.* New York: Funk & Wagnalls, 1976.

Ellis, A., & Harper, R. *A new guide to rational living.* Englewood Cliffs, N.J.: Prentice-Hall, 1975.

Fernandez, J. P. *Racism and sexism in corporate life: Changing values in American business.* Lexington, Mass.: Lexington Books, 1981.

Hennig, M., & Jardin, A. *The managerial woman.* New York: Pocket Books, 1977.

Jakubowski, P., & Lange, A. J. *The assertive option: Your rights and responsibilities.* Champaign, Ill.: Research Press, 1978.

Lazarus, A., & Fay, A. *I can if I want to.* New York: William Morrow, 1975.

Maltz, M. *Psychocybernetics.* New York: Pocket Books, 1969.

Maltz, M. *The search for self-respect.* New York: Bantam, 1973.

Rubin, T. I. *Compassion and self-hate: An alternative to despair.* New York: Ballantine, 1975.

Tavris, C. *Anger: The misunderstood emotion.* New York: Simon & Schuster, 1983.

Trahey, J. *Jane Trahey on women and power: Who's got it? How to get it.* New York: Rawson Associates Publishers, 1977.

Tubesing, D. *Kicking your stress habits.* Duluth, Minn.: Whole Person Associates, 1981.

Williams, M. *The new executive woman.* New York: New American Library, 1977.

Woolfolk, R. L., & Richardson, F. C. *Stress, sanity, and survival.* New York: New American Library, 1978.

CHAPTER SIX

Assertive Techniques

In this chapter you will:
- Learn the critical role of active listening in assertiveness;
- Learn techniques for stating expectations clearly;
- Become aware of the importance of saying no assertively;
- Become aware of the importance of giving positive recognition;
- Become aware of the importance of "I" statements in assertive interaction;
- Learn when and how to use the technique of "calling the process";
- Learn when and how to use "given that" statements;
- Learn when and how to use the emergency measures of the broken-record technique, selective ignoring, and assertive withdrawal;
- Learn techniques for leading meetings effectively.

Supervisory effectiveness depends not only on an assertive style, but also on the supervisor's repertoire of assertive techniques for accomplishing supervisory tasks. This chapter describes some of the techniques that may be useful in creating a climate of communication and involved teamwork. Style of delivery and context in which the techniques are used have a major impact on how they are received. All of the techniques discussed in this chapter need to be delivered with assertive word choices, voice characteristics, and body language in order for them to seem assertive rather than aggressive or nonassertive.

Active Listening

Since most people feel that they listen effectively, developing good listening skills seems like a trivial assignment. Ironically, listening is probably one of the most difficult assertive skills to master. One reason that listening is so difficult is the communication process itself. The words people use can express their meaning clearly or very indirectly. If a speaker is nonassertive (indirect) or unclear, it is much harder for a listener to understand the underlying message. For example, if a supervisor feels that a certain employee needs to monitor patient care in addition to his current job, he could say: "We're really hoping to encourage people to become more committed to the organization," "We would like some of the employees to take over the job of monitoring patient care on this unit," or "I would like you to take over the job of monitoring patient care on this unit." An employee trying to understand what this supervisor meant would have to do much more translation to understand the underlying meaning of the first two messages than he would to understand the last message. And even with the last message, the listener could hear: "He thinks I'm a good employee so he wants me to take over this important job," "He thinks I'm not providing good patient care and is punishing me," or "He thinks there is a terrible problem and wants me to confront other employees."

One technique that maximizes the opportunities for effective communication is a technique called "active listening." This technique is described in more detail in Thomas Gordon's book, *Leader Effectiveness Training* (1977). In active listening, the listener tells the speaker his understanding of the speaker's message as a way to make sure he understands and as a way to let the speaker know he is listening. In order to understand the speaker's message, the listener must do more than listen to the words. He must also observe body language and listen to voice tone as a way to understand the speaker's real message. Understanding the message means listening for the feelings and thoughts that are behind the speaker's words. The listener asks himself, "What is this person really telling me?" He can express what he understands the message to be by this formula: "You are feeling or thinking x because of y." For example, he could say, "You are convinced that we should work on the McGowen case before we do the others because that one is so complicated." The following is a more extended example of a supervisor using active listening to respond to an employee.

Supervisor: John, I've noticed that you seem frustrated with the customers lately. The last several weeks you've been very curt when they have questions. What's happening?

Employee: How am I supposed to be patient when they call and ask stupid questions? It just wastes my time.

Supervisor: So you believe that many of the questions are ones you should not have to answer.

Employee: I'll have three people in the same day call to ask when we will be shipping the new machinery. Besides, with this new project added to our other one, I'm up to my ears in work.

Supervisor: Then the problem is not just customer questions. You're feeling less willing to listen to customers because you feel overloaded with work.

Employee: Yes, I guess it is a problem with workload more than anything else. I just don't know how to deal with the pressures that have come with this new project.

Supervisor: The sense I get is that you and I need to sit down and take a look at your workload and maybe talk about time-management strategies. You're essentially saying that you could be much more responsive to customers' questions if you weren't feeling so pressured.

Employee: Yes. That's true.

In this example, the employee's attitude has been a problem. Through active listening, the supervisor was able to help the employee identify more clearly the source of the problem. Once the problem was clearly identified, the supervisor had a starting point for the problem-solving process. If he had lectured the employee about the need to be courteous to customers before really listening to him, he could have aborted the problem-solving process.

Active listening can be used as an adjunct to all other assertive techniques. For example, a supervisor could say no in a more positive manner by indicating first that he understood the reasons for the request: "I understand that you want me to do the report because I have more skills in this area than others do; however, I still have to say no." As will be shown later in Chapter Seven, active listening is a very important part of the process of giving criticism. Although repeating the message can initially seem stupid, clumsy, and redundant, practicing active listening will make the technique a more natural part of your repertoire. You will then be able to use active listening whenever you need to open communication channels or to correct miscommunication.

Think of someone who does not seem to listen very effectively. What does he do or not do that makes you feel he is a poor listener?

Think of someone who seems to listen very effectively. What does he do that makes you feel he is a good listener?

When to use active listening

Active listening is useful in several situations. It is important for the listener to use active listening when he may be distorting the speaker's message because of cultural differences or strong emotional reactions. The more differences there are between the speaker and the listener, the more likely it is that a misunderstanding will occur. For example, a young Chinese technician in an electronics firm might say to his supervisor, "Sometimes we need to recheck the specifications after the first step in the process." A supervisor who does not understand this polite way of raising an issue might miss the message. Clarifying his understanding by stating "Are you saying that we should check the specifications on this project?" can help him to make sure that he has really gotten the message. When the speaker is criticizing the listener or stating a view that the listener strongly disagrees with, it is also important to use active listening. Bach and Wyden in their book *The Intimate Enemy* (1968) insist that, in a fight, each person should summarize the other person's message before reacting to it. This provides an opportunity for clarification: "No, I didn't mean that you are a total idiot. I only meant that you didn't handle that customer in the most effective way." Forcing himself to slow down and really understand the speaker also helps the listener combat angry feelings. This can aid the listener if he is inclined to respond too quickly in a way he later regrets.

Active listening is also helpful for clarifying the message when the speaker is unclear or confusing. For example, a supervisor listening to an involved and fuzzy set of directions from his superior might want to use active listening to make sure that he clearly understands the directions: "Let me see if I've got this. First you want me to adjust the timing on the conveyor belt and then shift the workers to different locations. Is that right?" When the speaker is very nonassertive, he may state his message very indirectly. The listener can use active listening to check out his guesses about the speaker's meaning: "You would really like me to talk to Tina about the loudness of the radio in the office. Right?"

Active listening also makes a very powerful statement that the listener respects the speaker enough to make the effort to listen carefully and try to understand. Communicating this may be especially important in a conflict. The speaker will often repeat the same thing over and over in a conflict because the listener never lets the speaker know that he has been heard. If the speaker summarizes the listener's position before stating his own, the listener will feel that he has been understood even if the speaker disagrees with him. For example, a supervisor responding to an employee with a very different view of the supervisor's job might say, "I understand that you feel very strongly that I should be involved in the production process. I don't believe that I can do an adequate job of supervision if I am doing production." When a speaker has been listened to, he feels valued even if his wishes are not met.

Active listening also is a powerful tool for creating a climate in which people feel free to express their opinions and discuss problems. A climate of involved teamwork requires open communication. People will often express much more information when the other person is using active listening than they ever would if he were just asking questions. Both Gordon (1977) and Carkhuff (1983) have discussed the use of active listening as a way to draw people out and to encourage them to creatively solve their own problems. Often the supervisor can help employees to solve problems if he can serve as a good "sounding board." Even when the employee needs some advice from the supervisor, active listening helps to clearly define the problem so that the supervisor can offer advice that is really on target. Thus, active listening assists in the problem-solving process.

Reducing conflict in tense situations is one of the most powerful uses of active listening. When the speaker is expressing angry feelings, active listening can help to defuse the tension and calm the speaker down. Feeling as if someone understands can help the speaker to be less angry and defensive.

Barbara had developed a very combative relationship with one X-ray technician in her lab. One day when she was discussing a problem in the lab, she stopped to really listen. "It sounds as if you're pretty angry about some things" she said. By opening the doors and really listening, she was able to discover that this employee felt clean-up duty was assigned quite unfairly. Since this employee often finished her work first, Barbara had been assigning her extra duties. She had concluded that Barbara didn't like her or value her work. Once Barbara understood her employee's feelings, she could let the person know how much her work was valued, and tension was considerably reduced.

When someone is expressing a great deal of resistance to suggestions or to requests for change, active listening can draw him out and help him to express the resistance clearly. Once the supervisor understands the resistance, he is in a better position to deal with it: "So you feel that you shouldn't have to work overtime because you didn't have to do this extra work when you first came here. One reason you are being asked to work overtime now is that you are more experienced and can therefore handle the office alone." Sometimes just expressing the resistance and knowing that someone understands helps the speaker to do the task he is resisting.

Active listening is part of the process that is required to change someone's attitude toward a situation. It is possible to confront an employee and insist that he change his behavior; however, it is unlikely that just saying "Change your attitude" will be very effective in changing the attitude behind the behavior. Feelings do not change just by deciding to change them; the reasons for the feelings need to be explored and the problem situation needs to be seen in a different way. Much of the information in Chapter Five was aimed at uncovering reasons for destructive feelings and bringing about change. Through active listening, the supervisor can draw out destructive beliefs and can then help the employee to look at the situation differently. For example, if an employee were very hostile towards a supervisor, the supervisor could insist that the employee behave in a more civil way. However, in order to change the employee's feelings about the supervisor that led to this behavior, it would be necessary for the supervisor to help uncover the reasons for the hostility and correct any problems.

Barriers to active listening
There are a number of barriers to active listening. One is that the listener may be waiting for a chance to express his opinions rather

than really listening. People often use the time while someone is talking to plan their own arguments. This is a shoot-and-reload conversation in which each person "shoots" his opinion and then "reloads" his mind with new arguments while the other person is talking. Obviously not much real listening occurs.

Another barrier to active listening is the tendency to ask too many questions or to ask questions before the speaker has had a chance to tell his story. Many times asking questions can help to clarify what the speaker is saying; however, asking too many questions too soon can make the speaker feel as if he is not being listened to.

Giving advice prematurely can also interfere with active listening. Advice is useful when the listener thoroughly understands the problem and the speaker is asking for advice. People often discuss an issue because they don't clearly understand the problem and may need to talk it out, not because they want advice. The listener may form some quick hypotheses about the speaker's problem and give advice based on these. Initial conclusions often don't capture the complexities of the problem. When he is sure he understands the problem, the speaker may ask if the listener wants advice as a transition into problem solving: "Are you looking for suggestions on how to handle this?"

Another barrier to active listening is the tendency to let feelings and values get in the way of listening. For example, an insecure person may interpret what he hears as disapproval while a defensive person may hear every statement as an attack. If the listener strongly believes that the speaker is wrong or bad, he will have trouble listening and may filter the message through his own prejudices. As stated earlier, cultural biases will also make it hard for the listener to really understand the speaker.

> Kerry was having trouble with the new postal meter in the warehouse and approached his supervisor about the problem. Before he could even explain what the problem was, his supervisor angrily cut him off by saying "What do you mean you're having troubles with the postal meter? I picked out that meter and it's the best that money can buy. You just don't know how to run it." Since Kerry's supervisor wouldn't listen to him, Kerry approached someone else in management about his problem.

Active listening requires intense concentration and involvement by the listener. In order to listen well, a person has to shut out all distractions and really struggle to hear the underlying message.

Some listeners either cannot or will not commit themselves to fully concentrate on what someone else is saying. For further information on listening and its importance in management see Atwater, 1982.

◆

EXERCISE

Ask a friend to discuss a problem with you. Promise yourself not to ask questions, give advice, preach, or moralize. It will be a lot harder to do this than you may think. Simply summarize the meaning you are getting from what he says. Carry on the dialogue for 5 minutes. Your goal is to get as clear an understanding as possible of your friend's perception of the problem. At the end of 5 minutes, discuss the following with your friend:

1. What was it like for you to try to really listen for 5 minutes. What kinds of behaviors or feelings got in the way?
2. What was it like for your friend to be listened to? Did he feel as if you understood? Did he gain a different understanding of his problem?

◆

SELF-TEST

For each of the following statements, how could you respond using active listening?

1. "I can't seem to do anything right. I loused up this assignment. I did yesterday's project wrong. It's just hopeless."
2. "I can't believe you're handling this project in such a ridiculous way. I would have called each contact person at least twice by now."
3. "Helen doesn't work any faster on those tallies than I do."
4. "Things used to be a lot better when Mr. Jones was leading this department."

ANSWERS

1. "The problems you have had with the last two projects have left you pretty discouraged."
2. "You feel that I should be making more contact calls."
3. "You think I'm being unfair in asking you to work faster."
4. "You're pretty frustrated with how I'm running some things in the department."

◆

Techniques for
Stating Expectations Clearly

One of the most serious supervisory problems is the failure to let
people know what is expected of them.

> Herb, the house director in an in-patient alcoholism treatment
> center, complained to a consultant that the people on his staff
> were simply not doing their jobs. He would walk into the
> house and find bathrooms without toilet paper and with dirty
> baseboards. The staff complained that Herb rarely scheduled
> staff meetings and that they didn't realize cleaning base-
> boards was one of their duties. Herb didn't realize the staff
> wanted meetings. The consultant asked staff members to
> write down their expectations of Herb and Herb to write
> down his expectations of staff members. Herb and his staff
> were then encouraged to share these expectations with each
> other and discuss them to create a set of shared expectations.

It is hard for people to shed the belief that what they expect is
so obvious that others should know without being told. Failure to
know what is wanted is seen then as a fault, rather than a realistic
inability to read minds. Good communication not only requires
good listening; it also requires that the speaker find clear and direct ways to say what she means. However, in order to express
expectations clearly, a person must know what she expects. In
order for an organization or a department to function effectively,
managers and supervisors must establish clear goals and then
make specific plans for how to reach these goals. If the supervisor
has not given thought to what she expects, she will confuse her
employees by constantly demanding that they drop tasks to take
care of crises, by defining tasks in a fuzzy way, by constantly shift-
ing priorities, or by punishing employees for not doing what she
never clearly asked them to do. Thus, the first step in stating expectations clearly is a good goal setting and planning process.
There are a number of excellent books on managing time and
setting goals that describe planning skills in more detail (Lakein,
1973; Scott, 1980; Tec, 1980).

After setting goals and making plans, the supervisor must state
expectations to employees. For people to carry out a task in the
way the supervisor wants, they need three pieces of information:
what they should do, why they should do it, and when it should be
done. The more experienced the employee, the more likely it is

that she will be able to do the job with minimal specification of what, why, and when. The more similar the supervisor and employee are in age, value system, and previous life experience, the more likely it is that the employee will do the job the way that the supervisor wants without specific information about the supervisor's expectations. When an employee is inexperienced, unmotivated, or very different from the supervisor in her value system or previous life experience, the supervisor cannot assume that the employee will do the job the way she wants it done without clear directions. Confrontations can often be avoided by clearly spelling out expectations in the first place: "Mina, I want to sit down with you and talk about my expectations for you, and I'd like to hear what you expect from me as your supervisor."

Telling employees why they should do a job is a good way to motivate them, and yet often tasks are assigned with no discussion of the reason why the job is important. The supervisor almost always has a clearer perspective on the reasons why a task is important than an individual employee does. This is because she is generally better informed about overall organizational goals and priorities than her employees are. Informing the employee about the thinking behind the assignment of certain jobs can be a powerful way to build commitment and involvement.

> Nicole is the state special services coordinator who supervises school psychologists. She is aware that there will be a legislative hearing about the placement of special education children in a month. She also knows that parents who have not been informed about placement test results for their children could create problems at the hearing. Letting her staff know the reasons for pressure to complete all backlogged cases in the next 3 weeks can help to motivate them to meet the deadline.

Supervisors also have an obligation to let employees know how important each task is relative to other tasks. For example, a supervisor may give an employee an assignment and may know that the task has a higher priority than anything else the person could be doing (an A-priority task). Other assignments may be B or C priority (to be done when the most important work is finished or when there is the time). Employees do not generally know how important a particular task is. Supervisors need to help employees manage their time by letting them know clearly which are A-priority tasks. Supervisors can also help employees with time management by letting them know how much time a particular task is worth. For example, an employee might be able to generate a sketchy report in an hour, a more detailed report in half a day, and a really detailed report in 3 days. Sometimes productivity suffers because employees spend more time on routine tasks than the tasks merit. This is especially true of very perfectionistic employees. With this type of employee, the supervisor may need to encourage the employee to do a less thorough job on tasks that are not worth a great amount of time.

The supervisor, however, should not be establishing all of the objectives. A work environment in which all of the direction comes from the supervisor is not designed to encourage maximum employee involvement. The more motivated and experienced the employee, the more she should be participating in, or setting, her goals (see Chapter Ten of this book and also Hersey & Blanchard, 1982). The effective supervisor knows when to provide most of the direction herself, and when to say "Pete, the Williams project is ready to go. You decide what needs to be done and follow through on it yourself."

What are the most important goals in your department for the next 6 months? Think of a specific task that might be relevant to one of these goals. If you were to assign this task to one of your employees, what would you tell her to do? Why would the task be important? When would the task have to be done?

SELF-TEST

Which of the following remarks are good statements of expectations? Which are not?

1. Park supervisor to young summer employee: "You need to maintain the lawns in the park playground."
2. Supervisor in state agency to clerical personnel: "I need all of you to put aside your other projects and begin typing our grant proposal. The deadline is Thursday morning at 9:00 and without everyone working on it, we won't make the deadline and may lose our funding. I want the proposal to be typed by Wednesday evening."
3. New restaurant manager to kitchen staff: "I'd really like you to turn out better quality food from now on. Our reputation stinks and it will never improve unless you produce something of higher quality than you do now."

4. Supervisor to claims adjuster: "I would like you to take care
    of all of our outstanding claims over $500 so that we can
    report on our costs for the next department meeting at the
    end of the month. I think that having all of our claims
    backlog taken care of will help in the evaluation of our de-
    partment next month."

ANSWERS

1. This is a poor statement of expectations for a young and
    inexperienced employee who probably has quite different
    perceptions of the job than the supervisor does. It is not
    specific enough in what, why, or when.
2. This is a good statement of expectations. It specifies what,
    why, and when.
3. This is not specific enough in what is expected. If a res-
    taurant has always produced poor quality food, a transition
    to better food will require education of the staff in what is
    required. The expectation of immediate results is also
    unrealistic.
4. This statement has a good specification of what, when, and
    why.

Saying No

Another essential assertive technique is the ability to say no. The
ability to say no is essential because every supervisor is confronted
with many requests that are inappropriate (such as an employee
asking to take vacation in a tax accounting firm on April 12, 13,
and 14), are generally appropriate but conflict with priorities of
the moment (such as a colleague's asking a supervisor to help with
a project in her department when the supervisor is trying very
hard to get all client accounts up to date in his own department),
and simply demand more resources than are available (such as a
tempting board invitation offered to a supervisor when he is in the
middle of critical work in his own office).

Since the need to say no for effective time management is so
obvious, why is it hard to say no when it is necessary? In the first
place, there are many situations in which the need to say no isn't
as clear-cut as it is in the preceding examples. For example, an
employee may ask for time off at an unreasonable time to meet
personal needs that the supervisor feels are legitimate, there may

be almost enough time to help the colleague, or the colleague may have been very helpful in the past, which creates a sense of owing some support. Deciding whether it is necessary and appropriate to say no can be complex. To say no a supervisor needs to clearly decide on his priorities.

Walter was the manager of a small store with a number of energetic and creative employees. Several of the employees asked if they could rearrange the displays in the store. Although he wanted to encourage employee creativity, Walter knew that a single Sunday would not be enough time to complete the job. He also knew that he could not afford to have the store disrupted on Monday. As a consequence, he had to say no; however, to maintain his employees' involvement in improving the business, he suggested that they find ways to rearrange small sections at a time.

The request that needs to be evaluated is also often made with little warning: "Can I take Thursday off? I need to know right now." An immediate answer may not take into account how saying yes will interfere with other priorities. To say no assertively in some situations it is essential to take time to consider how the decision will affect other personal or departmental priorities: "I really can't let you know this minute. Let me take a look at the situation and I'll get back to you in 10 minutes." Saying no assertively requires that the supervisor take a few minutes to weigh the request in light of the question "How will my agreeing to this request affect my other priorities right now?"

Most people can quite comfortably say no the first time a request is made, but have difficulty continuing to say no when the person making the request persists and applies pressure. In this situation, almost everyone is vulnerable to manipulation. To hold firm in saying no, a supervisor needs to recognize and deal with her own feelings (Chapter Five). Some people find it very difficult to hold their ground when the person they say no to becomes extremely angry. Other people find it difficult to resist the pressure to be helpful: "But if you don't do it, who will? We will just never be able to do it without you." If someone is programmed to feel guilty if she upsets or inconveniences anyone else, it may be impossible for her to say no without some guilt. People may also avoid saying no because they feel sorry for the other person. There will always be some employees whose personal lives seem to be in one crisis after another. Flexibility and sympathy is appropriate in these cases; however, these employees' requests still need to be considered in the light of other critical priorities.

There are several things to keep in mind in saying no effectively. Voice characteristics, body language, and word choices are extremely important in how the no is received. Saying no in a hesitant, wishy-washy tone, with no eye contact, and with minimizing words like "I don't really think so" or "Probably not" invites the person making the request to ask again and again. To say no effectively, forceful, assertive voice characteristics, body language, and word choices are needed. This is why it may be more useful to take a few minutes to consider the decision and then to come back with an answer than it would be to think out loud about the decision. Considering pros and cons verbally may communicate a lack of clarity and firmness that invites argument.

When a supervisor says no, it is helpful for her to let the other person know what she will do as well as what she will not do. This kind of compromise allows firmness while at the same time communicating responsiveness to the other person's needs. For example, she could say, "I will not talk to Mr. Jones for you. I will call Mr. Jones and let him know that you will be in to talk to him" or "I can't give you this week off, but I can give you the last week of the month."

There may be times when assertive withdrawal, a technique discussed later in this chapter, will be necessary when saying no. For example, if a supervisor has said no to an employee several times and the employee applies more pressure, the supervisor may legitimately say, "I can certainly understand that you might be frustrated by my decision, but I really am not going to change my mind, and I'm unwilling to discuss it anymore."

———————◆———————

Think of a time in which you did not say no and wish you had. How did you get pressured into saying yes? What could you have done or said to counter this pressure?

Has there been a time when you have said no and had others continue to argue with you? If so, could there have been hesitation in your voice characteristics, body language, or word choices that could have invited argument?

———————◆———————

Giving Positive Recognition

Everyone needs acknowledgment or recognition. When there is no way to achieve positive recognition, even a negative reaction from others is better than no attention at all. This deep-seated human need for recognition is the reason why the concept of "stroking" is so important in supervision. Stroking is a term used in transactional analysis to refer to either positive or negative recognition or acknowledgment. Saying "hello" is a stroke; so is a verbal reprimand, a hug, a punch in the nose, a smile, or a frown (Jongeward & Sayer, 1978).

Positive strokes motivate and encourage employees. The positive recognition techniques of highly successful organizations are described in the study *In Search of Excellence* (Peters & Waterman, 1983).

> We all think we're tops. We're exuberantly, wildly irrational about ourselves. . . . The message that comes through so poignantly in the studies we reviewed is that we like to think of ourselves as winners. The lesson that the excellent companies have to teach is that there is no reason why we can't design systems that constantly reinforce this notion; most of their people are made to feel like winners. (p. 57)

Blanchard and Johnson, in their book *The One Minute Manager* (1983), emphasize the critical importance of praise in effective and encouraging management. It is surprising how many supervisors still don't believe that strokes are essential to developing employee commitment and involvement, but think instead that no positive strokes are needed because it is an employee's job to do a task well. These supervisors think, however, that if an employee is doing poorly, he should be told. What this means is that in many organizations the only way to get strokes is to do something wrong. Since people crave positive recognition, the lack of it can result in very discouraged or negative employees. A climate of commitment and involvement is probably impossible without many opportunities to receive positive recognition.

Most effective positive recognition has three characteristics: the first is that it is genuine. Phony praise is not an effective motivator; however, the alert supervisor can probably find something to genuinely acknowledge even with relatively limited employees. Giving some genuine positive recognition can build better working relationships even with enemies.

Aretha was really struggling to relate to one older employee in her department. She felt that his unwillingness to change was causing her tremendous difficulty. When she stopped to think about his work, she was able to acknowledge him by saying "Sam, I know that you have really worked hard here to see that everyone follows procedures and policies. I want to find ways to utilize that steady consistency in developing some new approaches that can work with the old."

Second, positive recognition is more effective when it is specific. General positive comments like "You are a really nice person" or "You do a good job" are better than no positive strokes at all but are not nearly as powerful as specific comments about what the person did that is being recognized. "Your skillful handling of Mary's mother in that last counseling situation really helped Mary and her mother to resolve some of their differences" is a good example of specific praise.

Third, positive recognition should be free of implied criticism. Although aggressive people believe that they give positive strokes, their comments often include criticism. For example, "At last, you did a good job in the Barber project" or "You handled *that* case well."

It is essential in assertive supervision to give positive strokes for good work. The effective supervisor uses every opportunity to acknowledge employees' contributions to the organization. He may say something like "James, I really appreciate the extra effort you made on that project last week. The time you spent checking the final results paid off for all of us" or "Karim, your thorough critical analysis of the current grant proposal was very important to our obtaining that grant." He also uses every means at his disposal within the organization to point out his employees' work to others. For example, he might make sure employees' names get into or on reports; mention employee contributions in meetings; tell upper management about effective work his employees are doing; support career development through promotions for his staff; and utilize any company recognition mechanisms such as awards. Sometimes he will use the technique of telling someone how pleased he is with an employee's work when that employee can overhear the remark. In general, he is constantly alert for opportunities to recognize and acknowledge his employee's contributions.

There are two other uses of stroking in assertiveness. One is to stroke positive intentions in order to establish a climate conducive to teamwork and problem solving. Chapter One discussed the value of assuming that most people want to do a good job. To stroke people's good intentions, the supervisor states that he knows they mean to cooperate or to do a good job. Approaching someone as if he is, of course, willing to cooperate in solving a problem can make it much more difficult for that person to be utterly resistant. For example, a supervisor might say, "Greta, I know that you want to make productive use of your time. That's why I want to speak to you about ways to find work when you finish an assignment" or "Mickey, I think that you want to do as thorough a job in your analytical work as possible. Lately I've noticed some errors in important calculations, so I would like to discuss it with you and solve any problems that are interfering with high quality work."

The other use of stroking is to acknowledge a manager's authority. This means to acknowledge up front that the "boss is the boss." This can reduce tension when being assertive with a supervisor. An example of this is "Renee, I know that you are the person who has to decide how the money is allocated for training. That's the reason I wanted to talk to you about a proposal I have for another way to allocate funds." This will be discussed in more detail in Chapter Nine.

Think of a supervisor who seems to be especially good at motivating his employees. How does he provide strokes?

What positive and negative strokes have you given to others in the last week? What are two positive strokes that you could give to each of your key employees?

"I" Statements

Since one of the goals of assertive interaction is to communicate with others in a way that generates open discussion rather than defensiveness, it is important to look for effective ways to express a point of view. One technique that has been developed as a way to express opinions without arousing defensiveness is the "I" statement. In an "I" statement the speaker describes his view about something without making judgments about the other person's point of view. In contrast, in a "you" statement the emphasis is not on expressing what the speaker believes but rather on making judgments about what the other person is doing or saying. For example, "I'm really having trouble following what you are saying" is an "I" statement. "You're confusing" is a "you" statement. "I think it's more helpful to look at the problem this way" is an "I" statement. "You're not looking at the problem in a realistic way" is a "you" statement. It may seem as though the difference between an "I" and a "you" statement is a trivial matter of wording, but the impact of a "you" statement is to arouse a defensive argument while an "I" statement often encourages an open discussion of differences in opinion. "I" statements express an opinion without putting the other person down. If a supervisor finds that his discussions often turn into arguments, he probably expresses his opinions in "you" statements.

> Rosa did not like the fact that every time she expressed an opinion to others in the office, an argument started. When she took a communications course, she discovered that rather than expressing her opinions, she was making statements that put the other person down. For example, instead of saying "I think that when we meet more than once a week we lose some time that could better be used in completing some backlogged reports," she would say something such as "These ridiculous meetings are a complete waste of time. How can you tie us up twice a week?" When she was able to use more "I" statements to express opinions, she found that others reacted less defensively and arguments were less likely.

Using *you* as a way to introduce an observation about something that has happened does not necessarily make that observation a "you" statement. "When I try to discuss a problem with you, you get up and leave the room" is an observation, not a "you" statement. In a "you" statement, *you* is used in the context of expressing an opinion about what someone has said or done. It is a great deal more clear when expressing an opinion to use an "I" statement. An "I" statement describes your opinion and implicitly states, "This is my opinion and, although I may disagree with your opinion, I recognize your right to have a different point of view." This self-clarity coupled with respect for others' opinions is the essence of the assertive stance. "I" statements get the point across and encourage people to listen and cooperate.

"You" statements can be converted to "I" statements that say the same thing by stating the effects of a particular action on the supervisor or by expressing an alternative view. For example,

"You are always late" could be converted to an "I" statement like this: "I find it very frustrating to have to wait for you." "Your way of doing that project is all wrong" could be converted to "I can see several other ways of doing that project that I think might be more effective."

Do you find that other people are defensive or argumentative when you express opinions? When you express your opinions, do you use "I" or "you" statements?

SELF-TEST

Convert each of the following "you" statements to an "I" statement that says much the same thing.
1. "You never listen to anything I say."
2. "Your way of looking at that situation is idiotic."
3. "You are so slow it's a wonder you ever get anything done."
4. "You are the problem in this situation."

ANSWERS
1. "I'm feeling as if you're not listening to me."
2. "I look at this situation quite differently than you do."
3. "I really need you to complete your work rapidly."
4. "I'm having trouble with your way of handling this situation."

Calling the Process

In any interaction between a supervisor and an employee, there are two components: the content of the interaction, such as what is being spoken about in a conversation, and the process of the interaction—all of the unspoken things that are going on between the supervisor and employee while they are talking about or acting out the content. In most situations, major attention can remain focused on the content. This is true as long as the process (the interaction) does not present a problem that needs to be dealt with. Voice characteristics, body language, general interactional quality, and how a particular task is being carried out are examples of process variables that may signal there are unspoken issues that need to be addressed directly. For example, if someone is looking at her watch every few seconds during a discussion, the process is calling for attention. If there is a great deal of tension and conflict within the office since some new policies were introduced, the process needs attention. If an employee is producing work at half her normal speed, the process must be discussed. Calling the process means talking directly about the unspoken aspects of an interaction. It consists of two steps. The first step is to make an observation. The second step is to ask a question, to state a hunch, or to make an "I" statement.

Calling the process means making the process the major topic of conversation. In other words, if a supervisor were discussing a project with an employee and the employee sighed every few seconds, calling the process would involve saying "I notice that you're sighing," then saying something like "What's going on?" Calling the process is a way to respond to interruptive behavior so that the focus can shift back to the task.

Calling the process is also useful to check out assumptions about a particular activity. It is important for a supervisor to state assumptions about the meaning of an employee's behavior as hunches, and not as if they were proven fact. For example, there is a difference between saying "I notice that you haven't said anything to me for several days and I wonder if you are angry at me" and saying "You haven't said anything to me for several days, and I know you are really angry about the way I handled your vacation request." Hunches should always be stated tentatively with "I wonder if . . ." or "Could it be . . ." or "I have a hunch that . . ." All of these ways of stating hunches can raise potential concerns without making the other person feel defensive. If a supervisor is convinced that her hunch is right and the other person simply denies it, the most appropriate response may be to back off and raise the issue again if the behavior continues. Sometimes it is appropriate to say something like "You say you aren't angry and yet I notice that you aren't speaking to me. What is going on?" Since very defensive individuals may not be aware of what they are doing or how they are feeling, asking them open-ended questions (What's going on?) may work better than stating hunches.

Calling the process can also be used to diagnose the cause of a problem and resolve it. Often when a problem begins to occur in an employee's work, calling the process is a more appropriate intervention than is criticism or confrontation. For example, it might be more appropriate to say "I've noticed that in the last few weeks you have been making many more errors in balancing your accounts. What's happening?" than to say "You've been making too many mistakes in balancing your accounts." Stating observations and then asking a question can help a supervisor to understand enough about a problem to know what action to take.

Hidden conflicts and tensions can also be uncovered and discussed through calling the process. Every office has conflicts that come up periodically and cause uncomfortable feelings. Often everyone in the office knows that the conflict is there but avoids facing it. This can take a great deal of energy and can sap productivity within an office very rapidly. People often assume that a conflict will go away if no one talks about it. On the contrary, one way to insure that problems created by a conflict will not be resolved is to avoid talking about the conflict.

In one organization, there was serious conflict between the clerical and professional staff members. Both groups felt that the other group was sabotaging their work. Even though she was well aware of the arguments and name calling that were occurring, the organization's director ignored the conflict hoping that it would resolve itself. During a training program, a consultant was able to say to the director and to the staff members "I think you have a problem that you need to bring into the open and discuss." Once everyone was able to actually discuss the problem, the whole staff and the director could uncover some of the causes of the tension and begin to work out a plan to solve the problem.

When there is underlying tension and conflict, calling the process is a necessary assertive intervention because problems in the process can interfere with whatever tasks need to be accomplished.

Think of a situation in which you were seeing some behaviors that would alert you to an underlying problem that needed to be discussed. What did you notice? How could you have called the process in this situation?

SELF-TEST

For each of the following situations, what would be an appropriate statement calling the process?

1. During a problem-solving session with an employee, the employee turns her back and avoids eye contact.

2.   You overhear your boss talking to another worker about the complaints he gets from wives when he sends his female employees to conferences with male employees. You (a female employee) are not sent to the next conference.
3.   You are auditing the books and find that you need additional data. The manager gives you another page of data and then you discover that you need still more data. After several repetitions of this, you are getting rather frustrated.
4.   One of your staff members has missed the last three staff meetings. You assume he's avoiding other staff members.

ANSWERS

1.   "I notice that you're turning away from me. Are you upset with what I'm saying?"
2.   "I have heard that there have been complaints about sending female employees to conferences with male employees, and I notice that you didn't send me to the last conference. Is there a connection between these two events?"
3.   "I notice that I'm getting data I need for the audit a page at a time. What's going on?"
4.   "I'm aware that you haven't been to the last several staff meetings, and I'm assuming that this means that you don't want to interact with the rest of the staff for some reason. Is that a correct assumption?"

"Given That" Statements

There are many factors that interfere with maximum productivity by employees. For example, a work unit might be overloaded with work, understaffed, short on financial resources, staffed with too many new employees, burdened by organizational rules and policies, forced to do jobs that should be assigned to other units, or run by ineffective and insensitive upper management. Employees also come to the work place handicapped with personal problems, poor preparation for the job, and personality problems. It is impossible to eliminate all of the factors that make it more difficult for an employee to do a superior job; however, it is possible to help an employee become more productive in spite of problems. These problems prevent good employee performance only when they become excuses for not trying to improve performance. "Given that" statements involve acknowledging real handicaps to effective performance and insisting that the employee find a way to be more productive given the handicaps. "Given that" statements are a powerful way to remove all excuses so that a productive discussion about how to improve performance can occur.

> Alvarez was the language arts curriculum supervisor for a large urban school district. He had been asked to meet with a teacher who had been having great difficulty in following district curriculum guidelines. In the discussion, the teacher first said he could not follow district guidelines because of class size. Alvarez said, "Given that all teachers have a greater than optimum-size class right now, what would you need to do to cover the basic curriculum writing projects?" The teacher then pointed out that the real problem was the unruly and poorly trained minority children in his classroom. Alvarez then said, "I know the job would be easier if all your students had the same academic background, but since they don't, what would help to bring the students with poorer backgrounds up to the minimum so you could complete the writing curriculum?"

One strategy that does not work in dealing with real handicaps to effective performance is to try to argue them away. If the workers in an office are overloaded because the unit is understaffed, the supervisor will not accomplish anything by saying "We're not really that understaffed. You only have a caseload of 380." An effective supervisor might say something like "Given that each staff member does have a very high caseload, what do you think we could do to provide better service to the clients?" or "Given that you do have a lot of problems finding adequate care for your children, what could you do so that this problem does not interfere with your getting the job done?" In this kind of interaction, the supervisor is essentially saying "I'll grant you that one. Now what?" This technique can eliminate long and generally unproductive discussions about how bad things really are or about whether the employee is justified in being frustrated with the situation. It also puts the responsibility back on the employee not to allow these handicaps to serve as an excuse for not trying to improve performance.

What are some of the limiting factors in your work situation that others might use as excuses? Have you needed to use "given that" statements in any of these situations?

For each of the following situations, what would be an appropriate "given that" statement?

1. Your employees must use a computer to complete data summaries at the end of the day. The computer is often down. Data summaries are essential for department productivity figures.
2. Your secretary has been misfiling client records so that in some cases records are not available. She claims that the telephone calls she must answer distract her too much for her to file accurately.
3. Your technician claims that he cannot do accurate analyses because he is going through a lot of stress at home; however, your final grant report is due soon, so you must have accurate data.

1. "Given that the computer is often down, what would you need to do so that the data summaries could be done by the end of the day?"
2. "I can understand that telephone calls are distracting; however, it is essential that we be able to find client records. What could you do so that the phone calls don't lead to misfiling?"
3. "I'm sure that the stress at home does make it more difficult to do accurate analyses; however, since accurate data are essential for the completion of this grant report, I need you to be more careful anyway."

The Broken-Record Technique

This technique (Smith, 1975) is used most appropriately as an emergency technique for maintaining control of an interaction when the other person is either unwilling to listen or is attempting to sidetrack the conversation. When used too frequently or when used in the course of a normal conversation with someone, the technique is aggressive because it involves consciously not listening. The classic example of an aggressive use of the broken-record technique is the salesperson who will not take no for an answer. In the broken-record technique, a supervisor acknowledges what the other person says but goes right back to the point of her message as if she were a broken record. By refusing to respond to the points the other person raises and repeating the central message, the supervisor can forcefully keep the conversation focused on a particular issue. This may be very important in getting an aggressive employee to listen to a confrontation about a problem.

Jurgen had one employee who would not listen when he attempted to discuss a problem. He found that the broken-record technique helped him to keep the conversation focused on the essential issues. For example, when confronted about lateness, the employee said, "The supervisor in the department next door isn't such a stickler about promptness." Jurgen then said, "That may be, but right now I'm concerned about finding ways for you to be here at 8:00." "But Helen doesn't always get here on time," the employee said. "Perhaps I need to talk to Helen about that, but for the moment I'm most concerned about finding a way for you to be on time," Jurgen replied. The employee then tried to change the subject by saying "Did I tell you about the trouble I've been having with Mrs. Jones?" Jurgen said, "I'm interested in hearing about Mrs. Jones, but first let's settle the issue of lateness." Finally, the employee listened to Jurgen and agreed to change his behavior.

Refusing to enter into a dialogue with people about issues of concern to them is quite aggressive; however, in dealing with aggressive people it may be very necessary to use aggressive measures so that the other person cannot control the interaction to such an extent that assertiveness is impossible.

Think of a situation in which you were distracted from the important assertive issue. What did the other person say to distract you? How could you have used the broken-record technique to keep the interaction on target?

Selective Ignoring

Selective ignoring is another assertive technique that seems aggressive if overused or used inappropriately. Selective ignoring is similar to the broken-record technique in that it involves a refusal to respond to certain issues. It is useful when a topic of conversation has been closed or an interaction has been ended and the other person tries to reopen the issue.

Selective ignoring involves ignoring attempts to initiate discussion on a particular topic. This can be done by reiterating the refusal to discuss an issue in a particular way, by not responding at all when certain topics are raised, or by changing the subject. Suppose a supervisor has told an employee that expanding lunch hours from 1 hour to 1½ hours is not a negotiable issue and is therefore a closed topic. The employee might then say, "I really think that employees would work more efficiently in the afternoon if lunch hours were longer. We have all agreed to work longer at the end of the day." If the supervisor then responds to these comments, he has agreed to continue the conversation. He could more effectively say, "I'm not willing to discuss lunch hours."

Selective ignoring is also useful when the other person is interacting in an unacceptable way. It is important not to discuss issues of concern under that condition. For example, if an employee were cursing at a supervisor in the lobby of the building within earshot of other employees and customers, the appropriate response would be for the supervisor to say something like "I'm willing to discuss the issue with you if you will come into my office and sit down." If the employee continued to rant and rave, the supervisor would need to continue to refuse to discuss the issue until the person came into the office. Selectively ignoring any attempts by the employee to discuss the issue in the lobby is an essential part of this intervention because it indicates unwillingness to talk to the employee when he is being abusive.

> Lacey was the supervisor of a substance abuse program. Drunk clients would sometimes create a scene in the lobby of his office building. He found that in order to gain control of the situation he would have to selectively ignore the client's comments about the program and then use the broken-record technique to insist that the client leave and return when sober. For example, he would say, "Mr. Dean, we cannot talk about these issues today. You will have to leave today and we can talk tomorrow. Mr. Dean, either your counselor or I will talk to you tomorrow when you return." He had discovered that responding to any of the accusations or questions about the program while a client was drunk was simply ineffective and often led to an unpleasant confrontation.

Selective ignoring is a difficult technique to carry out because most people believe that it is rude not to respond to someone's questions. Under some circumstances, selective ignoring certainly is inconsiderate, especially when used aggressively to avoid listening to others at all. It is not inconsiderate to use this technique when someone refuses to acknowledge or accept another person's unwillingness to continue to discuss a particular topic. For example, it would be aggressive to say "I'm not interested in your views on this new procedure. I don't want to talk about it." The assertive use of the technique comes after someone has had an opportunity for a fair hearing and still refuses to drop the issue.

◆

Think of a situation in which you responded to a conversation when you felt you shouldn't have. What kind of statements drew you into the discussion?

◆

Assertive Withdrawal

Another problem that some supervisors have in controlling interactions is getting trapped in conversations that are either inappropriate or not appropriate at the time. They may also find themselves being pressed to make decisions immediately and then later regret these spur-of-the-moment decisions. Assertive withdrawal may sometimes be necessary in order to avoid these problems. Assertive withdrawal involves a clear nonverbal signal, which may be accompanied by a verbal signal, indicating the desire to postpone or terminate a conversation. Usually assertive withdrawal is accompanied by selective ignoring of attempts to draw the supervisor back into a conversation. This technique is based on the assumption that the supervisor has the right to use her time in a productive way. Walking away, hanging up the phone, or nonverbally removing attention by starting other work reinforces a verbal message that the conversation is ended.

There are several situations in which assertive withdrawal may be useful. When the supervisor needs time to consider a request or think through an appropriate reaction to a problem, it may be useful to terminate the conversation with an agreement to reach a decision later. When the supervisor is too angry to be assertive, withdrawal for a time may be far preferable to continuing an unproductive or destructive discussion: "I'm too angry to talk about this productively right now. Let's talk at 2:00 this afternoon." When the supervisor has already verbally indicated an unwillingness to continue a topic, or when the discussion is unproductive, leaving the room, asking the employee to leave, or nonverbally withdrawing attention may be necessary in order to actually end the conversation.

Velma could not find time during her work day to do the planning that was necessary to manage time efficiently on long projects. She wanted to be available to her employees but realized that she was making herself so available that it was undermining her effectiveness. To solve this problem, she established 45 minutes of planning time each day. When anyone would approach her with a problem during this time, she would acknowledge his presence, tell him when she would be available, and then assertively withdraw back into her work. She had discovered that when she attended to the other person for a more extended time, she would lose her focus, and the other person would be encouraged to continue to interrupt her.

Think of a situation in which you were trapped in a nonproductive discussion. What happened? How could you have used assertive withdrawal to help you to develop a more effective response?

Techniques for Leading Meetings

Every supervisor will at some time be responsible for leading meetings within his work unit or with other units of the organization. In leading meetings he may need to use many of the assertive techniques described in this chapter.

Since meetings use productive time, it is essential that they be well structured. Many meetings are very poorly run. The meeting leader's word choices, voice characteristics, body language, and overall approach set the climate for a meeting and have a powerful influence on its productiveness. Aggressive supervisors may control a meeting so much that people don't get a chance to express themselves. They may dominate the discussion, insist on doing things their way, not listen to others, and blame and judge instead of solving problems. This type of meeting doesn't utilize everyone's contributions. In addition, people who do not get an opportunity to speak may become disgruntled and less involved in the organization. Nonassertive supervisors may, on the other hand, not have enough personal power to be able to adequately control and structure a meeting so that it is productive. A supervisor who is nonassertive in groups robs the organization of his perspective, fails to clarify goals and objectives when necessary, does not raise problems that need to be addressed, and does not intervene to avoid wasting time and energy. Since decisions affecting the work of every unit are made in committee or in groups, the ability to speak up in a powerful way is essential to the health and productivity of each unit and to the organization as a whole.

Participatory organizations work most effectively when everyone can be appropriately assertive because assertive people can clearly express their perspectives without attacking others. They can also take action to control and focus the discussion.

A meeting can be directed toward telling people information about procedures and policies (a command meeting), having people share information with each other about their work or the work of their unit, blowing off steam, identifying problems, diagnosing causes, generating solutions, making decisions, or developing plans. A single scheduled meeting may include several of these purposes. The leader of a meeting needs to be clear before the meeting starts which purposes are to be served by that particular meeting. He then needs to continually refocus the meeting so that everyone is working for the same purpose at the same time. One way to refocus is to ask "What are we trying to accomplish right now?" Another way is to say "Let's share information now. Later we can identify some problems that need to be solved."

> Linda could never figure out why the meetings in her unit were so ineffective. As she began to watch, she discovered that one person would be sharing information, another would be identifying a problem, someone else would be suggesting solutions to a problem, and another person would be developing a plan for how to implement some solution that had been suggested earlier. Because there were so many "meetings" going on at once, nothing was accomplished. Once she realized the problem, she could intervene by saying, "It seems like we are trying to do several things at once here. John is identifying the problem, Jean is suggesting solutions . . . Let's focus for the moment on identifying the problem, then we can all go on to develop some possible solutions."

The leader needs to keep the meeting focused on each topic long enough to reach some kind of closure in the group but must move the group on when they are spending too much time on a single topic. He can focus the group by saying something such as "I wonder if we're really ready to move on to making a decision. Is there anyone else who hasn't had a chance to express an opinion?" To help the group move on, he might say, "We've been discussing this procedure for quite a while, and I have a sense that we're stuck. Let's go on and talk about what we would need to do to implement it."

The leader also summarizes the issues that are being discussed so that everyone knows what is going on: "It seems as if there are three main issues here. Should we extend the treatment phase of the program for 3 weeks? Do we need to shift two staff members from intake to treatment? And, do we need to revise the last phase of our program?"

The leader must also call the process or intervene when destructive processes are interfering with the group's achievement of its purpose. A leader might want to intervene when someone dominates, when people don't participate, when subgroups are off task, when people seem uninvolved in the meeting, when people are attacking others rather than expressing their opinions, or when people do not seem to be listening to each other. Calling the process is a good way for a leader to handle these interactions. For example, he might say, "Doris has had a chance to express her opinion. Helen, how do you feel about the profitability of this new product?" or "I think it might be helpful if we could stay with expressing our own opinions without attacking others."

Think of a very productive meeting you have attended. What did the leader do to make the meeting so effective? Think of a very unproductive meeting you have attended. What did the leader do or fail to do?

Self-Test

For each of the following situations in a meeting, what would be an appropriate assertive statement?
1. The group has just spent 15 minutes of a 1-hour staff meeting complaining about clients, the agency, and the newspapers. Four items need to be discussed at the meeting.
2. For the last 20 minutes everyone who speaks has introduced a new problem to discuss.

3. One person has been very judgmental about everything others have said. You notice that others are participating less.

4. Several participants in the meeting are suggesting ways to solve the problem of too few staff people in the evenings while others are trying to find out how serious a problem this is.

5. John has come in late to a meeting in which the discussion has focused on the cost of purchasing a new building and opening a branch office versus the cost of adding a wing onto the existing office building.

ANSWERS

1. "I'm concerned because we have four items we need to discuss at this meeting. I would like to move on."

2. "I'm noticing that each person who speaks is introducing another important topic. I would like to see us pick one of the topics that has been introduced and see if we can make a decision on that topic before we move on."

3. "I notice that people are starting to participate less in this meeting. I think it would be helpful if each person who has a comment would give his reasons for his own view rather than being critical of others" or "Ted, I think it would be more helpful if you could tell Karen what your views are rather than criticizing her."

4. "Let's focus for a couple of minutes on talking about how large this problem is and then move on to discussing solutions."

5. "To summarize for you, John, the main issue is what would be more cost effective—purchasing the Dean building for a branch office or adding a wing onto our present building."

Summary

This chapter examines several assertive techniques that may be necessary in order to accomplish supervisory tasks. In the technique of active listening, the listener tells the speaker his understanding of the speaker's message. Some of the important uses of active listening include: to clarify the message when the listener may be distorting it because of cultural differences or strong emotional reactions or when the message is unclear or confusing, to make a statement that the listener respects the speaker enough to really make the effort to listen, to create a climate where people feel free to express themselves and problems can be solved, to reduce conflict in tense situations, and to help others change their attitudes and behaviors. There are many barriers to active listening including the shoot-and-reload conversation, too much questioning and advice giving, and letting feelings or values get in the way of listening.

Techniques for stating expectations are important because it is hard for people to shed the belief that what they expect is so obvious that others should know without being told. To express expectations clearly the supervisor must know what he wants, set goals, and make plans. Employees need to know three pieces of information in order to do what the supervisor wants: what they should do, why they should do it, and when it should be done.

Another essential assertive technique is the ability to say no. Every supervisor may need to say no to demands that are inappropriate, are not in keeping with present priorities, or need more resources than are available.

Giving recognition is another assertive technique. Everyone needs recognition, or strokes. Positive recognition should be genuine, specific, and free of implied criticism. Positive strokes motivate employees. Two other uses of stroking are stroking someone's good intentions to establish a climate conducive to teamwork and problem solving and stroking a manager's authority to reduce tension when being assertive with supervisors.

Using "I" statements is an assertive technique that lets the speaker describe his view about something without making judgments about the other person's point of view. "You" statements judge and blame and often arouse defensive arguments, while "I" statements encourage open discussion of differences of opinion.

Calling the process is another assertive technique. The unspoken aspects of a situation such as voice characteristics, body language, general interactional quality, and how a particular task is being carried out are all process variables. To call the process, first make an observation, and second ask a question, state a hunch, or use an "I" statement. Calling the process can be used to shift focus back to the task, check out assumptions about a particular activity, diagnose the cause of a problem and resolve it, or uncover and discuss hidden conflicts and tensions.

"Given that" statements can be used to deal with factors that interfere with employee productivity but cannot be changed. They acknowledge real handicaps to effective performance and insist that employees find a way to be more productive given the handicaps. Responsibility is put on the employee to try to improve performance in spite of handicaps.

The broken-record technique, selective ignoring, and assertive withdrawal are techniques that should be used only in emergencies for controlling destructive interactions, as they can be aggressive if used too frequently. The broken-record technique can be useful to keep from being sidetracked in a discussion. In this technique, a supervisor acknowledges what the employee says but goes right back to the point of the message. Selective ignoring involves ignoring attempts to initiate discussion on a particular topic. This can be done by reiterating the refusal to discuss an issue in a particular way, not responding at all when certain topics are raised, or by changing the subject. Selective ignoring is useful when a topic of discussion has been closed, and when the other person is interacting in an unacceptable way. Assertive withdrawal involves a nonverbal signal, and sometimes a verbal signal, to postpone or terminate a conversation. It may be necessary to avoid inappropriate conversations or to withdraw to make a decision.

Techniques for leading meetings are important because much of the work of organizations is conducted in meetings. Leading meetings assertively contributes to open communication, cooperation, and productivity. A meeting can be directed toward one or several of the following purposes: telling people information, having people share information, blowing off steam, identifying problems, diagnosing causes, generating solutions, making decisions, or developing plans. The leader of the meeting needs to be clear before the meeting starts what the purpose is and must continually refocus the meeting so that everyone is working for the same purpose. He needs to keep the meeting focused on each topic long enough to reach closure, move the group on when they are spending too much time on one topic, summarize the issues being discussed, and call the process or intervene when destructive processes are interfering with the group's achievement of its purpose.

Bibliography

Atwater, L. T. *I hear you: Listening skills to make you a better manager.* New York: Prentice-Hall, 1982.

Bach, G., & Wyden, P. *The intimate enemy: How to fight fair in love and marriage.* New York: Avon, 1968.

Blanchard, K., & Johnson, F. *The one minute manager.* New York: Berkley Publishing Group, 1983.

Carkhuff, R. *Sources of human productivity.* Amherst, Mass.: Human Resources Press, 1983.

Gordon, T. *Leader effectiveness training.* New York: Wyden Books, 1977.

Hersey, P., & Blanchard, K. *Management of organizational behavior: Utilizing human resources.* Englewood Cliffs, N.J.: Prentice-Hall, 1982.

Jongeward, D., & Sayer, P. C. *Choosing success: Transactional analysis on the job.* New York: Wiley, 1978.

Lakein, A. *How to get control of your time and your life.* New York: New American Library, 1973.

Peters, T. J., & Waterman, R. H. *In search of excellence: Lessons from America's best run companies.* New York: Harper & Row, 1982.

Scott, D. *How to put more time in your life.* New York: New American Library, 1980.

Smith, M. *When I say no I feel guilty.* New York: Dial Press, 1975.

Tec, L. *Targets: How to set goals for yourself and reach them.* New York: New American Library, 1980.

CHAPTER SEVEN

Giving Assertive Criticism and Solving Problems

In this chapter, you will:
- Learn the purpose of assertive criticism and the reasons why assertive criticism is such an important aspect of the supervisory role;
- Learn the steps in problem solving;
- Learn some of the feelings and beliefs that make giving assertive criticism difficult;
- Learn about the DESC Script for giving assertive criticism;*
- Learn to deliver criticism effectively;
- Learn to continue the problem-solving process after delivering criticism;
- See an example of the process in practice.

One of the most important functions that a supervisor performs is to monitor the work that is being done and to correct problems that are interfering with quality work. To do this, the supervisor must be able to give assertive criticism.

The Purpose of Giving Assertive Criticism

Assertive criticism's purpose is to confront problems in a way that elicits the employee's cooperation in the problem-solving process. As has been shown in Chapter Two, nonassertive supervisors do not

---

*The DESC scripting method was first developed by Bower and Bower in *Asserting Yourself* © by Addison-Wesley, 1976.

confront problems in a way that leads to cooperative problem solving. They will often avoid confrontation and allow problems to become quite serious before they intervene at all. When they do intervene, they are inclined to be very apologetic and to describe their concerns in general, indirect ways. They may also save up grievances and explode inappropriately, confusing employees with this sudden change in style. Their voice characteristics and body language are hesitant, pleading, or questioning and they use minimizing words like "This is a little bit of a problem." With a highly motivated group of employees, this low-key approach might be quite sufficient to correct the relatively infrequent problems that will occur. However, given the normal range of employees, the supervisor will find that some employees need more assertive correction and control (Hersey & Blanchard, 1982). For these employees, the nonassertive approach would be a case of "too little and too late." The nonassertive word choices, voice characteristics, and body language fail to convey to them the importance of the issues and therefore may not motivate these employees to put forth serious efforts to change.

The aggressive supervisor, on the other hand, doesn't hesitate to point out problems and to demand that employees correct the problems. As shown in Chapter Three, the aggressive style is one of accusation and blame. Criticisms are personal and threatening. Requests for change are stated as demands. Voice characteristics and body language are attacking and demanding and often send a "you dummy" message. The language used to describe problems is loaded and may involve name calling or judgmental labeling of the person. Unfortunately, while this approach may intimidate an employee into quickly correcting a problem, it creates defensiveness and resistance rather than involvement and teamwork. When people feel attacked or feel as if they are being forced to comply with demands, they may cooperate on the surface, but their underlying resentment saps energy and could lead to passive-resistant heel dragging. Also, people listen less effectively when they are on the defensive. The employee who is subject to aggressive criticism literally stops listening. Instead of examining the issues to see what can be done to solve the problem, he directs his energy primarily toward protecting himself. Thus pointing out to an employee how a problem is his fault may interfere with, rather than enhance, the problem-solving process. Although aggressive criticism often does solve the immediate problem, it does not contribute toward developing a work climate in which the supervisor and the employee work together to solve problems and to get the work done. Neither does it lead to the kind of open discussion that allows the supervisor to uncover the causes of the problem so that further problems can be prevented.

Assertive criticism is the first step in the problem-solving process. The assertive supervisor uses criticism as a way to open up communication with an employee. The purpose of this communication is to uncover the causes of the problem and to remove these blocks to effective performance. The assertive supervisor approaches an employee's failure to perform as an opportunity to help that employee to do a better job. He assumes that most people don't intend to be ineffective, understands that people need to save face, and recognizes that fixing blame stimulates defensiveness rather than an effort to search for solutions to the problem. In this approach, even if the employee never admits that he is wrong, the criticism is considered effective as long as the problem behavior changes.

> Jenine had been involved for several months in a power struggle with one of the receptionists she supervised. No matter how hard she tried, Jenine could never get this woman to admit that she was doing an inadequate job. Finally, she decided to simply describe to the employee how her frequent trips away from her desk were creating a problem in the office and specify how she wanted the behavior to change. She also granted that the employee was clearly trying to do what she felt to be a "good job." Once the employee did not have to admit that she was incompetent, she was willing to alter some of her behaviors.

Assertive criticism focuses on the situation (the behavior) and not on the person. It is objective rather than judgmental. The specific behaviors that are creating problems, the reasons why these behaviors create problems, the behavior that the critic expects to replace the problem behavior, and the consequences for the employee if the problem behavior continues are all clearly and objectively described. Voice characteristics and body language are neutral, strong, and direct. The words used to describe the problem are carefully chosen so as not to put the other person on the defensive. Once the problem has been explained to the employee, the supervisor listens and asks questions to help uncover the causes of the problem and to help the employee to generate solutions to the problem. Together the supervisor and employee discuss the problem until they are able to develop a plan of action to solve the problem. The supervisor then asks the employee to commit himself to carrying out a specific plan to solve the problem and follows up to see if the plan is working. To summarize, the steps in assertive problem solving are:

1. Call the employee's attention to the problem with assertive criticism.
2. Discuss the causes of the problem with the employee and elicit his perspective on the problem.
3. Develop a plan of action to solve the problem.
4. Get a commitment from the employee to the plan.
5. Follow up to see that the plan is working.

This chapter will deal in detail with how to call an employee's attention to a problem through assertive criticism. In particular, it will describe an assertive technique called the DESC Script. The DESC Script, which advocates giving criticism through describing problem behaviors, expressing why they are problems, specifying expected behaviors, and outlining consequences, was developed by Bower and Bower in *Asserting Yourself* (1976). The script is the first step in problem solving, which is covered in this chapter.

◆

Which way of giving criticism (nonassertive, aggressive, or assertive) do you use most often?

How satisfied are you with your way of delivering criticism? What do you think needs to be changed?

◆

Feelings and Beliefs that Create Problems in Giving Assertive Criticism

Giving good criticism seems to be one of the most difficult assertive skills to learn. One reason is that very few people are given a good model for dealing effectively with problems in their families. In some families, all conflict is ignored or denied. The message in this family is "If you can't say something nice, don't say anything at all." Attempts to express anger or let others know when something is upsetting are met with a very clear message that conflict and disagreement are unacceptable. In other families, the norm is to express criticism but never to do it directly. In this kind of family, Mother may have complained to everyone about Aunt Helen but then been very nice to her in person. The message given is that criticizing someone directly will be devastating or catastrophic; however, there is at least a recognition that conflict and disagreement are a part of human relationships. In other families, any problems cause explosive fights characterized by verbal or even physical attack. Very few families demonstrate a way to solve problems through rational discussion. Thus, from the very beginning most people are hampered in their ability to solve problems through direct, open dialogue.

In addition, problems and conflict stir up many powerful emotions. When someone has been doing something that creates problems, you may feel angry and frustrated. Old feelings of guilt at expressing disagreement or criticism may crop up. Old fears that expressing criticism will result in some catastrophe and doubts that you are being fair and are justified in being critical may interfere with effective criticism. You may worry that being critical will be seen as mean or uncaring. You may have such a need to be perfect that you cannot imagine anyone being able to accept criticism without being totally devastated. Giving good criticism requires that you be able to be objective, calm, and confident of your right to confront problems directly. Sometimes it may be necessary to use the techniques described in Chapter Five to be able to deal with feelings that interfere with giving assertive criticism.

How were conflicts and problems handled in your family? What kind of messages did you get about being direct in expressing your feelings about a problem?

Think of a situation in which you either avoided criticism when you needed to be critical or criticized in a very aggressive way. What was the situation you needed to confront? What did you do? What do you wish you had done? What feelings and beliefs interfered with your assertiveness? How could you have disputed these feelings?

The DESC Script

The DESC script-writing technique, developed by Bower and Bower in *Asserting Yourself* (1976), is a clear, concise way to bring a problem to an employee's attention and to initiate the problem-solving process. It is called a DESC Script because in order to be effectively assertive, a supervisor must be able to *describe* (D) what the employee is doing that creates problems, *express* (E) why that behavior is a problem for the supervisor or for the organization, *specify* (S) what she wants the employee to be doing instead, and outline positive or negative *consequences* (C) for either succeeding or failing to change the problem behavior. Writing out or thinking out what she wants to say to an employee enables the supervisor to be clear and forceful and also insures that the problem will be described in a nonjudgmental way. Calling this assertive technique a script does not mean that the supervisor writes out her confrontation and reads it to the employee. It does mean that she must have thought through the presentation of the problem carefully before she talks to the employee. Sometimes the supervisor writes out the script, practices it, and then delivers it without the written notes. With practice, the steps in the script can become a kind of mental checklist that a supervisor can use to decide quickly on a way to express her criticisms clearly. Here is how the Bowers' DESC scripting method works.

Describe
The first step in making an employee aware of a problem is to describe what the employee is doing that is a problem. A good description expresses clearly and specifically what the other person is doing. It uses words, voice characteristics, and body language that are not likely to put the other person on the defensive.

A good description covers facts, not the supervisor's negative assumptions about what these facts mean. In other words, a good description is objective. As stated in Chapter Five, assumptions about another person's behavior are really guesses until they are checked out. There seems to be a common tendency to make the worst possible assumptions about someone's intentions or the meaning of a person's behavior when that behavior is frustrating. Thus, assuming can lead to a judgmental, blaming description of the problem. Using assumptions in the description tends to create defensiveness and also moves the focus away from the behavior and onto arguments about what the behavior does or does not mean. For example, suppose an employee is consistently late for staff meetings. The supervisor assumes that he is late because he is not committed to the organization. If the supervisor starts her script with "You are not committed to the organization," she points the conversation toward a discussion of whether or not the person is committed and away from changing the person's lateness to staff meetings. A script will be more likely to elicit a focus on the behavior to be changed if the supervisor can avoid introducing assumptions.

For finding out if assumptions about an employee's behavior are correct, calling the process, described in Chapter Six, can be used. Calling the process may still be followed by the express, specify, and consequences portions of the script when there is a need to change behavior as well as a need to understand the employee better.

> Sung-Lin was a supervisor in a matrix system that depended very heavily on communication between employees at all levels. One of her employees refused to communicate with the relevant personnel despite several conversations about the issue. She wanted to change the employee's behavior but she also wanted to find out how the employee felt about the job. She checked out her assumptions by saying "I've noticed that you haven't been telling Mark and Hannah when you finish coding and that you seem frustrated. I'm wondering how you are feeling about your job right now." When she had fully explored the employee's attitudes and had discovered that the employee really did not like the job, she was then able to deliver a script asking the employee to change the behavior despite the attitudes. She could also provide support in helping the employee to seek a more satisfying job.

It may be helpful to review the section on anger that deals with assumptions in Chapter Five before trying to describe the problem. This can aid in separating the facts from the assumptions so that your description can be objective.

A good description is not judgmental. One way judgmentalness is expressed is in the kinds of words that are chosen to describe the problem. If the description uses loaded language (described in Chapter Three), the employee is likely to begin planning her defensive retort and thus not even hear the rest of the script. Voice characteristics and body language also have significant influence on how a script is received.

The description should also be specific. There are two reasons for this. First, it is very hard for employees to change their behavior unless they know specifically what they are doing that creates problems. This is particularly true if the supervisor has identified a problem in behavior that the employee doesn't see as a problem.

Jane had been told in her 6-month evaluation that she wasn't able to sort priorities very well. She spent weeks trying to figure out which aspect of her nursing behavior was unsatisfactory. Was she spending too much time talking to patients, too much time working on nursing notes, not enough time talking to patients, not enough time on nursing notes, or not enough time on cleaning up the unit? In other words, she knew that her supervisor considered her behavior defective in some way, and she wanted to correct the problem. She simply could not be sure what aspect of her nursing behavior was the "real" problem.

Second, presenting the problem in general terms invites the employee to change what she thinks is the problem, not necessarily what the supervisor thinks is the problem. Usually a supervisor has a specific complaint in mind when she describes a problem. For example, an employee might be doing one or more things that could lead a supervisor to call her inefficient. She might not be turning reports in; she might not be returning phone calls; she might be away from her desk too much. When the supervisor expresses the general complaint of inefficiency, the employee might start spending more time at her desk, thinking this will satisfy her supervisor. However, if she is mainly concerned about the employee's failure to turn in reports, the supervisor will continue to be frustrated. Further, when she confronts the employee again, the supervisor won't understand why the employee feels that her efforts to change have been ignored. Thus both employee and supervisor feel frustrated.

◆————

SELF-TEST

Pick the better description of a problem from each of the following pairs of statements and specify what cues you used.

1. a. "You're supposed to be on top of all the samples in the lab, but at the rate you're going, you probably couldn't keep track of your own head if it weren't attached."

   b. "I checked the samples this morning and found that there are six samples that have been in the lab over 3 months."

2. a. "You don't communicate with me enough."

   b. "When you change a reporting procedure in the office without letting me know that you are making the change, you create problems for me."

3. a. "You don't seem to really care about the productivity of this unit. You have been placing fewer clients than other counselors."

   b. "I'm concerned because you have been placing five fewer clients per month on the average than the other counselors."

ANSWERS

1. *b* is the better description because it avoids sounding like a judgment and is more specific.

2. *b* is the better description because it is more specific than *a* and, therefore, is more likely to communicate the supervisor's concerns more clearly.

3. *b* is the better description because unlike *a* it avoids introducing assumptions that could sidetrack the discussion. It concentrates on behavior.

Express

The second DESC step that the Bowers propose is *express:* in calling an employee's attention to a problem, let the employee know why what he is doing is a problem. Expressing this is critical because this is one of the most important motivational steps in the script. People are much more likely to be motivated to change something when they understand clearly why others see the behavior as a problem.

> The director of training in one organization was extremely frustrated because one unit of the organization was not firming up a schedule for follow-up training. She would periodically call the manager of the unit and point out that the training had not been scheduled and ask for a decision to be made soon. Finally, she explained that she was holding up her whole training calendar to make sure that the follow-up could be scheduled. Once the manager knew why scheduling the follow-up now was important, he was quite willing to make a decision.

There are several reasons why a behavior might become a problem that needs to be confronted. The most important reason for confronting a behavior is interference with accomplishing the job. A supervisor needs to help employees understand how what they are doing might be interfering with their ability to get the work done. Also, specifying the effect that a particular behavior has on productivity forces the supervisor to separate personal preferences for a certain way of doing things from behaviors that clearly interfere with productivity. For example, a supervisor may strongly believe that it is more efficient to file materials once a week than to file every day. An employee may be doing excellent work and at the same time filing once a day. The supervisor can express his personal preference in this case, but he may not be able to make a good case for this personal style affecting output. On the other hand, if an employee's lateness means that he can handle significantly fewer clients per day, the supervisor can make a good case for how the behavior interferes with getting the job done. Employees also need to know that their behavior is a problem when it prevents others from getting their work done. For example, an employee might need to be reminded that stopping to chat with others on the way back from the Xerox machine interferes with others' productivity.

A second reason for confronting a behavior is if it is against the rules, is unethical, or is illegal. In some cases, employee behaviors violate the company rules without affecting productivity in any way that can be easily specified. For example, with some employees, it is hard to say how lateness interferes with getting the work done. In this case, the supervisor can simply state that the behavior is a problem because it violates company policy and failure to enforce company policy can establish a precedent that cannot be allowed. Another example is the frequent occurrence in human services agencies of breaches of confidentiality through discussions of cases in the halls. Counselors need to be reminded that such behavior is a problem because it is a breach of confidentiality and therefore unethical.

A third reason for confronting a behavior is that it creates interpersonal difficulties within the organization. For example, if a supervisor has to remind an employee several times to complete assignments, a working relationship is established in which the supervisor cannot trust the employee and then is always getting after the employee. Even if the employee produces the reports, a supervisor may want to help the employee understand that behaving in a way that creates this kind of personal relationship is not desirable. Behaviors may also need to be confronted because they create tension with co-workers or with higher management. Since employees may not really be aware of the interpersonal effects of their behavior, they may be motivated to change when they are told about the problem.

A fourth reason for confronting a behavior is that it is damaging that person's credibility or status in the organization. Since most people are highly motivated to protect their own interests, they will be more willing to solve problems that interfere with these interests. For example, an employee might need to be reminded that his failure to quickly return calls to important customers hurts his credibility and potentially damages his sales. The more a supervisor can focus on the self-interest of the person being confronted, the more likely it is that the person will be motivated to change. This is especially true when the person receiving the script is a manager rather than an employee. A careful expression of how changing a behavior is in the manager's self-interest may be the only way to motivate him to change. For example, a manager might need to know that his rewriting a supervisor's reports without consulting the supervisor means that the supervisor will never learn how to do the reports correctly, and therefore the manager will always have to make corrections.

A fifth reason for confronting a behavior is that it is creating a negative image of the organization or a unit within the organization. For example, an employee who complains about the organization in front of potential customers needs to know that his negative comments may hurt the organization and in the long run affect his job. In some cases, an employee's behavior may affect the image of other units of the organization. For example, the failure of the data processing branch to notify clients when refund checks are going to be late has negative repercussions for employees in other units, who then look as if they have not done their jobs.

All too often supervisors assume that the reasons why something is a problem are obvious and should not have to be pointed out. This is true only if those who are creating a problem have the same information and perspective as the supervisors do. A supervisor inevitably has a different picture of organizational needs than an employee because of different levels of involvement in management communication systems. Therefore, employees frequently don't have the background to see why doing something a particular way creates problems. Also, most people cannot see themselves as others see them and may not have considered the negative repercussions of their actions.

Most supervisors assume that any good employee shares their values about work and how it ought to be done. In the movie *What You Are Is What You Were When* (1976), Dr. Morris Massey points out important differences in values placed upon work in different generations. For example, for those people now in their fifties and sixties who experienced the Depression, job security is to be prized above everything else. Employees in their twenties consider security less important. Far more important are a sense of involvement in their work and good working conditions. In addition, some cultures place a stronger emphasis on the work ethic and on the relative positions of men and women in the work force. There are bound to be conflicts between supervisors and some of their employees just because differences in ethnic background, age, sex, and so on will produce inevitable differences in values. Thus, supervisors cannot assume that employees will always understand why their behavior is creating problems. The more different the employee is from the supervisor, the more necessary it will be for the supervisor to help the employee understand why a behavior is a problem.

> After working for many years as a technical librarian, Gina
> found herself supervising a group of newly employed high
> school students in a public library. Initially she simply as-
> sumed that these students were not very motivated because
> she would describe a problem and find that they did not seem
> nearly as concerned about it as she felt they ought to be. After
> several months on the job, she realized that they really did
> not understand why something was a serious problem. For
> example, she realized that she needed to help them under-
> stand that filing books under the wrong call number might
> really prevent patrons from finding books they needed. She
> found that she had to carefully express the reasons for her
> concern in order to motivate these employees to change.

Traditional human relations training suggests that what should be expressed when confronting a problem is the confronter's feelings about the behavior. For example, one model (Gordon, 1977) suggests a framework of "I feel x because . . ." or "When you do x, I feel . . ." In intimate personal relations where caring about each other's feelings is the essence of the relationship, expressing feeling reactions to another person's behavior is probably not only appropriate but necessary. In supervisor-employee relationships, however, the employee may not care how the supervisor feels. In fact, with some "problem" employees, making the supervisor upset may be a payoff for the behavior. For this reason, the expression of why the behavior is a problem needs to focus on effects of the problem behavior on getting the work done, interpersonal relationships, and so on, not just on the supervisor's feelings. Thus, saying "You have been a half hour late the last several mornings and that infuriates me" is likely to be less effective than "You have been a half hour late the last several mornings. When you are late, your customers are forced to call back to get information. I think that makes both you and the organization look bad." There are situations in which stating the supervisor's feelings about the behavior may be very useful. A supervisor may need to say to an employee "When you do x, I get very, very angry" when he needs to get the employee's attention. Some employees will not accept that they have over-stepped a boundary until the supervisor is angry.

Another way to motivate an employee to change his behavior is to express not only the negative effects of a particular action but also the positive hopes or goals that are being interfered with by the problem behavior. This focus on creating a picture of how things could be if the behavior described in the initial part of the script did not exist can help the employee to see how change can help him: "I would like to have the kind of supervisory relationship where I can allow you the freedom to organize your own time. Not completing projects on time forces me to control your work more than I think either one of us likes."

◆

SELF-TEST

Pick the better expression of why the behavior is a problem from each of the following pairs of statements and specify what cues you used.

1. a. "Your credibility in the organization is strongly influenced by the quality of your monthly reports. You will not be seen as a really competent worker unless the reports are good and in on time."

   b. "When you don't get your paperwork done, it drives me crazy."

2. a. "I hate it when you override my decisions with my employees. It makes me feel ineffectual."

   b. "When you override my decisions with my employees, I lose credibility and it creates a sense that you are the one to handle everything. That makes me less effective as a supervisor and creates more work for you."

3. a. "Not letting me know when you won't be in is really frustrating."

  b. "When I don't get the message that you won't be in, I
    can't make sure that someone covers for you and some
    of the students in your caseload don't get their needs
    met."

4. a. "I'd like to have a working relationship in which you
    and I can solve problems right away. When you let
    others know about problems but don't let me know, we
    don't get to solve the problems."

  b. "When you don't let me know about problems, we
    aren't able to put our heads together and come up with
    solutions."

ANSWERS

1. *a* is the better expression of why the behavior is a problem
because it tells the employee how the behavior affects his
status in the organization.

2. *b* is the better expression of why the behavior is a problem
because it explains how the behavior affects working relationships in the organization and shows the listener how it
would be to his advantage to change the behavior.

3. *b* is the better expression of why the behavior is a problem
because it describes the effects of the action on the productivity of the unit.

4. *a* is the better expression of why the behavior is a problem
because it describes more fully the positive hopes that the
behavior interferes with.

Specify

The third DESC step in the criticism process is to let the employee
know what behavior change is wanted. A confrontation with an
employee will be ineffectual if the supervisor is clear about what is
wrong and very vague about what she wants to have happen instead. This often happens because the supervisor has not decided
what she wants to accomplish by confronting the employee. Unless
the goal of the confrontation is clear, it will be very difficult to
develop a concrete plan of action to solve the problem. In developing a script, the supervisor needs to decide what she wants the
other person to stop doing, start doing, or keep doing. She also
needs to decide what she herself wants to stop doing, start doing,
and keep doing.

A social work supervisor was very annoyed because a case worker would come to her four or five times a day for advice on cases he should have been able to handle himself. The supervisor decided that she wanted to quit spending 20 minutes discussing an issue she felt the employee could handle. She wanted the employee to try several strategies for solving the problem himself before bringing it in for discussion and to stop bringing in more than a few cases a week. However, she still wanted the employee to keep bringing in cases that he had tried to solve and couldn't.

It is helpful for the supervisor to explore changes she could make in her own behavior that might lead to solving the problem because people have more control over themselves than anyone else. Bringing about almost any change in an employee will require some change in the supervisor's way of responding to that employee. Sometimes the supervisor can change the situation quite radically simply by altering her behavior. For example, a supervisor may find herself trapped in extended conversations with an employee about personal problems when she asks a dejected-looking employee "What's wrong?" One way to alter the situation is not to initiate that type of conversation with the employee.

When specifying the outcome wanted from the confrontation, the supervisor should usually let the person being confronted suggest the means to achieve the outcome. There are several reasons for this. In the first place, people are more committed to plans they are involved in developing. Eliciting the employee's involvement in the process of developing a plan of action can increase the employee's willingness to follow through with the plan. It is also important not to be patronizing to employees. Outlining a specific plan for solving a problem may be experienced as a put-down. For example, saying to an employee "I would like to have letters typed accurately enough so that I don't have to return more than one or two a week for correction" is a specific description of the desired goal or outcome. Saying "In order to do this you should proofread every letter at least twice and then put the letters aside and proofread them again" would be insulting to a secretary with experience. The more motivated the employee, the less the supervisor should be suggesting the means to an end and the more the details of the plan should come from the employee (Hersey & Blanchard, 1982.) However, with an employee who is either unwilling or unable to do the job, it may be necessary to specify not only the desired results but also the specific means to get to those results. (See Chapter Ten for more on this topic.)

> Bart found that his employees were constantly annoyed by his specific requests for change. All of his employees had at least a master's degree, were highly motivated, and knew their jobs thoroughly. In an effort to be specific, he was leaving no room for their creativity and knowledge.

It is important to be specific and behavioral in the wording of the desired outcome. General terms, such as *try harder, be more considerate, be more efficient,* and *communicate more* leave too much space for the employee to interpret for herself what the supervisor expects. Not only does this increase chances of misunderstanding, it also makes it difficult to develop a specific plan for solving the problem.

It is also helpful for the supervisor to decide before confronting the employee not only the desired outcome but also what she would settle for (the bottom line). For example, suppose a supervisor has an employee who takes 3 months to develop an engineering plan that others can complete in 2 weeks. The ideal might be for the employee to do a report in 2 weeks, but the supervisor might settle for a month. Defining the bottom line ahead of time can help the supervisor know how much she is willing to compromise with the employee and can also help to define how far the supervisor is willing to carry the consequences if the behavior doesn't change. For example, would the supervisor be willing to fire the employee if the behavior does not change? What behavior change is the minimum acceptable change? There are many objectionable behaviors that are already above the bottom line, ones that the supervisor would prefer to change but could live with. One device for figuring out how much to invest in a given change is for the supervisor to ask herself "How important is this change to me on a scale of 1–5 (with 5 being the most important)? How invested is my employee in not changing on a scale of 1–5 (with 5 being the most invested)?" If the supervisor rates the behavior change at 5 and the employee also rates it at 5, there may be a very difficult nonnegotiable situation. If the supervisor rates the behavior at 1 and the employee rates it at 5, it may not be worth the supervisor's trouble to press for change. For the issues the supervisor rates at 5, she might use all levels of consequences.

Lee felt that all of his staff members should be able to analyze data using microcomputers. One staff member had very strong feelings against microcomputers (a rating of 5). When Lee evaluated his feelings, he recognized that although he preferred that each staff member learn to analyze data (a rating of 3), he would be willing to have some people who would simply carefully prepare data for analysis. This was his bottom line. Thus, Lee encouraged all staff members but this one to use the microcomputers. He recognized that to push this employee to use the computer would not be worth the trouble.

Think of one of your supervisory problems. What behaviors do you want yourself to stop doing, start doing, and keep doing in the situation? What behaviors do you want the other person to stop doing, start doing, and keep doing? What is your bottom line for behavior change in this situation?

SELF-TEST

Pick the better specification of desired behavior change from each of the following pairs of statements and specify what cues you used.

1. a. "I'd like you to try harder to do a good job on new accounts."
   b. "I'd like new accounts to be contacted at least every 2 weeks for the first 3 months."
2. a. "I'd like you to be considerate when I am on the phone."
   b. "I'd like you to wait to speak to me until I am off the phone."
3. a. "I would like to reduce the number of incident reports on the unit by 20 percent. How could we do this?"
   b. "I want to reduce incident reports on your unit by 20 percent. I want you to check all medication orders personally, talk to each patient, and check all special orders."

ANSWERS

1. *b* is the better specification of desired behavior change because it is more specific and behavioral.
2. *b* is the better specification of desired behavior change because it is more specific and behavioral and it does not imply that the employee is inconsiderate as statement *a* does.

3. *a* is the better specification of desired behavior change for an employee who is experienced and motivated and who would be insulted by overly explicit instructions. It is also more cooperative. *b* is the better specification of desired behavior change for an employee who is unmotivated to do the job.

Consequences

The fourth step of the criticism process suggested by Bower and Bower in the DESC Script is to let the employee know the positive consequences for changing his behavior or the negative consequences for failing to change his behavior. Often during the first intervention with an employee consequences can be left out altogether; however, this stage of the interaction presents a powerful opportunity to motivate the employee to choose to change. Thus, stating the positive consequences that will happen for the employee if he changes his behavior is the best first approach. People are more likely to do something if they feel that it is in their self-interest to do so. In one sense, they are always asking "What's in it for me?" If the supervisor can describe how it is to the employee's advantage to change his behavior, the employee may be more willing to carry out the change. It sometimes requires creativity on the part of the supervisor to think of ways in which the change would be beneficial to the employee. Sometimes the major positive benefit for the employee is to get the supervisor off his back: "If you do this, I won't be bugging you all the time." Other positive consequences might be to reduce tension in the office, to make the employee look better at his annual review, or to help the employee be able to organize time better.

Chapter Three discussed muscle level in an interaction. At Muscle Level I, the supervisor politely requests what he wants. At Muscle Level II, he states his position with more forceful word choices, voice characteristics, and body language. At Muscle Level III, he states the negative consequences that will occur if the behavior continues. At Muscle Level IV, he carries out the consequences. The assertive supervisor starts with the lowest possible muscle level but is willing to apply more serious consequences if the behavior does not change. It is not aggressive to raise the muscle level with an employee, but it is aggressive to raise the muscle level too soon. With employees who are unmotivated, it is often necessary to apply Muscle Levels III and IV to motivate them to change. With more motivated employees, Muscle Levels I or II may be sufficient to bring about the desired changes, and higher muscle levels at an early stage of intervention would be counterproductive and threatening.

If the behavior does not change after several low-level interactions with the employee, or if the problem is very serious and cannot be allowed to occur again, it is appropriate to state clearly the negative consequences that will occur if the specified behavior continues. It is very important that the supervisor not state a consequence that he would not be willing to carry out. This is one reason that threats like "We don't want people who act like you around here" are generally ineffective motivators. If the supervisor states a consequence for continuing a behavior and the behavior continues without the supervisor's following through, he has lost much of his power for later interactions. This is one reason that it is important for a supervisor to decide how far he is willing to go to get a particular behavior to change.

> Ellen, a head teller, supervised an employee who was often 5 to 10 minutes late. The employee did an outstanding job when she did arrive. Despite several confrontations, the employee's lateness had not improved significantly. Since the employee was otherwise competent, Ellen was clearly not willing to fire her for lateness. She was willing to make a written comment in the employee's annual review.

There is a whole range of potential negative consequences that a supervisor could apply to problem behavior. Generally, verbal reprimands have less power than written reprimands. Written reprimands that become a permanent part of the employee's records have more power than memos that can be destroyed. Letting the manager or others in the organization know about the problem is a higher power consequence than just discussing the problem with the employee on a one-to-one basis. Reprimands that will directly influence the employee's promotability or salary are higher power than reprimands that will have no concrete influence on his position in the company.

At this point it is important to be realistic. There are many situations in which supervisors only have access to relatively low-power consequences. For example, in some organizations, firing (the consequence with the most power) is simply not available. Even in companies where employees can be fired with cause, special circumstances may make it very unlikely that a particular employee could be demoted or fired: the employee may have many years of satisfactory service to the company, he may have political connections that protect his position, or the branch manager may be unwilling to take a stand where a court suit is a possibility.

This lack of firing or demotion as a consequence has three implications for supervisors. First, the supervisor must often struggle to develop consequences short of firing or demotion that will be sufficiently powerful to influence a particular employee. Asking "What would affect this employee's working life? Is it something I have control over?" can help to define these alternative consequences. One supervisor, in working with an employee with many years of satisfactory service who had stopped producing at work, started meeting with the employee every Monday morning. At this meeting the employee was to document his performance for the previous week. This intensive follow-up offered an opportunity to help the employee to improve his performance and also served as a negative consequence for continuing to perform poorly. Second, the supervisor must often assert himself with others in the organization to get the backing that makes it possible to apply serious consequences. What this means is that any decision to change an employee's performance rating or to apply any other very serious consequence should be discussed with and supported by management. Third, the supervisor should realize that documentation is the key to having access to high-power consequences. Union officials have made it clear that, even in organizations with a strong union, an employee who is carefully documented to be incompetent and given plenty of opportunity to improve can be fired.

Since the Bowers' DESC Script is a clear and objective way to describe employee problems, it forms a strong base on which to build documentation of an employee's failure to improve. The more specific and well defined the problems and expectations are, the more likely that the supervisor will be able to demonstrate failure to solve problems.

Voice characteristics in delivering consequences can strongly influence the way the statements are received. If the tone of voice is threatening, the consequences statement may sound like a challenge or a dare. It is vital that the consequences be stated calmly and matter-of-factly. It is sometimes helpful to state the consequences along with a statement that the employee has to make a choice. In other words, the consequences are presented as information that the employee needs to take into account in deciding whether to work to change his behavior. As said in Chapter One, when the supervisor implies he can make an employee do something, it tends to set up a power struggle. For example, saying "You'd better begin to proofread more accurately or you're going to lose your good rating" can be quite different in effect from saying "Not proofreading your work more accurately will lower your rating on your next review. You need to decide whether you want to keep your present rating."

With a very difficult employee you may need to use Muscle Levels III and IV several times. Each time the consequence that the employee must face should be a more serious one. This corresponds to the normal steps in disciplinary action that are included in many company personnel policies. For example, an employee might first have a note about his behavior entered into his personnel file. If the problem continues, it might result in a change in the employee's performance rating or in a meeting with the employee, the supervisor, and the manager. It is helpful when dealing with a difficult employee to consider the range of consequences that are available if the behavior does not improve. Since these consequences differ with each company, it is vital that the supervisor know the company's personnel policies thoroughly.

Eugene was working with a clerk who was often late, did sloppy paperwork, and was rude to customers. His first step was to clearly confront each problem with a script. In the first few confrontations he avoided negative consequences and expressed his hopes that the employee would become a fully productive member of the department. When no improvement occurred, Eugene warned the employee that failure to improve would be noted in her personnel file. When her performance still did not improve, Eugene met with the employee and the manager to discuss the problems and let the employee know that failure to improve would influence her rating. At the same time that he confronted her, Eugene looked for and acknowledged positive performance. After several months, there was gradual improvement in the employee's behavior.

Pick the better statement of consequences from each of the following pairs of statements and specify what cues you used.

1. a. "If you cannot decrease your absenteeism, I will have to decrease your rating from a very good to satisfactory. You need to decide if you want to keep your present rating."

    b. "You had better come to work more regularly if you don't want to get into a lot of trouble."

2. a. "If you don't stop interrupting me when I'm on the phone, I'm going to scream."

    b. "If you cannot wait until I am off the phone before asking me questions, I will have to alter my open door policy and ask you to make an appointment before you come to see me."

3. a. "If you can make the next three meetings, I think we can lay the groundwork to complete the whole project by May. That would mean that you could move on to the bridge designing project that you are interested in."

    b. "If you can't get to the next three meetings, don't bother showing up here at all."

ANSWERS

1. *a* is the better statement of consequences because it states consequences as a choice, is specific, and does not make threats as statement *b* does.

2. *b* is the better statement of consequences because it is specific and states more realistic consequences than statement *a*.

3. *a* is the better statement of consequences because it states positive consequences and does not make threats as statement *b* does.

For each of the following examples, how effective is the script? If the script is not effective, what needs to be done to make it more effective? (These scripts intentionally do not include consequences because consequences vary among work settings.)

1. "Your design work lately has been incompetent. We need your kind of incompetence like three holes in the head."

2. "You have been spending time each day making and receiving phone calls having to do with your other business. I
   want you to stop it."
3. "You haven't been charting some of your patients lately before you leave. This means that the nurses on the next shift
   do not have detailed information about the patients' conditions to use to evaluate changes. This could clearly adversely influence patient care."
4. "You don't seem to be too interested in your work lately.
   The last several samples you have run have been reported
   with serious errors in the calculations. Since some of these
   results are used in determining potential hazards, this kind
   of error could result in a very serious problem. I would like
   you to check your calculations more carefully so that this
   kind of error does not recur."

ANSWERS

1. This script has a number of problems. First, it is very aggressive. "Incompetent" is a word that cannot be used in a
   nonloaded way. Second, it is very general. The person receiving the script still would not know exactly what needed
   to be corrected about his design work nor would he know
   what the person criticizing the work wants him to do instead.
2. This script is fairly specific and nonloaded about the description and specifies the behavior change desired but
   does not attempt to motivate the employee to change behavior. There is no expression of why the behavior is a
   problem at all.
3. This script has a clear description of behavior and an excellent expression of why the behavior is a problem but does
   not specify clearly what the script deliverer wants the
   employee to do about the problem. Although the desired
   behavior is obvious here, not stating it clearly and getting a
   commitment to do something about it could lead to a failure
   to change.
4. The last part of this criticism is an excellent script. The
   problem is that the first part of the script interprets the
   employee's motives in a negative way. This is likely to shift
   the focus from solving the problem to whether the employee
   is interested in the work.

◆

PRACTICE DESC SCRIPT

Now, choose a supervisory problem and write a good DESC Script.

D =

E =

S =

C = (Include four consequences of increasing seriousness.)

Evaluate the script by asking someone else to read the script and answer the following questions.

1. If I were the person receiving this script, would I be clear about what I am doing that's a problem, why it's a problem, and what my supervisor wants me to do about it?
2. Is the script written in a way that would be sure to put me on the defensive?

◆

Delivery of Criticism

Writing out or thinking out the four steps in the DESC Script encourages supervisors to clarify their complaints and to carefully consider their choice of words. However, as outlined in Chapters Two, Three, and Four, the way in which the supervisor delivers the script to the employee also strongly influences the employee's reactions. Voice characteristics, body language, and the pacing of the script influence how the message is received. Since the purpose of the script is to communicate "We have a problem that we need to put our heads together to solve," it is vital that the script be delivered in an even, strong voice tone, with eye contact, and with a relaxed posture rather than in an overly meek or overly aggressive style. If the script is delivered in a wishy-washy, questioning tone of voice with no eye contact, the receiver can ignore the importance of the message. If the script is delivered in an attacking tone with a pointed finger, the receiver is just as likely to be on the defensive as if the script were worded in loaded language. Chapter Nine of *Asserting Yourself* by Bower and Bower provides some exercises that are useful for delivering a DESC Script assertively.

If you are too angry to be objective when delivering criticism, do something to discharge some of the anger first. Someone who is enraged is not likely to deliver a script in a neutral, objective tone of voice. You may need to write a nasty memo and tear it up, blow off steam to someone else, or release enough of the angry feelings in some other way to be able to deliver the script relatively calmly.

Clayton had been avoiding delivering a script to Tom about talking to his girlfriend on the only phone in the office on company time. One day when Tom made his usual 10:00 call to his girlfriend, Clayton could no longer contain his rage. He shouted at Tom to hang up immediately and told him he was forbidden to use the phone again for any personal calls. Tom was very resentful and defensive about the way Clayton had confronted him, and although he stopped making calls to his girlfriend, his working relationship with Clayton became very hostile.

When delivering a script, describe the problem behavior, express why it is a problem, and specify the desired behavior before allowing the employee to interrupt. There are several reasons for this. First, you need to maintain control of the interaction. If the employee reacts before you are finished, you have lost control. Second, until you finish, the employee really doesn't know what she is going to be asked to do. The employee's reactions before you specify the behavior may be out of proportion. For example, an employee being confronted about a need to complete one project before starting another may imagine that she will be asked to do all projects in less than a week. Knowing that all that she is being asked to do is to finish may be quite acceptable. Third, once you have delivered the script, your job is to listen to what the employee has to say in response. If you are just listening for an opening to finish the confrontation, you are unlikely to be really listening to the employee.

Of course, it may be difficult to stop some employees from interrupting you. Finishing the script with a very defensive employee may require three things. First, don't pause or give the employee any opportunities to sidetrack the conversation. Second, if necessary, use the broken-record technique, described in Chapter Six, to get back on track. It is important to remember that the DESC Script should not be a monologue but a frame for a conversation. However, it may be necessary to use the broken-record technique or assertive replies, as covered in Chapter Eight of Bower and Bower's *Asserting Yourself*, to get the employee back on track. For example, if an employee said, "What about Mary? She never answers the phone on the first three rings," her supervisor might say, "That may be, but right now I want to talk about what's happening with you." She might also say, "I want to hear your reaction but let me finish first." With a very aggressive employee it might be necessary to repeat the broken-record statement several times in order to finish describing, expressing, and specifying. Third, make these sections of the script short. Overly long scripts are not good with any employee, but they are especially prone to failure with very aggressive employees because such employees will not sit still for a long confrontation.

An initial negative reaction to a script does not mean that the criticism will not work in changing the employee's behavior. As stated previously, most people have a need to save face. One way that some people have learned to save face is to sulk or bluster when they are criticized. Other people will almost always cry. As you learn each of your employee's common strategies for responding to criticism, it becomes possible to just let the blustering or the tears happen without taking those reactions personally. Supervisors who back off from confronting an employee because of a negative pattern of response to criticism may be inadvertently training the employee to be negative. For example, suppose every time a child had a temper tantrum in the grocery store, the mother gave the child a lollipop. What would happen to the incidence of temper tantrums in grocery stores? If every time an employee cries, sulks, or gets angry the supervisor backs off, what is likely to happen to the incidence of crying, sulking, and getting angry when criticized?

> Whenever Lois confronted Kim about her rude behavior with other employees, Kim blustered, saying her co-workers didn't deserve better treatment, and then sulked for days. After the first confrontation, Lois felt it was hopeless to talk to Kim but decided to try again. When Kim's behavior did not improve in a week, Lois talked to her again and continued to confront her and explore the reasons for the behavior until Kim changed.

What to do with particular kinds of problem employees will be discussed in more detail in Chapter Ten. In brief, there are several assertive things that you can do when confronted with a strong negative reaction to a script. First, simply allow the employee to have the negative reaction and go on with the problem-solving process. Second, help the employee to express her distress in clear verbal terms by calling the process: "You are yelling at me. Can you tell me what upsets you so much about what I said?" Third, present the script, then back off for the moment with a commitment to discuss the problem again later. Fourth, if the employee's reaction to criticism is always so negative that it is impossible to do problem solving, you may need to deliver a "metascript"—a script about what happens when the person is criticized. In one instance, a supervisor had an employee who would simply get up and walk out of the room whenever the supervisor started to say anything the least bit critical. This supervisor needed to find a time when some other problem was not too pressing and call the employee in for a conference to deliver a metascript something like this:

D   "Whenever I try to talk to you about a problem, you walk out of the room and refuse to discuss the issue."

E   "I think that creates more problems because it leaves me feeling as if we have no way to solve anything. I feel that you could really work with me if we could just sit down and discuss some things."

S   "I would like you to at least stay and hear me out, and then if you think I'm being unfair, let me know."

C   "If you will do that, I think we can solve problems before they become real crises."

When you deliver a script and you sense that the other person did not hear or understand you, ask her to paraphrase or summarize the criticism before reacting. Clarifying communication problems in the beginning can prevent some long and futile arguments based on misunderstanding. For example, if an employee seems to be acting as if the supervisor said she was a completely incompetent employee when all the supervisor said was that she needed to rewrite the last paragraph of her report, it would be helpful for the supervisor to say either "I'm not saying you are incompetent, I'm just saying that you need to rewrite the last section" or "What did you hear me saying to you?"

It is helpful to confront only one or a few issues at a time with a script. Since the script is a problem-solving process, script delivery needs to focus on a problem that can be solved by some specific plan of action. Outlining a long list of problems scatters the focus of the confrontation so that little real problem solving can go on. What about the employee with a long list of behavior problems? In this instance it may be helpful to say something like "I'm concerned about several problems relating to your work; however, right now I'd like to see if we can take a look at x and come up with a plan for solving that problem."

Helping an employee to understand that this particular problem is only one of a number of concerns is an example of providing a "frame" for the script. A frame helps the employee see how the behavior described in the script fits into the bigger picture of the employee's overall performance. An appropriate frame when dealing with a very sensitive employee who has a tendency to overreact to criticism could be a statement like "I am very pleased with your work in general. However, I am concerned about this one problem. I'd like to see if we can solve it and bring this part of your work up to the excellent standards you have set in the rest of your work."

Timing is very important when presenting a script. Choose the moment of confrontation carefully. For a script to have maximum impact, it must be delivered, whenever possible, at a time when the receiver can listen wholeheartedly. This means that delivering the script when an employee is just leaving for lunch or at the end of the day or the week may not be the most effective timing. Although it is often best to confront a problem immediately when it happens, there are some circumstances in which it would be better to wait to confront an employee. When an employee chronically does something that creates problems, the best time for confrontation might be when the behavior is *not* happening. When a problem is occurring, you are likely to be angrier and less in control and the employee is likely to be defensive (the "hand-in-the-cookie-jar" phenomenon). For example, suppose a supervisor has an employee who chronically interrupts meetings. Catching the employee between meetings, the supervisor might say, "I'm concerned because you often come in to talk to me when I'm in a meeting. At those times, I don't really listen to what you're saying, and I can't pay attention to the meeting either. Next time I want you to wait until after the meeting is over before you ask questions."

When the problem behavior is a long-term habit, do not assume that if the problem recurs the employee is unwilling to change.

People are often unaware of habit behaviors. When she is confronted about a habit, the employee will pay attention and bring the behavior into awareness. While she pays attention, the behavior is controlled. When she stops paying attention, the old behavior will start to return. This is why a confrontation will sometimes lead to 2 or 3 weeks of change followed by a recurrence of the same problem. Long-term habits or deeply ingrained styles of acting require many confrontations before lasting change occurs. Lateness is a prime example of this kind of problem. People who are naturally prompt find it very difficult to understand why anyone would be late. People who are chronically late are usually late not only to work but to many other activities in their lives. They often are also very poor at estimating how long any task will take. These habitual ways of dealing with time are pervasive and difficult to change. That does not mean that a supervisor should not confront and attempt to change chronic lateness. It does mean that the supervisor needs to be braced for a relatively long struggle. It may take 6 months or a year for permanent change in habit to occur. Sometimes it isn't necessary to deliver a whole script to remind an employee to pay attention to a problem. In some cases, just an "oops, it's happening again" is enough to direct attention to the problem so that the employee can bring the behavior under control.

SELF-TEST

Say whether each of the following would be an effective delivery of a script and specify what cues you used.

1. Ralph confronted his manager about the new scheduling procedures the day before a hearing with the budget committee.
2. Martha had allowed herself to get very angry at one of her employees. She decided to talk over her anger with another supervisor and then sit down and develop a script when she had cooled down.
3. Arlene was very concerned about developing a dialogue with her employees. When she confronted them, she would describe the problem and then elicit a reaction from them.
4. Wanda was learning to confront one of her employees who responded to all criticism by sulking for several days. When she ignored the sulking, she found that the confrontation would work anyway.

5. Louis had an employee with many problems. His strategy was to include these multiple problems in one script.
6. Jefferson found that with certain employees who were particularly sensitive to criticism, it was very helpful to let them know what they were doing right as well as letting them know the problem.
7. Bennett would get furious because one employee with an overly loud voice would quiet down for a week when Bennett confronted him, but would then start to talk loudly again.
8. Candice didn't explain her criticisms to employees even when they asked for clarification.
9. Ernie developed very clear and specific scripts but delivered them in a loud and demanding voice and often pointed his finger or slapped his hand on his desk while talking.

ANSWERS

1. Ineffective—A manager faced with a budget hearing will not be as available to listen as usual. Ralph needs to choose a better time to confront his manager.
2. Effective—Martha has recognized that she needs to get her anger under control so that she can effectively confront the problem.
3. Ineffective—Arlene may lose control by asking for reactions before she has completed the script. If she wants to uncover the causes of the problem rather than focusing on solving it, calling the process is more helpful.
4. Effective—Wanda is learning that even though the first reaction to a script is negative, it may still work.
5. Ineffective—Scripting too many issues at once loses the focus.
6. Effective—Letting the employee know how the problem fits in overall behavior is useful.
7. Ineffective—Bennett doesn't recognize that changing long-term habits requires many confrontations.
8. Ineffective—It is important to make sure the other person understands the criticism.
9. Ineffective—Ernie is using aggressive voice characteristics and body language that may make his listener defensive.

Problem Solving After Giving Criticism

Giving criticism is the beginning of the problem-solving process, not the end. A great deal of time has been spent outlining ways to approach the employee about the problem because how the problem is initially broached has a lot to do with how the employee will participate in the problem-solving process. The script is a way to initiate a mutual problem-solving process. After presenting the script, you need to continue the problem-solving process by:

Step 1.   Discussing the causes of the problem with the employee and eliciting his perspective on the problem,

Step 2.   Developing a plan of action to solve the problem,

Step 3.   Getting a commitment from the employee to the plan,

Step 4.   Following up to see that the plan is working.

Discuss the causes of the problem
and the employee's perspective on the problem

Since the script is not an attempt to fix blame, it ideally leads to some real exploration of the issues creating the problem. Before any solutions are developed, both the supervisor and the employee need to understand exactly what is going on. At this point, even if you feel that the employee is being defensive, it makes sense to listen to the employee carefully. It is often helpful to use the technique of active listening (Chapter Six) to open communication with the employee. Listening is one of the ways that an assertive interaction differs from an aggressive one. An employee confronted assertively may not feel happy about the confrontation, but he will feel heard. Mutual dialogue is a very important part of building involved teamwork.

Even if the employee's response is to argue that he doesn't see the behavior as a problem and that he thinks you are being totally unfair, it is far better for the employee to have an opportunity to express his disagreement verbally than to have it expressed later through passive aggressive resistance to carrying out the plan of action. If an employee were to say "I don't see how you can be upset about my working in the stockroom so much. You keep telling me that keeping the shelves clear is important. I think it's unfair that I should have to keep the stockroom clear and be at my desk," the supervisor might summarize and let the employee know he had been heard by saying "So, you feel at this point like I'm giving you contradictory instructions." Responding to the employee's views, even when they are negative, helps to create open dialogue and communicate respect for the employee.

The employee's reactions to the script will often uncover some causes for the problem that may need to be corrected before the problem can effectively be solved. In the situation just described, it is possible that the supervisor hadn't clarified to the employee that he should be at the desk unless another employee is available to take over for him. In another example, an employee was failing to get monthly reports in on time because he wasn't getting the data from another unit of the organization on time. He needed supervisory help to get the data. Once the supervisor really understood the employee's concerns, it was possible to devise a good plan to solve the problem. Sometimes the employee's protests provide you with information that will allow you to devise a better description, expression, and specification in your script. In the previous example, knowing that the employee feels a conflict between parts of his job, the supervisor might say, "The problem isn't that you work in the stockroom. The problem is that you leave the desk uncovered when you are working in the stockroom. That means that customers may leave before they find someone to wait on them. It sounds as if you and I need to talk about ways for you to do both parts of your job without a conflict."

Employees may just need an opportunity to run through their repertoire of excuses for not doing the job. Once the supervisor knows what the excuses are, he can then use a "given that" statement to move the discussion back to problem solving: "Given that you don't like Helen, what could you do so that your dislike of her does not interfere with your job performance?"

One of the problems that most supervisors encounter when an employee is resistant to confrontation is letting their own frustration and annoyance interfere with their ability to problem solve. In other words, they may be perfectly capable of calmly and assertively stating the problem through using a DESC Script, but when they start to listen to the employee they find that they disagree so strongly with what is being said that they react to the resistance instead of handling it. As stated previously, some employees will learn which kind of resistance causes the supervisor to have trouble remaining objective. They can then use this reaction to get control of the interaction, or at least to cause the supervisor to lose control. Handling resistance rather than reacting to it requires that you put aside your emotional reaction to the resistance, listen carefully to the employee's point of view and let the employee know you understand, and then either restate the expression of why the behavior is a problem to make a stronger case or clarify the description of the problem behavior or the specification of the desired behavior. In this method of responding to resistance, you use the employee's perspective on the problem to strengthen your statement of the problem.

Develop a plan of action

This step of the problem-solving process requires asking the employee to develop a plan to solve the problem. As said earlier in the chapter, plans that employees develop themselves elicit more commitment than plans that come from the supervisor. Since the goal of the whole problem-solving process is to develop a plan that will be carried out, eliciting employee participation can be a vital part of problem solving. The more motivated the employee, the more important it is that you elicit some employee involvement at this point. This involvement of the employee in the planning helps to create an environment in which problem solving becomes the employee's, as well as the supervisor's, responsibility. For example, a supervisor might say, "I need you to find a way to balance your accounts more accurately at the end of the day. What would you need to do to accomplish this?" If the employee says he doesn't know, the supervisor has two alternatives. He can make suggestions ("You could do x. Would that work for you?") or he can say, "Since you are the one who will have to carry out the plan, it's important that you help to come up with a plan that will work. What are some possible ways you could see for overcoming the problem?" In this second instance, the supervisor simply refuses to take full responsibility for solving the problem. Giving suggestions as in the first instance is appropriate when the employee probably honestly does not know what to do about the problem. When the failure to participate in the problem-solving process represents an attempt to evade responsibility for solving the problem, the supervisor's assertive refusal to solve the problem for the employee may be an important part of the confrontation. Of course, it is very tempting at this point for the supervisor to say "You should do x, y, and z to solve the problem." Resisting the temptation to take over the responsibility and saying "Why don't you think about some possible ways to solve the problem and we'll get back together this afternoon" may be difficult.

With a very motivated employee, it may not be necessary to discuss all of the specific elements of the plan of action. The end result of the process in this case may be a general agreement that the employee will solve the problem by a certain time. The less motivated the employee, the more necessary it is that the plan of action be very specific. With a very unmotivated employee the supervisor will need to supply many more of the specific details of the problem solution: "I need you to do x, y, and z by 3:00 this afternoon." The development of the plan of action then becomes a negotiation in which both the supervisor and the employee make suggestions, evaluate these suggestions, and then decide on the most feasible plan. In some cases, the supervisor's role may be to question unrealistic plans; for example, "John, I wonder if it's really realistic for you to plan to do six sets of notes a day when you have not been able to get any done this week." It is also the supervisor's responsibility to search for obstacles that might interfere with carrying out a particular plan, perhaps asking "John, can you think of anything that might interfere with carrying out this plan?" The goal is to have a workable plan that will be carried out. This may require that the supervisor step in and remove some obstacles: "So, John, you're saying that you can't work on the case notes when you are being interrupted so much by the phone. If I have your calls held for an hour every day, will you be able to get the notes done that day?"

A good plan of action should specify what the employee and the supervisor are going to do and when they are going to do it. If other people are to be involved in the solution of the problem, the plan needs to specify how they will be informed of their role: "So we will meet every Monday starting next Monday to go over the backlog of reports and see which ones will be priority for the week. I'll let Mary know and you can let Bob know about the meeting."

Get a commitment from the employee to the plan

Once you and the employee have discussed the problem and developed a mutual plan of action, you need to ask the employee to make a commitment to the plan: "Are you willing to do this?" If the employee says something like "I guess so" or "I'll try" or "Maybe," it may be important to ask again, "Does that mean that you are or are not willing to do this?"

The supervisor's and the employee's commitment to carry out particular behaviors within a given time constitute a kind of verbal contract. This clear specification of expectations is quite different

than the usual vague "You should try harder to be more efficient."
Although this kind of verbal contract doesn't carry legal weight, it
certainly carries with it more demand for performance than a
general understanding would. With a difficult employee with whom
multiple confrontations have been required, it may be useful to
write out an actual behavioral contract and have the employee sign
the contract.

> John's supervisor needed to have him finish his client case
> notes by the end of March. He wrote this behavioral contract
> with John and had John sign it. "I, John Jones, will complete
> case notes on 42 clients by the end of March. This will require
> my completing 6 cases per week. My supervisor will assist
> me by having all of my calls held for 1 hour each day."

It is useful at this point to summarize what both you and the
employee have agreed to do and by when you have agreed to do it.
For example, a supervisor could summarize by saying "So I'm
going to have your phone calls held every day for 1 hour. You are
going to then finish 6 sets of notes a week until you have caught up
with the backlog."

Follow up to see if the plan is working
Most traditional performance appraisal systems build in a 6-month
or 1-year follow-up period. For evaluating the effectiveness of a
plan, it is often best to follow up in 2 or 3 weeks to see if the plan is
working. That way, if the plan is not working, some changes can
be made along the way. For example, John's supervisor set a deadline of 2 months for all case notes to be complete. After 1 month
and 2 weeks, he still did not have any of the notes. In this case, the
plan was clearly not working and needed to be revised, but too
much time had gone by before this became obvious. Short-interim
follow-up periods may strongly communicate that actually carrying out the plan is important. Again, with a very motivated employee, it may not be necessary to build in very specific follow-up
periods. However, with an extremely unmotivated employee, very
frequent follow-up periods may be critical.

It is usually more useful to confront a problem frequently over
short periods of time than it is to confront the problem every now
and then over a longer period. There is a story told in management
circles of a town that was struggling with violations of its regula-
tion against overnight parking on streets. The police would ticket
once a month, and everyone still parked on the street. When police

began to ticket every night, the incidence of overnight parking dropped 75 percent in 2 weeks. Confronting an ongoing problem every several months may inadvertently communicate to the employee that the problem is not that important. With difficult employees, continuing to do the problem behavior may be worth infrequent conferences with the supervisor. As a supervisor, you may say, "I don't have time for all of this follow-up." But as time consuming as this process is, you need to ask yourself how time consuming the problem is over an extended period. The time spent in the short run to really solve the problem may save time in the long run.

The Process in Practice

Since the purpose of giving criticism is to initiate a problem-solving process, it may be helpful to see an example of how an interaction might look from beginning to end.

Dee is the office manager of a large insurance company. She has been a supervisor for about 3 years and in that time has built a good working relationship with most of the workers in the office. Recently, however, a new employee has been transferred into her unit from another office. This employee does very good work when she works, but she is frequently talking to other employees away from her desk or talking on the telephone. For this reason, her output is lower than that of the other workers.

Dee: Jesse, I wanted to talk to you about a problem that I have begun to observe with your work. You do a very excellent job when you sit down and work on reports. I've noticed though that you often . . .

Jesse: Wait a minute, I . . .

Dee: Just a minute, Jesse. Let me finish. Then I want to hear your reaction. I am concerned about the fact that you get up and talk to others or make phone calls and as a result are not getting as many reports done as you could. (describe) This makes you look bad and it also creates tension in the office because others either can't work when you are talking to them or are forced to do more to get work out. (express) I'd like you to limit your talking on the phone or to other employees to breaks. (specify) Are you willing to do this?

Jesse: At the other office where I worked, they weren't such slave drivers. All of us used to talk. That's what made the job fun.

Dee: So the change in rules in this unit is a little hard to get used to.

Jesse: Yes. I don't see why you have to be so rigid about it.

Dee: If it were not interfering with getting reports done, I probably wouldn't be, but it is. I know that you can be an excellent employee here and I don't want this problem to interfere with that. (positive consequences)

Jesse: Well, I think that I do enough reports anyhow.

Dee: How many reports do you complete in a day?

Jesse: About 10.

Dee: We try to get at least 60 reports a day out of the office. That means each person will probably have to do at least 15 per day. Are you willing to limit your conversation and work on increasing the number of reports you complete each day?

Jesse: What about the times when I have to go to the stockroom for supplies?

Dee: Certainly going to get supplies is legitimate, but I would prefer that you not stop to chat with others on the way back. You will have time to talk on breaks and at lunchtime when it won't interfere with anyone's work.

Jesse: I guess if I have to do it, I will. It just seems like a pain.

Dee: I can understand that it is a pain to be in a job that demands more than you are used to. I'm hoping that you can find a way to get the work done here and still enjoy yourself because I think we could have a good working relationship if you can get used to this way of doing things. Are you willing to limit the talking and work on getting out more reports?

Jesse: OK.

Dee: Let's get together in 2 weeks and see how it's going.

This dialogue shows a number of things that may be useful to the supervisor in her work with this employee. The first is that she has not been sufficiently clear about her output expectations for the employee. At this point, the employee does not see anything wrong with what she is doing and needs to be helped to understand what's required. Second, the rules in the employee's previous job were quite different. This means that the supervisor will have to watch for other differences and help to keep the employee aware of new rules. She may also have to continue to give the employee opportunities to express her frustration about the new policies and procedures. Third, the approach described here is Level II muscle —quite firm but no adverse consequences are stated. Of course, if the behavior were to continue it would be necessary to state adverse consequences in the next interaction with the employee. The approach is also fairly specific, as it would need to be with the relatively unmotivated employee depicted here.

Summary

The purpose of assertive criticism is to confront problems in a way that elicits the employee's cooperation in the problem-solving process. Nonassertive criticism is too little, too late, and aggressive criticism creates defensiveness and resistance. Assertive criticism is the first step in the problem-solving process. It opens up communication, does not fix blame, focuses on behavior, not personality, and is objective.

The steps in assertive problem solving are: calling the employee's attention to the problem with assertive criticism, discussing the causes of the problem with the employee and eliciting her perspective on the problem, developing a plan of action to solve the problem, getting a commitment from the employee to the plan, and following up to see that the plan is working. Poor models for giving criticism in most people's families and destructive feelings and thoughts make delivering good criticism particularly difficult for most supervisors. Working to become calm, objective, and confident may be an important part of learning to criticize assertively.

The DESC Script, developed by Bower and Bower in *Asserting Yourself* (1976), is a model for assertive criticism. With the DESC Script, you *describe* (D) what the employee is doing that creates problems, *express* (E) why that behavior is a problem, *specify* (S) what you want the employee to be doing instead, and outline positive or negative *consequences* (C) for either succeeding or failing to change the problem behavior.

A good description of problem behavior is objective, nonjudgmental, and specific. Behaviors need to be confronted if they interfere with productivity, violate rules or ethics, create problems in work relationships, damage the employee's position in the organization, or damage the image of the organization. Expressions of why a behavior is a problem are more effective when they focus on the effects of the behavior, rather than just your feelings. Expressing positive feelings or hopes about the relationship can be helpful.

When specifying the desired behavior, you need to know what you want the other person and yourself to stop doing, start doing, and keep doing. It is usually better to let the employee suggest ways to bring about the changes in her behavior. The desired behavior should be expressed specifically and behaviorally.

The consequences of not changing behavior are stated using the four muscle levels. In early interventions, it is best to state positive consequences for change. However, if change does not occur with low-power interventions, you must apply consequences of increasing seriousness to help bring about change. You must try to develop consequences that matter to the employee, get backing from others in the organization to apply serious consequences, and closely document employees to have access to high-power consequences. Consequences should be outlined matter-of-factly and be accompanied by the statement that the employee has a choice to make about changing her behavior.

To deliver criticism successfully there are several things you should remember: use voice characteristics and body language that are assertive and deal with your anger before beginning the criticism; when delivering the script, go through at least the describe, express, and specify portions before allowing interruptions by the employee; realize that an initial negative reaction to the script does not mean that the criticism won't work; if the employee did not understand the script, ask her to summarize and then clarify misunderstandings; confront only one or a few issues at a time; give the employee a frame for understanding where the problem fits in her overall behavior; choose the time of the confrontation carefully; and recognize that changing long-term habits will require a number of confrontations.

After delivering the criticism, continue with the problem-solving process. Discuss the causes of the problem with the employee and elicit her perspective on the problem. This lets the employee express resistance or frustration, uncovers causes for the problem, provides information for devising a better script, and allows the employee to get beyond excuses for behavior to problem solving.

Next, ask the employee to develop a plan of action to solve the problem. The less motivated the employee, the more specific details of the plan you will need to supply.

Then, get a commitment from the employee to the plan. The commitment is a verbal (or sometimes written) contract between a supervisor and employee to carry out certain behavior. You need to follow up to see if the plan is working. It is usually more useful to confront a problem frequently over a short period of time than every now and then over a longer period.

Bibliography

Bower, S. A., & Bower, G. *Asserting yourself.* Reading, Mass.: Addison-Wesley, 1976.

Gordon, T. *Leader effectiveness training.* New York: Wyden Books, 1977.

Hersey, P., & Blanchard, K. *Management of organizational behavior: Utilizing human resources.* Englewood Cliffs, N.J.: Prentice-Hall, 1982.

Massey, M. *What you are is what you were when.* New York: Columbia University, 1976. (Film)

CHAPTER EIGHT

Responding to Criticism

In this chapter, you will:
- Learn the purpose of responding to criticism assertively;
- Learn to recognize mistakes that make it difficult to respond assertively to criticism;
- Learn to recognize different kinds of criticism;
- Learn to respond to teasing;
- Learn to respond to blowing off steam;
- Learn to respond to criticism that attempts to solve a problem;
- Learn to uncover hidden criticism.

The last chapter examined the difficulties that you can encounter in giving good criticism to others. Confronting someone's behavior without making the confrontation seem like a personal attack requires careful thought and assertive skill. It is hardly surprising that the criticism you receive from others can be frustrating or painful. However, even though criticism may be stated in a vague, attacking way, people who criticize you are doing you a favor by letting you know about problems so that you can solve them. When problems are not openly discussed, the person who is bothered by the problem may withdraw, complain to others, become resentful, or lower his opinion of the person whose behavior bothers him.

The Purpose of Responding
to Criticism Assertively

Responding to criticism assertively is necessary to get the information that is needed to solve problems, to defuse tensions, and to maintain open lines of communication. Problems that are not discussed do not go away; they persist and damage productivity and interpersonal relationships.

Nonassertive supervisors are ineffective when dealing with criticism because when they are criticized, they feel hurt, frightened, or guilty. Their response is often either apologetic or defensive. Sometimes they go on and on explaining themselves. Often they will dwell on criticism and worry about it, tending to blow it out of proportion. They accept all criticisms at face value and do not probe or question to find out what the criticism really means. They try to avoid criticism, ignore tension and conflict, and do not work to uncover hidden conflict.

Aggressive supervisors can also be ineffective in responding to criticism because when they are criticized, they often feel angry and tend to attack the critic rather than really listen. They often feel that others have no right to criticize them and that most criticisms are so unfair or biased as to be worthless. They do not probe criticisms but rather are inclined to react emotionally to what is said. They escalate tension and conflict through their emotional reactions and ignore hidden conflict.

Assertive supervisors can deal effectively with criticism because they feel calm and self-accepting. They rarely feel very guilty or very angry when criticized. They are able to sort criticism and calmly discard criticism that does not fit. They try to clarify criticism through questions and try to understand what is creating problems for the other person, so that a mutually agreeable solution can be found. They defuse tension and work to uncover hidden conflict and open discussion with others.

> Jesse was the assistant director of a library system. He had noticed that the director seemed somewhat unhappy, but until his annual performance appraisal, he had no idea that the director had some significant problems with his work. During his appraisal interview, he asked the director to let him know right away when there was a problem. He also realized that when he sensed some tension between himself and the director, he would need to call the process by saying "I notice that you seem unhappy about something. Am I doing something that you don't like?" Jesse often wished that his superior would be assertive enough to let him know where he stood.

Which way of responding to criticism (nonassertive, aggressive, or assertive) do you use most often? How satisfied are you with your way of responding to criticism? What do you think needs to be changed?

<hr>

Mistakes in Responding to Criticism

There are several common mistakes that make it much more diffi-cult to respond appropriately to criticism. Many of these are based on feelings and beliefs that make it hard to receive criticism.

Not distinguishing
the other person's problem from your problem

Someone may criticize you for two reasons: because you are doing something wrong, or because she has a problem. For example, an employee might accuse a supervisor of being uncaring because the supervisor insists that she get the job done. In this case, the prob-lem is not in the supervisor, but rather in that employee's definition of *caring*. If her definition of *caring* is "someone who never con-fronts or pushes," then she may see the supervisor as uncaring just because the supervisor is doing her job. The supervisor receiving this criticism needs to check it against her perceptions of herself, what she knows about that employee, and feedback she has gotten from others to see if the criticism is accurate. At one end of the spectrum are nonassertive people who always believe that the crit-icism is accurate. They never see criticism as a reflection of the other person's problem. Rather than carefully examining criticism and seeing if it fits, they indiscriminately accept all criticism. At the other end of the spectrum are aggressive people who always believe that criticism is a reflection of the other person's problem. They discard all criticism without trying it on to see if it fits. They are not sufficiently open to feedback about their behavior. Either indiscriminately accepting criticism without considering whether it might be the other person's problem or indiscriminately dis-carding all criticism without examining it is very ineffective.

Laura Huxley, in her book *You Are Not the Target* (1963), has described in detail the negative cycle that can take place when you cannot distinguish between criticism that results from the other person's mental state and criticism that really refers to something you are doing. You might visualize the following scenario:

> Helen gets up in the morning and her daughter misses the school bus. On the way to work she is upset and in a hurry and tailgates John. John is frustrated and as he walks into

the building he works at, he stops at the newsstand for a paper. The newsman is slow in delivering change. John says, "Don't take all day." The newsman is upset and when he stops next door a little later for a cup of coffee, he snaps at the waitress. The waitress is frustrated and is irritable at lunch when Mary is ordering lunch. Mary is annoyed by the waitress and is irritable with the secretary when she returns from lunch. The secretary is irritable with another co-worker, who is irritable with her husband when she goes home. In all, seven people were irritable because Helen's daughter missed the school bus.

Sometimes people are critical simply because of their own internal state, not because of something you are doing that is inappropriate. This is especially true of the quick off-the-cuff criticisms that happen in day-to-day life. You are not really the target in many of these cases. Customers, supervisors, and employees all have frustrating lives of their own. Their frustration may get carried into the work environment in the form of unfair criticism. Recognizing that someone is in a bad mood and simply allowing the criticism to go by without reacting is as essential sometimes as is learning to respond assertively.

Seeing criticism as a personal attack

Another mistake in responding to criticism is to take all criticism personally and to feel as if you are being indicted or condemned. Assertive supervisors recognize that even criticism that sounds like a vicious personal attack may be the critic's fumbling attempt to solve a problem. Assertiveness in responding to criticism requires not only assertive responses but also an attitude of objectivity about yourself and the world. If every criticism is experienced as a personal attack, it is obviously going to be hard to respond in a non-defensive way. The assertive person listens to criticism and says, "This is not a personal attack; this is simply information about myself or the other person that I need to examine and assess."

Distorting criticism

Distorting the criticism or hearing it inaccurately is another mistake. You may have a tendency to hear more criticism than is there. For example, your superior might say, "I want you to rewrite the last paragraph of your report." You might hear, "You are an incompetent idiot who never does anything right." On the other hand, you may minimize criticism. When your superior says,

"That report really needs some work. There are major problems in the organization of the report, section two needs to be expanded, and the last part needs to be completely rewritten with some corrections in the grammar," you might hear, "There are a few picky criticisms about the report."

The objective approach is to listen to the specific comments and hear each comment as it is stated. There are two ways that the meaning of the criticism can be checked. One way is the use of the assertive technique of active listening to make sure that the criticism is clear before reacting to it. In the first example, you might say, "Let me make sure I understand you. Are you saying I'm not doing anything right or only that you don't like the last paragraph of the report?" or "You're saying that you don't like the last paragraph of the report, not that you don't like the report at all. Is that right?" The other way is to force yourself to listen carefully to what people actually say and to respond only to the criticism that they actually state. In this case the message to yourself is "What did she really say? Did she say that I am an incompetent idiot or only that she doesn't like the last paragraph of the report?" If you minimize criticisms, you may have to think "What did she really say? Was this a major or minor criticism?" It is extremely important in reacting appropriately to criticism to hear the criticism accurately and to react to what the critic actually states, not to all of the imagined or assumed feelings that might be behind the criticism. This "reading-into" process is one of the things that makes it so difficult to accept criticism as information. For example, a supervisor may hear complaints about the changes she has made in procedure as complaints about her overall effectiveness as a supervisor. This misperception then leads the supervisor to overreact and become defensive rather than maintaining a problem-solving orientation toward the criticism.

Seeing criticism as a reflection of worth
Another error in responding to criticism is to have such a rigid concept of yourself that any fault is a reflection on your worth as a person. Chapter Five covered the perils of perfectionism as a belief system. Unless you can genuinely accept failure to be competent and effective all of the time, it will be impossible to react nondefensively to criticism from others, particularly when this criticism is correct. For example, if a supervisor knows that she can be very disorganized sometimes and is very unforgiving of this behavior in

herself, criticisms that focus on her disorganization become an invitation for her to berate herself: "You really are disorganized. What a jerk you are. Can't you ever get your act together? How can you ever be a good supervisor when you are disorganized?" The more effective way to approach this fault is for her to say to herself, "I'm disorganized sometimes, but I'm still a worthwhile person." The effective way to approach a mistake is as a "mis-take." In a movie there are usually many takes before a scene is finished. Each take is viewed as an opportunity to learn something about how to do the scene more effectively the next time. A mistake is thus seen as an opportunity to learn something so that the mistake won't happen again, not as an opportunity to berate and "kick" yourself. This fundamentally accepting attitude about yourself makes it much easier to accept criticism as information.

Believing that everyone
must have a good opinion of you

You may respond to criticism with the belief that everyone must hold a good opinion of you at all times. This attitude can lead you to feel a very strong need to prove that others who hold incorrect opinions are wrong in their opinions. Of course, there are some situations in which it is very important to correct someone else's misperception of your character or abilities. If a negative opinion or an incorrect criticism will seriously influence your life, as, for example, an inaccurate criticism in a performance review, it is very important to persistently insist that the misperception be corrected.

> Dixie was a clinical psychologist in a private consulting practice. One of her colleagues informed her that another consultant had been telling others in the professional community that she did not have any of the credentials to do what she was doing. It was clear that this kind of talk could damage her professional reputation. For this reason she knew that she had to do something about the criticism. She spoke to the person who had been saying she was unqualified and by doing so was able to clarify this person's misunderstanding of her credentials.

However, there are many situations in which it is neither necessary nor possible to change other's negative opinions of you. Others have a right to their opinions even if you happen to strongly disagree with those opinions. Unfortunately some people become very

invested in having everyone think well of them. They spend large
amounts of time and effort arguing with others in an attempt to
change their negative opinions. They also feel very upset when they
are not successful. Feeling an obligation to argue with every criticism almost inevitably leads to a defensive response. The assertive
posture is that criticisms are information that may or may not be
relevant. When the information is not relevant, assertive people
can state their point of view but they can also live with not being
able to persuade the critics that they are wrong.

> Craig, a supervisor, worked in the same department with a
> supervisor with a very different supervisory style. This su-
> pervisor would often criticize him for being "overly soft" on
> his employees. Craig was satisfied with not trying to change
> this supervisor's opinion of his work. He knew that the criti-
> cism reflected their differences in style and not his ineffec-
> tiveness as a supervisor; but he also knew that he probably
> would not be able to persuade his colleague that this was so.

The inner message for an assertive person is "No matter what you
say or do to me, I'm still a worthwhile person."

◆

Think of a time when you responded to criticism in a nonassertive
or an aggressive way. What was the problem your critic wanted to
confront? What did you do? What do you wish you had done? What
mistakes did you make in dealing with the criticism?

◆

SELF-TEST

Pick the statements that reflect mistakes in responding to criticism
and specify what mistakes.
1. "I'm really interested in hearing what my employees might
   have difficulty with so we can correct problems early."
2. "I can't stand it. No matter how many times I explain the
   situation, she still thinks I handled the Smith case completely wrong."
3. "He says I should learn to listen more carefully when others
   are critical. Nothing he tells me is worth hearing. He really
   has no right to criticize me."
4. "I know that I sometimes do make mistakes and every criticism is an opportunity to learn more about how to handle
   the situation better next time."

5. "I'm so upset. My boss hates me. He thinks I'm completely incompetent and useless."
6. "She's right. I don't run the film projector very well. What an idiot I am. I can't even master a simple thing like that."

ANSWERS

1. Not a mistake—This statement reflects a healthy attitude of taking criticism as information rather than a personal attack.
2. Mistake—This statement reflects the mistake of needing to have everyone hold a good opinion of you at all times.
3. Mistake—This statement reflects the mistake of seeing all criticism as the critic's problem and not examining it to see if it's accurate.
4. Not a mistake—This statement reflects a healthy attitude of self-acceptance and objectivity.
5. Mistake—This statement could be an accurate reflection of a criticism but because of the extreme reaction probably represents a distortion and the mistake of seeing criticism as a personal attack.
6. Mistake—This statement reflects the mistake of seeing criticism as a reflection of worth.

Recognizing Different Kinds of Criticism

One of the reasons that it is difficult to respond appropriately to criticism is that there are several types of criticism and each type requires a different kind of response. Some assertiveness training books talk about criticism as if all criticism were the same (Smith, 1975). This is not the case.

Teasing

Some criticism is just teasing. Responding to teasing as if it were a serious criticism gives the teasing much more weight than it deserves and usually encourages the critic to continue or to escalate the teasing. Learning to recognize when someone is teasing is an essential social skill because teasing is the norm in some organizations. Reacting as if all of the teasing criticism is serious can leave the person being teased constantly defensive. The author's first job after graduate school was as a management consultant for drug-free therapeutic communities in Manhattan. All of the co-workers were ex-addicts and they had gotten into the habit of putting down college-educated professionals. Their opening comment of the day was often something such as "You're here to give us some more irrelevant book learning, huh?" Although these people certainly had some past experience that would lead them to distrust professionals, their comments were not real criticisms of the author and needed to be treated in a much lighter way than would have been appropriate if the comments expressed their personal concerns. Voice tone, facial expression, or words often reveal when a person is teasing. It is also possible to recognize teasing from the context (e.g., the person has not had enough contact with you to make real criticisms) or from your knowledge of the issues that are likely to be of real concern to the critic (e.g., teasing about a messy desk from someone who is not overly concerned about neatness). When it is not clear whether someone is teasing, it may be necessary to probe the criticism to see what it means. How to probe criticism will be discussed later in this chapter.

Blowing off steam

The second type of criticism is "blowing off steam." Blowing off steam is usually easy to recognize because it has the quality of a temper tantrum. In this type of criticism critics are frustrated and want to vent their frustration. They do not necessarily expect you to do something about the problem. In fact, in many cases they know that you cannot do a great deal to solve the problem. In other cases they need to express their anger in order to calm down enough to solve a problem.

> Cora was the supervisor in a data processing department in a bank. Because of a great increase in the volume of credit card business, the data processing staff was being required to work at least two weekends a month. Several staff members were very critical of Cora for asking them to work weekends; however, they knew that she was responding to orders from her superiors. Letting her know about their frustration made them feel a little better even though nothing could be done to solve the problem.

Blowing off steam can serve three purposes in an organization. First, a great deal of tension can be released by blowing off steam. This is particularly important when there are real problems that cannot be changed. Morale can suffer and tension can build when there are no appropriate outlets for frustration other than complaining to co-workers. Second, blowing off steam can reveal important misunderstandings of organizational policy and of the reasons for certain policies. Listening carefully to this kind of criticism can provide the supervisor with an understanding of the other person's point of view so that these misunderstandings can be corrected. Third, blowing off steam can open communication on some important problems that can be solved. A heated description of all of the critic's frustrations with the supervisor or with the organization can bring into the open some specific concerns that need to be examined much more carefully.

Attempting to solve a problem

The third type of criticism is an attempt to call someone's attention to a problem so that the problem can be solved. As noted in Chapter Seven, effective criticism is objective, nonjudgmental, and specific. It includes a description of the problem, an explanation of why that behavior is a problem, and some specification of what needs to be done to solve the problem. However, since most people have not thoroughly studied ways to give effective criticism, their attempts to solve problems are often judgmental, loaded with assumptions, and quite general. For example, criticisms might be something like "You're flighty," "You're disorganized," or "You just don't seem to want to pay attention to your work." These criticisms still refer to behaviors that the critic either states or implies need to be changed. Since an assertive supervisor wants to encourage open dialogue about problems, it is probably best to treat any criticism that is not clearly recognizable as teasing or blowing off steam as if it were an attempt to solve a problem. Although problem-solving criticism is usually delivered calmly, some people blow off steam whenever they criticize. With these aggressive individuals, attempts to solve a problem are presented in an irrational manner that makes problem solving difficult.

SELF-TEST

Which of the following criticisms are likely to be teasing? Which ones are blowing off steam? Which are attempts to solve a problem?
1. "Don't tell me you're talking on the phone again? It's a wonder it doesn't grow to your ear."
2. "You don't communicate enough with other departments."
3. "I can't stand it. You just keep telling me that I have to work the problem out. Why don't you ever offer some help when a person needs it?"

4. "Your operators are totally incompetent. There have been nothing but errors lately in their work."
5. "Smile, smile, smile. You're so friendly it makes me wonder if you're selling life insurance."
6. "This organization drives me crazy. All you supervisors do is sit in your offices. You never do any real work."

ANSWERS

1. This comment is likely to be a tease. The way it is worded and the tone of voice in which it is delivered could confirm this diagnosis.
2. Even though this criticism is quite vague, it is probably an attempt to solve a problem. Further clarification would uncover the specific behaviors that are causing problems.
3. The "I can't stand it" sounds like the person is blowing off steam. Some exploration such as "So you are feeling that my insistence that you work on the problem yourself means that I don't care about you" is needed. You might also need to do some problem solving when the person calms down.
4. This person is probably blowing off steam and describing a real problem that needs to be solved. Certainly the need for some problem solving is apparent.
5. This comment is probably a tease.
6. This comment is probably blowing off steam. The person sounds quite frustrated but may not be referring to a specific problem.

Responding to Teasing

One of the first experiences most children have is the struggle to learn to deal effectively with teasing. Some people learn this lesson well and never find teasing a problem in adult life. Other people are very uncomfortable with teasing and are at a loss for a response. The key factor in responding to teasing is not to take the comments too seriously. Reacting defensively to teasing invites more teasing. Several types of responses are effective as long as they communicate, "I hear you and so what."

One of the best ways to respond to teasing is with humor. Humor effectively acknowledges what the other person says and at the same time communicates, "I don't take your remarks seriously."

For example, the author's response to "So you are here to give us some more of your irrelevant book learning" was "Yeah, I thought I would add it to some of your irrelevant street learning and see what we can come up with." A favorite humorous response to criticism was one shared by a workshop participant whose mother-in-law used to run her finger across the mantle in the woman's home and say, "My, it's dusty in here, isn't it?" The woman's response was "Yes, I'm trying for the antique look. How do you think I'm doing?" The humorous approach is most effective when you want to respond to the teasing but don't necessarily want to stop it completely.

> Sylvia found herself fuming because of the constant teasing of another staff member about the piles of paperwork on her desk. She found that when she was able to lighten up a little and tease back by saying something like "I'm hoping I can bury my desk deep enough so no one will be able to leave any more work for a while" she was less upset and the teasing subsided.

Since teasing is often designed to produce some sort of reaction, another way to respond is simply to ignore the teasing criticism completely. An example of this kind of response would be to answer the comment "You're always talking to someone. Can't you turn off your mouth?" with a comment about any other topic: "How's your project going, John?"

You can also ignore a criticism by "fogging" (Smith, 1975). This technique can be very useful for situations in which someone is delivering a criticism that seems designed to elicit an argument along the lines of "yes, you do; no, I don't." When someone is criticizing to elicit an argument, you can "fog" by agreeing with the criticism in principle without necessarily agreeing with the implied judgment. For example, if someone said, "Your supervisory meetings are really a bore. Why don't you pep them up with a slide show every week?" a fogging response would be "My supervisory meetings probably could be jazzier" or "You may be right." If the critic is trying to start an argument, she may want you to say "Boring! Supervisory meetings aren't supposed to be exciting." When you agree with the critic, the argument often fades away before it starts. Although some assertiveness training materials recommend fogging as a technique to use for all criticism, this technique is a very destructive way to respond to real criticism.

The technique stops communication and interaction rather than uncovering and solving problems. Humor, ignoring, and fogging are all techniques that should be used only for responding to teasing or attempts to start an argument, not for situations in which someone is criticizing to solve a problem.

Sometimes teasing is sufficiently painful or annoying that you may want to stop the teasing altogether. The simplest way to stop teasing is with some variation on "Hey, knock it off" or "Stop it!" When the teasing has become a more serious issue, it may be very important to confront the teasing using a DESC Script: "You are teasing me at nearly every staff meeting about being a woman and therefore emotional and flighty about my work. This undermines my credibility with my employees, and I feel that it's damaging our relationship. I would like you to stop making jokes about my sex." Using the script format makes a serious issue of teasing. For this reason it is not an appropriate strategy to use with all teasing criticism. Using a script may make a serious issue of what should be treated lightly.

If you suspect that the teasing is an indirect or hidden way to express a real criticism, it is important to call the process to find out what the critic means by the teasing. As outlined in Chapter Six, calling the process is a two-part intervention. The first part involves making an observation, for example, "I notice that you have been teasing me about my effectiveness." The second half involves a question or a statement, such as "Is there a problem we need to discuss?" As you remember, calling the process is particularly useful when there are unspoken messages that need to be brought into the open. Criticism disguised as teasing is a perfect example of this kind of situation. Sometimes the person who is making an indirect criticism will deny that there is any problem. At that point you can either back off by saying "I would like to solve problems before they become crises so if you do have problems with something I'm doing, I would like to know" or can continue to confront by saying something like "If you aren't having a problem, I can't understand why you are teasing me about my effectiveness in front of others." If the critic acknowledges that the teasing is expressing a real criticism, it is then appropriate to question the critic further to find out what you are doing that is a problem, why it is a problem, and what the critic wants you to do about it. Once the problem is clear, it is appropriate to initiate a problem-solving dialogue.

In summary, you can respond to teasing by:
1. Humor.
2. Ignoring.
3. Fogging.
4. Saying stop it.
5. Using the DESC Script.
6. Calling the process, questioning, and problem solving.

Think of a time when you were teased on the job. How did you respond? Were you satisfied with the results of this kind of response? If not, how would you like to have responded?

Responding to Blowing Off Steam

In responding to blowing off steam, you should provide an opportunity for the critic to release tension and at the same time be alert to opportunities to correct misperceptions and to solve underlying problems. When the person is blowing off steam because of distorted information about the situation, it is important to correct these misperceptions first.

Aretha was the supervisor in a dietary department in a hospital. One of her employees came in to see her in a state of outrage. The employee understood that a large number of employees were going to be laid off in an austerity move. Aretha quickly let the employee know that the rumor was incorrect. Once the situation was clarified, the employee's anger faded.

Sometimes, however, a person who is blowing off steam because of distorted information is too angry to listen to an explanation of the facts of the situation. In this case and with blowing off steam that is not based on incorrect information, the best response to the criticism is often to ask "What else?" or to use active listening to allow the person to express his frustrations until he is no longer so angry. Listening to the initial blowup can allow the release of enough tension to prepare ground for a more considered discussion. It can also be very helpful to ask the person to describe specifically what has happened that he is upset about. Recounting the detailed facts in a situation requires the person to calm down and use his "adult" information-processing self.

If you watch a person blowing off steam, there is often a moment when the person leans back in the chair, sighs, lowers his voice, or in some other way indicates that some of the anger is gone. At this point, it is often possible to provide an explanation or to do some rational problem solving that would not have been accepted earlier.

> Dale was the president of a small company that provided supplies used in many other manufacturing processes. Customers would sometimes visit the company in a rage to complain about the product or about service. Dale's strategy was to invite the person into his office, provide the person with a comfortable chair, and then lean back and say, "What else do you think we are doing wrong? What else don't you like about our company?" When the person had calmed down enough to really discuss the problems, Dale would then explain or work with the person to develop ways of handling problems.

To move the person to problem solving after he has blown off steam, the supervisor might say, "Among your other frustrations, it sounds as if there are some problems with x that we need to take a look at" or "What can we do at this point to improve the situation?"

When the critic is addressing a legitimate problem, it is often helpful to acknowledge the person's right to be frustrated at the start of the conversation and to agree with the criticism: "I can understand why you would be frustrated. You really didn't commit yourself to working every weekend" or "You have a right to be angry. You were counting on having the product by now." For some reason, granting the person the right to be angry often reduces tension. The critic can then sometimes be more reasonable because there is no need to provide a justification for the anger.

There are times when it is essential that you set some limits on the expression of anger. First, you must set limits when the frustration is being expressed in a violent and abusive way. Not setting limits in this situation can cause you to lose credibility and respect. Repeated confrontations and even raising the muscle level may be necessary in order to bring about a different approach with an employee whose habitual style is aggressive. It may even, in some cases, be necessary to elicit the support of a superior in helping an employee to recognize that aggressively attacking her superior is simply unacceptable. Both clients and employees may become so angry that they become abusive. In most cases one of the worst things to do in this situation is to become abusive back. The only time that an aggressive reaction may be useful when someone is being abusive is to shock the person out of an almost hysterical state. However, the aggressive response may simply make the critic angrier.

In Chapter Six, the technique of selective ignoring was discussed. Abusive criticism is one situation that calls for selective ignoring. For example, an irate customer who was cursing the supervisor might be told, "Calling me names isn't the best way to work on solving the problem. Let's sit down and talk about it" or "I can understand that you are angry because you expected to get a response to your letter much sooner. I'd be happy to discuss it if you will sit down and tell me what happened." It is then very important not to discuss the complaint until the person becomes calm. With some people it may require many repetitions of the statement before they will become calm. If the person will not calm down enough to discuss the problem, it may, in some cases, be necessary to have the person removed. Generally, however, granting the person's right to be angry and setting limits will calm the person down enough to allow the situation to be defused through further discussion.

Second, you should set limits when people attempt to blow off steam at an inappropriate place or an inappropriate time.

> Clarissa was a nursing supervisor in an out-patient unit of a hospital. One day one of the doctors started to rant and rave about the record keeping in her unit in front of a patient. Clarissa was able to say "Dr. Jones, let's discuss the charts as soon as you are through with Mrs. Ames." When he started his tirade again, she repeated, "Clearly there are some problems with charts that we need to discuss. Let's talk about them when we are through with Mrs. Ames." Although he fumed through the rest of the examination, he did wait to discuss the issue until later.

Third, everyone has personal limitations on time, energy, and resources. Just because a person needs to blow off steam does not mean that you must be willing to be the audience. For example, sometimes the assertive supervisor must say, "I understand that you are frustrated; however, I can't listen right now" or "I understand that you need to blow off steam, but I'm not willing to be the person you blow off steam to." Sometimes this refusal to discuss an issue with someone needs to be reinforced by selective ignoring or withdrawal.

Blowing off steam can be useful to an organization when it is properly managed. Improperly managed, blowing off steam can be explosive and destructive. Proper management means responding in a calm and rational way that allows the other person to finish blowing off steam and to calm down. Most particularly it requires that the assertive supervisor stay calm and powerful while others blow off steam. In summary, you can respond to blowing off steam by:

1. Correcting misperceptions.
2. Using listening and asking for details to allow the person to release tensions and to calm down.
3. Being alert for problems that need to be solved.
4. Acknowledging the other person's right to be angry.
5. Setting limits when the person is violent or abusive, when the time or place is inappropriate, or when you are not willing to listen to the person blow off steam.

Think of a situation in which someone was blowing off steam to you. How did you handle the situation? How effective was your response in relieving tension and in uncovering problems that needed to be solved? What else could you have done?

Responding to Criticism
That Attempts to Solve a Problem

As said earlier, people who call your attention to problems are doing you a favor. By letting you know about the problem, they are giving you an opportunity to solve it rather than keeping conflict and tension hidden. Open discussion of problems is one of the hallmarks of productive organizations (Herman & Korenich, 1977).

It is clear, however, that most criticism requires some translation to put it in a usable form. Many attempts to direct attention to problems will be too general, too attacking, and filled with assumptions. In order to solve a problem, you need three pieces of information: what specifically you are doing that's causing a problem; why it is a problem; and what the other person wants you to do about the problem. In other words, you need to ask questions that elicit good describe, express, and specify portions of the DESC Script.

At an employee's annual review, Alma asked the employee if there were any problems she wished to discuss. After some hesitation the employee said, "You're too flighty." Alma asked the employee to describe the behavior further by saying "What am I doing that makes you say that I'm flighty? Give me an example of something you would call flighty." The employee responded by saying "When you suggest priorities for tasks, you often change your mind and reassign priorities." Alma asked, "What bothers you about that?" The employee answered, "I get confused by the changing priorities. I'm never sure when I start to work on a task that the priorities won't change." Alma asked the employee to specify the desired behavior by saying "What do you want me to do about the problem?" and the employee answered, "I'd like you to keep the same priorities once you assign a task."

It is very important to probe general criticisms even if the criticisms happen to be the same as your self-criticisms. For example, an employee might call a supervisor "disorganized." Even though the supervisor may agree that she is disorganized, she does not know from this description of the problem what is specifically bothering the other person. Agreeing to general criticisms about yourself does not lead to a concrete plan of action for solving a problem. When you glibly agree with a criticism without exploring what you are doing that causes a problem, why this is a problem, and what the critic wants you to do, you are short-circuiting the problem-solving process.

Once the person has said what behavior is causing a problem, why that behavior is a problem, and what she wants done about it, you have all the information that is necessary to begin to solve the problem. Then you need to evaluate the criticism to see whether the description of the behavior is accurate. As stated earlier, it is sometimes important to disagree vigorously and use documentation when inaccurate criticism will adversely affect your standing in the organization. Sometimes you may disagree with the critic's formulation of the problem but accept the fact that there is some problem that needs to be solved. For example, the supervisor in the preceding example might say, "I don't believe that I change priorities that frequently, but clearly there is some problem between us. Can you say some more about what's bothering you?"

Once you have examined the facts and have come to some agreement about the situation, you must decide whether you accept the criticism as your problem and are therefore willing to change. You may try on the criticism and decide that although you agree with the facts, you disagree with the evaluation that the particular behavior is bad. The supervisor could, for example, say, "I agree that I sometimes change my assessment of priorities after I assign a task; however, it is clear to me that in this line of work priorities do change frequently. I will probably continue to shift priorities. Given this reality, is there anything we can do to make the situation more livable for you?" It is not necessary to change something just because a particular behavior causes problems for others. The only obligation of an assertive supervisor is to listen to criticism with a relatively objective point of view and to decide whether it is in her best interests and the best interests of the organization to change. It is helpful when possible to offer to find some way to assist the critic in dealing with the behavior as it stands; however, it is clearly not always possible or appropriate to make this offer.

If you agree with the need to change, explore with the critic mutually acceptable solutions to the problems. Although the critic may suggest particular solutions, those solutions may not be acceptable to the person being criticized: "I can't guarantee that I won't ever change the priority on a task after I make an assignment. I am willing to talk to you about how to rearrange priorities of other tasks when I assign a new high-priority task." Developing an acceptable plan of action is a negotiation process. At the end of a problem-solving session, there should be some agreement on a specific plan for solving the problem or a clear understanding that the critic will have to live with the problem. As in a session designed around criticizing others, it is helpful to summarize any agreements that come out of the discussion.

One very difficult problem for most people is responding appropriately to criticism that is delivered in a very hostile or aggressive way. This is particularly difficult when the criticism comes from a superior because it is hard not to react emotionally to the childlike position that such criticism creates for the person receiving the criticism.

It is important when dealing with a hostile critic to detach yourself emotionally from the criticism and recognize the aggressiveness as the critic's problem: "Helen doesn't know how to criticize without being aggressive. Her criticism is not a reflection of my worth." You need to listen objectively for the problem the critic is trying to address. Some aggressive critics may be ready to

discuss the problem after they have calmed down. Others may refuse to provide any clarification of the problem. When asked to
clarify the problem they may say something such as "You're just
flighty. You should know what I mean." This is particularly true
of the threatened superior who feels cornered when questioned in
any way by an employee. With a highly threatened superior it may
be impossible to question or probe the criticism at all without
arousing defensiveness. One strategy that can be helpful is to ask
for feedback frequently. Asking for frequent feedback prevents a
buildup of tension and may reduce the occurrence of attacks.
However, sometimes the only alternative may be to learn to detach
yourself from the other person's hostility. If you cannot get any
clarification of a criticism, a legitimate response could be "I'd
really like to do something to solve the problem but I can't when I
don't know specifically what is bothering you. The next time I'm
doing something flighty, point it out and let's talk about it."

When a critic is consistently hostile, it may be important to deliver a script about the way in which the critic expresses concerns:
"When you feel I haven't handled a situation effectively, you will
often call me in and start to tell me how stupid I am before I've
had a chance to clarify the situation. This really puts me on the
defensive and makes it difficult for us to discuss a problem and
come up with some good solutions. I would appreciate it if you
would let me tell you my perceptions of the problem before you tell
me that I handled the situation incorrectly." With a threatened
superior, this kind of script may provoke so much defensiveness
that it will not be effective. With a superior who is an aggressive
bully, taking a stand may help her to give more useful criticism.
With employees, it is vital to establish appropriate boundaries in
the way they criticize. As mentioned earlier, it may be necessary
to repeatedly confront and raise the muscle level with habitually
aggressive employees.

Voice characteristics and body language are very influential in
determining how well the problem-solving discussion will go. Most
effective problem solving occurs when the criticism is treated as
information to be examined objectively. An assertive response to
criticism is delivered in a neutral tone of voice and with relatively
relaxed body posture. A defensive tone of voice in asking the question "What am I doing that's creating a problem?" or "Why is this
a problem?" can change the tone of the discussion from rational

problem solving to defensive argumentation. Listening to criticism with a clenched jaw, arms crossed rigidly, or hands on hips and leaning forward already communicates defensiveness about the criticism.

In summary, you can respond to criticism that attempts to solve a problem by:

1. Eliciting good describe, express, and specify portions of the DESC Script.
2. Evaluating the criticism for accuracy.
3. Deciding whether you accept the criticism as your problem and are willing to change and, when appropriate, clearly disagreeing with the criticism.
4. Exploring mutually acceptable solutions if you agree with the need to change.

EXERCISE

Think of a time when you were criticized and you felt that the underlying criticism was legitimate. How was the criticism expressed? How did you respond? Were you satisfied with the results of this kind of response? If not, how would you like to have responded?

Think of a time when you were criticized and you felt that the criticism was illegitimate. How did you respond? Were you satisfied with the results of this kind of response? If not, how would you like to have responded?

Ask a friend to criticize you. Try to respond nondefensively. Ask the friend for feedback about whether you were able to maintain a problem-solving rather than a defensive orientation.

Uncovering Hidden Conflict

Earlier, this chapter discussed the need to call the process in cases of chronic teasing to see if the teaser is indirectly expressing feelings about a problem that needs to be solved. Teasing is one kind of indirect criticism that needs to be confronted and brought out into the open. Employees may also indirectly express criticism by complaining to others about something; by expressing anger nonverbally through withdrawal, angry facial expressions, or tense body posture; or by being passive-resistant and failing to do jobs or doing poor work. Entire work units may express anger and frustration by lethargy, deficits in work performance, withdrawal, high turnover, absenteeism, or other symptoms of morale problems.

Employees may not openly criticize for two reasons. Employees who are nonassertive may have difficulty expressing their feelings directly to anyone. Other employees may have particular difficulties being assertive with someone in authority. Employees' internal problems may make it more likely that they will express criticism indirectly. The second reason employees may be indirect when they are having problems is that either there is no mechanism for discussing problems directly or there has been such a negative reaction to direct criticism in the past that they are afraid to bring up a problem. This is one reason that responding in an encouraging, assertive way when problems are expressed is so vitally important to developing involved teamwork. Your response as a supervisor establishes whether your unit is one in which problems can be discussed openly or one in which problems are expressed in ways that are indirect and are often damaging to productivity.

An effective supervisor is alert to the nonverbal cues that some negative feelings may be present but not expressed directly. He then calls the process by stating his observations and asking for feedback: "I've noticed that you seem preoccupied this week. Is there some problem that I need to do something about?" It is important in eliciting clear feedback that the observations and questions be delivered in a neutral tone of voice. It is easy to call the process in a way that inadvertently communicates that the answer to the question had better be no. Body language can also have a powerful influence on whether people will say what they are feeling. It is important to create a safe climate for the expression of criticism. This also means that you must be able to listen to criticism in a nondefensive, problem-solving way. Responding in a defensive or angry way simply tells the employee that being direct is not safe and discourages open communication.

It is also important to have some mechanism for regular problem discussion within a work unit. This is handled in many different ways by different supervisors. Some supervisors schedule regular individual meetings with each employee. Other supervisors offer opportunities in regular staff meetings for employees to blow off steam and to bring up problems. Whatever mechanism you use, there needs to be some way to encourage employees to bring problems into the open for a unit to achieve maximum productivity.

In summary, you can uncover hidden conflict by:
1. Being aware of nonverbal cues of conflict.
2. Calling the process.
3. Having a regular mechanism for discussing problems within your unit.

━━━━◆━━━━

Think of a time when you noticed nonverbal signals of conflict in your work unit. How did you respond? Were you satisfied with the results of this kind of response? If not, how would you like to have responded?

━━━━◆━━━━

SELF-TEST

For each of the following criticisms, what would be an effective response?
1. "You're too patronizing."
2. "Oh, no! Here comes the memo factory."
3. "I can't believe that you did such a stupid, idiotic thing as calling her before you found the data. Can't you do anything right?"
4. An employee is glaring at you and saying nothing.

ANSWERS

1. This is a comment that needs to be probed to uncover the specific behaviors that make the critic feel that you are patronizing, why it is a problem, and what the critic wants you to do instead.
2. This sounds like a tease that could be handled with humor ("Better look out or I might hire three more memo writers"), calling the process ("This is the third time you have commented on my memos. Are you having a problem with them?"), or a request to stop teasing ("Hey, leave me alone about the memos, will you?").
3. This sounds like an aggressive, blowing off steam comment and as such needs to be handled by ignoring the aggressive, punitive message and responding to the content by asking the critic to express his concerns: "I understand that you are angry about that call. Can you explain more of what's making you angry about it?"
4. This nonverbal criticism indicates hidden conflict that needs to be uncovered by calling the process: "I notice that you look upset. Are you angry at me about something?"

━━━━◆━━━━

Summary

This chapter covers ways to respond to criticism directed at you. The purpose of responding to criticism assertively is to get the information that is needed to solve problems, to defuse tensions, and to maintain open lines of communication.

The nonassertive supervisor accepts all criticism and takes it personally. She feels apologetic, hurt, frightened, guilty, defensive, and self-critical when criticized. The aggressive supervisor is angry and attacking when criticized. She rejects all criticism because she feels others have no right to criticize her or are unfair and biased. The assertive supervisor is calm and self-accepting when criticized. She is able to sort criticism and accept accurate criticisms. She uses criticism as information and probes and questions to get specific information. The assertive person works toward open dialogue and problem solving, defuses tension and conflict, and uncovers hidden conflict.

Not distinguishing the other person's problem from your problem is a common mistake in dealing with criticism. Seeing criticism as a personal attack, distorting criticism, seeing criticism as a reflection of worth, and believing that everyone must have a good opinion of you are other mistakes in dealing with criticism.

To respond appropriately to criticism, it is necessary to recognize the difference between teasing, blowing off steam, and criticism that attempts to solve a problem. Teasing can be recognized from the way it is expressed, the mismatch between the criticism and the real problem, and the context. Blowing off steam is similar to a temper tantrum. It shows frustration and may reveal some real problems that need to be solved. Criticism that attempts to solve a problem may be judgmental, loaded with assumptions, and general.

You can respond to teasing with the techniques of: humor, ignoring, fogging, saying stop it, using the DESC Script, and calling the process, questioning, and problem solving.

You can respond to blowing off steam by: correcting misperceptions, using listening and asking for details to allow the person to release tensions and to calm down, being alert for problems that need to be solved, acknowledging the other person's right to be angry, and setting limits when the person is violent and abusive, when the time or place is inappropriate, or when you are not willing to listen to the person blow off steam.

You can respond to criticism that attempts to solve a problem by: eliciting good describe, express, and specify portions of the DESC

Script, evaluating the criticism for accuracy, deciding whether you accept the criticism as your problem and are willing to change, and if you agree with the need to change, exploring mutually acceptable solutions.

Often employees do not express their criticisms openly but express conflict through body language and passive-resistant behavior. You can uncover hidden conflict by: being aware of nonverbal cues of conflict, calling the process, and having a regular mechanism for discussing problems within your unit.

Bibliography

Herman, S. M., & Korenich, M. *Authentic management: A gestalt orientation to organizations and their development.* Reading, Mass.: Addison-Wesley, 1977.

Huxley, L. *You are not the target.* New York: Avon, 1963.

Smith, M. *When I say no I feel guilty.* New York: Dial Press, 1975.

CHAPTER NINE

Asserting Yourself
with Superiors and Colleagues

In this chapter, you will:
- Learn when to be assertive with superiors;
- Learn how to be assertive with superiors;
- Learn when to be assertive with colleagues;
- Learn how to be assertive with colleagues.

Most of the focus of this book has been on the need for a supervisor to be assertive with the people he supervises; however, it is also important for supervisors to be assertive with superiors and colleagues. One of the critical roles for a first-line supervisor is as an organizational link between his employees and upper management. It is impossible for a supervisor to gain real respect from his employees unless he is willing to take a stand within the organization as well as with them.

In a traditional hierarchical management system, most of a supervisor's communication was either down the chain of command to his employees or up the chain of command to his superior. A nonassertive supervisor could be productive if he had an assertive manager to handle relationships with other departments. In the newer management systems like W. L. Gore's network system, in which there is no rigid chain of command, or matrix management, in which any unit may report to several supervisors, a supervisor must be able to communicate successfully with many other people in the organization in order to get the job done. Not only must he be able to let others know what he needs, he also must be able to persuade them to respond to his unit's needs without some of the traditional leverage that was available in the old hierarchical system. In order to persuade superiors and colleagues in other departments to cooperate, he must clearly, forcefully, and assertively communicate needs and priorities directly to them, and then he must be able to negotiate skillfully to meet mutual needs. Involved teamwork is the essence of these more participatory organizations. Nonassertiveness and aggressiveness are more damaging in systems that depend on open communication and on cooperation between units.

> Carlos was working on a joint project with two other design groups in his organization. Successful completion of the project demanded that all three teams meet the deadlines. One team was several weeks behind schedule. Carlos needed to approach the supervisor of the other team to let him know that not meeting the deadline was hurting the whole project and to ask him to push his team to catch up.

When to Be Assertive with Superiors

There are a number of times when a supervisor might need to be assertive with a superior. These include when getting what is needed to do the job, when representing employees, and when responding to requests and behavior that interfere with work.

Getting what is needed to do the job

A supervisor must know what she needs to accomplish within what time frame in order to perform effectively. In some organizations, management is very poor at clearly defining a supervisor's objective. In that case, the supervisor must assert herself with superiors to get a clear definition of the goals and objectives for her unit. She may also need to have management define priorities for each objective. Putting primary emphasis on one set of objectives and helping her department achieve these objectives while management views other objectives as more important can hurt a supervisor.

> Ling was the assistant director of a small state alcoholism unit. She and her three staff members developed a very effective alcoholism prevention program for senior high schools. The problem was that the state alcohol agency that provided her funding had moved from an emphasis on school programs to an emphasis on alcohol education in business and industry. The state supervisor had never informed Ling of the priorities; nevertheless, her small agency lost funding to another group that emphasized alcohol education in business.

A supervisor also needs to be assertive with management to get resources that are needed to do the job. A supervisor is often more aware of the resources needed for a job than a manager is because she is more closely associated with the job. There are times when certain resources are so essential to getting the job done that the supervisor must develop a plan for getting these resources and must be willing to fight to implement this plan.

To get the leverage she needs to confront problems may also require a supervisor to be assertive with management. For example, many supervisors do not have the authority to directly influence an employee's performance rating, to alter job assignments, to place negative comments in an employee's personnel file, or to fire an employee. With a very difficult employee, there may be times when the use of strong negative consequences is necessary to bring about change. If the supervisor does not have authority to impose these consequences herself, it will be necessary for her to assert herself with her manager before she can be assertive with the employee.

Representing employees

When employees' needs must be communicated to upper management it is important for supervisors to be assertive with superiors. One of the problems with many organizations is that communication is one way down the chain of command. Policies and procedures are set at the top with almost no input from the people who will actually have to carry out these policies. The only way for a supervisor to get a message to management may be to communicate through her manager. Persuading the manager to pass on a message sometimes requires assertive action. This is most difficult when the manager is very nonassertive. The nonassertive manager will not confront problems, nor will she stick her neck out to communicate concerns to her manager. In some cases, it may be essential to find a nonthreatening way to get around this kind of person in the chain of command.

Valerie was a supervisor in a large community mental health center. In this center, the medical director and the board of directors established most procedures and policies. One center policy was that no staff member should see more than one member of a family. Since many staff members were getting training in family therapy, Valerie wanted to suggest a change in that ruling. For the change to be made, her manager needed to communicate this information at the next department head meeting. She knew he had a tendency to be nonassertive so she asserted herself by presenting a persuasive case to him. She also asked him if she could appear briefly at the board meeting to present her case.

A supervisor must also be assertive to get recognition for employees. To be motivated, employees must receive recognition when they are doing good work; failure to pay attention to good work discourages employees. Very often the supervisor does not have direct access to rewards and other forms of recognition. She may need to ask her manager to recommend employees for awards, push for promotions and merit pay for her good employees, work for training opportunities for employees, and press for opportunities for good employees to become visible within the organization. Employees know when a supervisor will fight for their interests and are more willing to go out of their way to make an effort for her. Supervisors who will not assert themselves with their managers to get positive feedback for their employees will seldom have the most motivated employees.

Maintaining visibility within the organization, and in some cases the community, is one of the most important ways for a supervisor to get recognition for her employees and for herself. Sometimes this visibility is necessary to insure the survival of the unit. Doing a good job is not always enough to guarantee that a unit of an organization will be maintained and supported by the larger organization or by the company. One classic example of this is the problems that school guidance counselors have had in maintaining funding. In several communities, exemplary guidance programs nearly lost funding because no one outside of the counseling department and the school knew what an outstanding job the counselors were doing (Orlando, 1981). Survival does to some extent depend on the supervisor's ability to make her unit's work known to people who have the power to support or maintain resources for that job. In other words, any job requires a certain amount of political and public relations activity.

Nonassertive supervisors are often passive about maintaining visibility. Their position is that good work will be recognized without any particular effort to be visible on their part or that they must depend on superiors to look out for their welfare by making their good work known to others in the organization. They don't try to become highly visible in the organization and may avoid opportunities for visibility that do arise. For example, the nonassertive supervisor will not usually speak up at an organizational meeting, nor will she go out of her way to present her department's work to others in the organization. The aggressive supervisor will lose no opportunity to compete with other departments for recognition or to make her unit's good work known to others within the organization. It is probably better to be aggressive rather than nonassertive in the area of maintaining visibility in the organization. The aggressive supervisor is conscious of the need to promote her unit. She has no hesitation about making successes known to powerful people within the organization. Of course, a very aggressive supervisor may find that in actively promoting her unit, her aggressive, self-promoting attitude will be so obnoxious that she will get negative recognition within the organization: "Oh, no. Here comes Shelly again." The politically astute assertive supervisor is alert to chances to promote her unit in the normal communication mechanisms of the company. For example, she uses routine meetings to tell managers about successes, uses opportunities to speak to other units of the organization or to the public about what her employees are doing, and summarizes successes in newsletters or reports.

How do you create organizational visibility for your unit or for your organization? What else could you do to build organizational visibility?

Responding to requests and behavior that interfere with work

A supervisor must be assertive and say no when her manager asks her to take on tasks that are not appropriately her role or asks her to assign tasks to her employees that are not appropriately part of their roles.

> Jeff was the guidance director in a secondary school. The principal of the school insisted that guidance counselors become disciplinarians as well as counselors. Jeff had to take a very strong stand in helping the principal to understand that counseling and disciplinarian roles were incompatible. He needed to describe the ways that taking on the disciplinary role would destroy the counselor's effectiveness in doing what he should be doing.

It may also be necessary for a supervisor to say no when the manager assigns a task that cannot be done with the available time and resources. In this case, it is useful to make the manager aware of other departmental priorities and let her reassign jobs if she thinks it necessary.

Another time a supervisor needs to be assertive is when her manager is doing something that undermines her authority.

Karen was a supervisor in a social services agency. When she would make a determination of eligibility to settle a disagreement between a client and a caseworker, her manager would often overturn her decisions without discussing the cases with her. This process was undermining her credibility with the clients and with her caseworkers. She needed to let her manager know how this behavior was affecting her functioning as a supervisor and to ask the manager to consult with her before she reversed decisions.

A manager can also undermine a supervisor's authority by being too involved in the work of the unit. The essence of effective management is delegation. Although there are situations in which delegation is not possible, there are many managers who cannot let go of the reins enough to allow someone else to do what she needs to do. These managers may constantly check up on work, interfere by making suggestions, or in other ways be overly involved in the tasks they should be delegating. This failure to delegate can also result in an overburdened manager who becomes an organizational bottleneck because she cannot get her legitimate managerial work done.

Supervisors may also need to be assertive when they are reporting to two managers with contradictory priorities. When the supervisor is not assertive about being caught in the middle, she may become the victim of a power struggle between the two managers. The supervisor may need to call the process and say to both managers, "I'm caught in the middle here. Joe says to do this. You say to do that. I need to meet with both of you to discuss priorities and settle on a way the three of us can work together."

If a supervisor is being unfairly criticized by a manager, it is also essential that she be assertive. It is necessary for the person who evaluates the supervisor's job performance to have a fair and realistic picture of work performance. The supervisor is obligated to call the manager's attention to work that might serve to change the manager's view of her performance. For example, a supervisor whose manager seemed to have overlooked several significant contributions she had made in the last year might need to say "You have been saying that I don't cooperate enough with other departments. As I recall, I've been involved in cooperative projects on the

Jones case, on the Smith case, and on several other projects. Can you tell me what else you want me to do in order to feel that I'm working enough with other departments?"

Another time that it is essential for the supervisor to be assertive is when a manager is treating her in an aggressive, bullying way. Failing to confront her not only encourages her to escalate the bullying; it may even lead her to lose respect for the supervisor. Bullies seldom respect or value the people that they can bully. It is far better to be somewhat aggressive with a bully than it is to be nonassertive. Being nonassertive with a bully is almost like waving a red flag in front of a bull; the bully cannot resist the temptation to attack. It is vitally important, however, to distinguish agressiveness that comes from a bullying approach to others and aggressiveness that comes from feeling threatened. The bully treats people who stand up to him with respect. The person who is aggressive because she feels threatened becomes more aggressive when anyone stands up to her. Since even ordinary assertiveness can be a threat to this type of person, she must be handled very carefully. Making every effort to inform this kind of supervisor about plans before taking any action can help to reassure her. Sometimes it is necessary to be almost nonassertive in voice characteristics and body language in order not to further threaten an anxious superior. A supervisor who works for this type of superior may need to build a power base elsewhere in the organization to protect herself from extreme aggressive attacks and then either learn to ignore the aggressiveness or to find somewhere else in the organization to work. Another source of ways to deal with difficult people is Bramson, 1981.

Although this list of reasons why a supervisor might need to be assertive to those above her in the organization is not exhaustive, it clearly indicates that assertiveness with superiors is a critical part of a supervisor's role.

How to Be Assertive with Superiors

Although assertive behavior patterns, word choices, voice characteristics, and body language are helpful when asserting yourself with superiors, there are some special concerns that need to be taken into account. Three important things to remember are: don't undermine the superior's authority, build a strong case for change, and recognize norms and power dynamics in the organization.

Don't undermine the superior's authority

One thing it is absolutely essential not to do in asserting yourself to a superior is to communicate to him that you are questioning his authority. The supervisor who graduates from an assertiveness training class and then goes back to his superior and says in one way or another, "Let me tell you how you ought to do your job" may be asserting himself into great difficulty. In asserting yourself with superiors, it is helpful to acknowledge the other person's authority right from the beginning: "I know that you are the boss and have the authority to decide how this ought to be done. That's why I want to discuss with you how to handle this situation."

A supervisor might be able to get away with being quite aggressive to an employee. It is much riskier to be aggressive to a superior. Aggressiveness can be easily misinterpreted as an attack on the superior's authority. If your superior feels that you are being disrespectful when confronting him, constructive dialogue could be impossible. This general rule is obviously not true in all cases. There are some superiors who are very secure in their authority and can respond in an assertive, nondefensive way to aggressive communication from their employees. With this kind of superior, it is not as important to be very careful in phrasing your comments. Bullies, as mentioned earlier, are another kind of superior who may not respond badly to an aggressive approach. In some cases, they may watch for aggressive reactions as a signal that it is time to back off. However, these exceptions aside, it is usually important in being assertive with superiors to be careful not to be aggressive in word choices, voice characteristics, and body language.

In a traditional hierarchical organization, bypassing your direct superior to assert yourself with someone higher on the chain of command may be seen as quite aggressive. At times, it is necessary to carry a request or a complaint to someone higher on the chain of command, but it is important to exhaust the possibilities at the lowest level first. An effective upper-level manager will usually ask whether you have tried to discuss an issue with your direct superior before he will even consider intervening. When you have discussed an issue with your direct superior, it may be quite appropriate to ask for a meeting with the next level of management. Usually it is appropriate to let your direct superior know about that meeting if he is not to be involved. When your direct superior is totally opposed to any assertiveness up the chain of command, it is necessary to weigh the risks and assert yourself anyway if the issue is important enough, or build a power base with someone in the organization who can make your concerns known to upper management. It is also possible and necessary to use regular communication mechanisms like newsletters, reports, and performance reviews to keep upper management informed about your concerns without infringing upon the normal chain of command.

Juame had a very anxious and nonassertive direct superior. He had great difficulty getting clear information about departmental priorities from this person. Juame made sure that his memos and reports reflected his understanding of departmental priorities as he had been able to define them in conversations with his direct superior. He also used regularly scheduled meetings with upper management to get information about priorities. Juame used contacts made in monthly meetings to build a strong relationship with someone who had the ear of upper management and communicated his concerns indirectly through this outer channel.

Build a strong case for change

When you need to assert yourself to superiors to bring about a change, you must build a strong case for this change. When asserting yourself with someone you supervise, you can use the weight of your position and whatever rewards and coercive power go with your role to motivate the other person. When asserting yourself with superiors, you rarely have the authority to apply much direct leverage. This means that you must be able to persuade your superior that whatever you are asking for is in the superior's or the company's best interest. If you use a DESC Script to present your case to a superior, it is essential that the express part of the script be clear and specific because your description of the reasons that a particular action is a problem will be the primary means for motivating him to take the problem seriously. For example, a supervisor asserting himself to a manager who doesn't regularly schedule staff meetings would need to make a strong case for why lack of meetings is a problem. He might say, "When I don't get a chance to meet with the other supervisors in this department on at least a monthly basis, I find that I often duplicate work being done elsewhere. I think all of us could make more efficient use of time if we could meet more regularly. I would like you to schedule monthly meetings." This script would be much more effective than one in which the supervisor said, "We're supposed to have regular meetings, and I wish we would." When using scripts with superiors, consequences will usually be positive instead of negative to avoid appearing aggressive.

Providing documentation to support a particular request can also motivate a superior. In asserting yourself with employees, it is possible, but not always the best course, to simply issue an order with very little explanation to support the order. In making an assertive request with a superior, the more data that can be provided, the better. Facts and figures that support a particular assertive position can be very important in having that position accepted.

> The planning staff in a social agency had been complaining to the director about the large number of service oriented phone calls that they were responding to. The director listened to the complaints, nodded responsively, and sympathized, but took no action. Staff members then started to keep records of the amount of time spent each day on service oriented calls. When they could demonstrate that they spent 20 percent of their time on service calls, the director began to seriously consider hiring someone to handle requests for service.

It is particularly important not to shoot from the hip in asserting yourself with superiors. Not only is there danger that a poorly considered response would be aggressive, but also it is difficult to make a convincing case for a particular position unless you have done some homework before presenting your case to your superior.

There will always be some resistance to change. You can make a better case for a particular change if you take into account and respond to other's resistance to the request. You should put yourself in your superior's position and try to imagine his potential objections to an assertive request. Empathy allows you to tailor your approach to your superior. Responding with empathy to a superior's resistance also communicates to management that you understand organizational constraints and organizational problems.

In large bureaucratic organizations, resistance at all levels of the organization means that any significant changes happen slowly. Some supervisors defeat themselves in trying to bring about organizational change by not recognizing this natural resistance to change and pushing too fast or by pushing in ways that ignore the resistance rather than taking it into account. Making changes in any organization requires a thorough understanding of the potential resistance to change. Once this resistance is clear, requests for change can respond to it. You can reduce a person's resistance to change by empathizing with him. Ignoring or discounting someone's resistance can make him more resistant.

Yukio was convinced that his family therapy staff at a child guidance clinic needed some additional training. The director of the agency was convinced that people with doctoral degrees should not need further training. He was also very concerned about staff time because training would cut the number of client hours each staff member could provide. Yukio presented his request for further training along with some descriptions of training programs at similar agencies. When the director expressed resistance to this request for training, Yukio became very angry. He accused the director of not being concerned about the development of the staff. Yukio's attempt to be assertive resulted in making the director feel that Yukio had no real understanding of organizational constraints. The director became, therefore, even less motivated to support the training.

One technique that is very helpful in assessing potential resistance to change is Lewin's Force Field Analysis technique (Lewin, 1947). Lewin assumes that there must be fairly equal forces pushing toward and resisting change for any situation to stay as it is. To bring about change, the first step is to identify the forces pushing toward and resisting change in a situation. Then, change can be brought about by increasing the push for change or by reducing the resistance. There is danger that the resistance will also increase if the pressure for change is increased. Therefore, it could be most effective to attempt to reduce the resisting forces.

Helena wanted to get her manager's support for more involvement by employees in goal setting in her unit. She analyzed the forces pushing toward and resisting change in the following way:

Current situation	Goal
All goals set by upper management	Employee participation in goal setting
Forces pushing toward change	*Forces resisting change*
Employees' desire to get involved	Too much time spent in meetings
Research showing that participation increases motivation	Fear by manager that employees don't really understand organization

Good experiences of other companies	Fear by manager of loss of control
Motivated employees	Fear by manager that meetings will become gripe sessions
Management's desire for enhanced creativity across organization	

Once Helena examined the forces for and against change, she could plan a strategy to best present her request to her manager. Thus, her assertiveness was based on a thorough understanding of her manager's possible objections. She was able to assure him that he would not lose control by acknowledging his authority, explain to him how the time invested in meetings in the short run could save time in the long run, and show him some goal-setting forms that would structure meetings and keep them from being gripe sessions. Her thorough analysis of the organization's needs and her assurances that she would help employees to understand organizational priorities spoke to his concerns in that area. She also was able to allay some of his concerns by suggesting a 6-month trial of the new process.

In building a case for change, you also need to recognize when to back off. There are times when no matter how assertive you are, it will be impossible to bring about change in particular aspects of an organization or in relationships with a particular superior. As stated in Chapter One, personal and organizational constraints maintain some very troublesome situations within an organization. No matter how assertive you are, you probably will not be able to change your superior's basic management style or your company's basic organizational philosophy, objectives, funding structure, and management system. It is useful to realize from the start things that you cannot change and to put your energy into working for changes that are possible. Some supervisors waste their energy and create tension and conflict within the organization by refusing to accept unchangeable situations.

Of course, some situations that can't be changed are not situations that you can accept. If your manager is mentally ill or alcoholic, it may be impossible to change that manager's behavior. In some organizations, you may be able to change a manager's behavior by asserting yourself directly or indirectly with upper management; however, the cost of this kind of assertiveness is often high. If people in upper management are not yet aware of the problem, they are unlikely to support an employee in any way that will ultimately improve the situation.

> Barbara was working for a manager who had been steadily deterioriating mentally over the last several years. Her rapid mood swings, her unpredictability, and her arbitrary decisions were making Barbara's life miserable. She was a constant buffer for her employees with the manager and was subjected to a great deal of pressure. Since upper management did not yet recognize the severity of the problem, there was no way that Barbara could assert herself to really help the situation. She finally acted by building bridges with another department and then getting a transfer.

If your manager is impossible to work for, the organizational philosophy is incompatible with your value system, your job is poorly designed, or the overall organization is poorly managed, then the only option may be for you to leave.

Recognize norms and power dynamics
in the organization

Two aspects of organizational politics that need to be taken into account in asserting yourself with superiors are norms and power dynamics. Norms are unspoken organizational rules (e.g., what people who are going to move into management should wear, who talks to whom informally about important organizational decisions, where and how it is acceptable to raise certain organizational concerns). Although these rules are never written in policy manuals, those who violate them will find that their organizational effectiveness is greatly reduced.

Although, in general, organizations function better when there is clear, straightforward communication, supervisors who work in organizations in which power maneuvers and power struggles are common may not be able to be direct with superiors. In this kind of organization, it may be necessary to be indirect, to keep your real agenda hidden, and to work behind the scenes using power maneuvers to bring change. Aggressiveness or nonassertiveness may be necessary in order to have some impact. In some organizations, the norms may sanction assertiveness from only a few individuals. The supervisor who wanted to request change from management would need to present his approach to the organization through the person sanctioned by the norms to be assertive.

Even in organizations that do not totally discourage direct communication, there may be times when the most direct approach will not work. Assertive communication needs to be examined in light of the political realities of your organization. When direct communication will not work, you need to search for other strategies for accomplishing your objectives. These organizational norms are another reason why assertive action with higher management requires preparation. Presentation of an assertive request to a manager without understanding of the "unspoken rules of the game" could inadvertently put you in jeopardy.

Kathryn was a new supervisor for an engineering consulting firm. In a meeting with management, the managers asked supervisors to let them know about any problems they were having. Kathryn had become frustrated with poor communication from upper management so she took this opportunity to bring up this problem. What Kathryn had not noticed was that no one else made complaints at this meeting. When she did complain, several managers quickly changed the subject. Another supervisor took her aside after the meeting and told her that this meeting was really a showcase for her general manager to look good in front of higher level management. Although managers had requested feedback, the request was not a real one. Her manager was, in fact, open to criticism, but only in private one-to-one sessions. Kathryn had violated an organizational norm and in the process had established a reputation as a troublemaker.

The second political aspect that a supervisor needs to be conscious of is power dynamics. Most organizations have a very clear organizational chart that specifies who, theoretically, has the power to make decisions within each area of the organization. However, the formal organizational chart rarely reflects the real distribution of power within an organization. People who would, according to the organizational chart, have a great deal of power may in reality have almost no influence in the organization; yet people who would have little power according to position may be very powerful because of connections, charisma, expertise, knowledge, access to rewards, or the ability to punish (French & Raven, 1959). For example, in some schools, the school secretary may be one of the most powerful individuals in the school because he controls access to the principal and strongly influences the principal's decisions. In other organizations, people who control certain budget items like travel may have more power than their position would indicate. Effective assertiveness within an organization requires awareness of the "real" organizational chart. Sometimes it may be more useful to pass information to someone who has a great deal of organizational power than it would be to assert yourself directly. Although this book does not deal with maneuvering for power in great detail, knowing who has power and how to build a power base through a mentor or through other relationships is very useful in addition to an understanding of assertiveness.

Bill was the supervisor of a production unit of a small plastics manufacturing firm. The way the plant equipment was arranged was quite inefficient, so he wanted to assert himself to change the arrangement. Although at one time his manager had been very powerful, he had lost his influence when a new vice-president was hired. This manager felt that the old ways were always the best ways. Bill realized that to rearrange the equipment he would need to get the vice-president's support. Bill explained the problem to another supervisor who had contacts in the vice-president's office and followed this initial contact with a discussion with the vice-president during one of his plant visits.

For further material on understanding office politics see DuBrin, 1978 and Kennedy, 1980. *How to Manage Your Boss* (Hegart, 1982) is also useful.

In summary, to be assertive with superiors:
1. Don't undermine the superior's authority.
2. Build a strong case for change.
3. Recognize norms and power dynamics in the organization.

Think of a situation in which you need to be assertive with superiors. What specifically is the problem? What do you want from management in this situation? Why should management do what you are asking? How could you build a strong case for change, and what documentation could you use? What is your manager's resistance to your request likely to be? Does your particular manager have the power to solve this problem? If not, who does and how could you reach that person without violating the chain of command?

SELF-TEST

Pick the attempts to be assertive with superiors that are likely to be effective and specify what cues you used.

1. "You just can't keep making changes in our department without giving us notice. It's driving everyone crazy."
2. A supervisor in a social services agency feels that her superior is undermining her authority by countermanding her decisions on eligibility. She goes directly to the director of the agency to complain about her superior.
3. "Since you are the one who decides how the paperwork is organized in this department, I want to talk to you about some problems my workers are having with the new forms to see if we can find some way to streamline their workload."
4. "I can understand that you don't want to adopt any plan that will reduce the amount of work that can be completed in a day; however, I think that my workers can be more productive over a week if we do take off that hour a week for staff meetings."
5. "This memo that you just issued on overtime is ridiculous. I can't believe that you expect me to tell my employees that they will have to work again on Saturdays."
6. "The last 3 months you have had to make many changes in the schedule you submit. Sometimes I already know about potential schedule conflicts. I think it would be helpful to let me see the schedule before it is finalized. It would probably save both of us time in the long run."

ANSWERS

1. Ineffective—This statement could be seen as aggressive because it implies that the supervisor questions the superior's authority—"You can't . . ." It also doesn't express well why the changes are a problem or offer documentation. It probably would not be very effective.
2. Ineffective—The supervisor in this example did not work within the chain of command. A good director would refuse to deal with the issue until the supervisor's direct superior is confronted.
3. Effective—This statement acknowledges the superior's authority so it could be effective. It expresses why the forms are a problem but needs to be more specific.

4. Effective—This statement could be effective because it shows empathy for the supervisor's view and works with the resistance to change.
5. Ineffective—This statement is quite aggressive and probably would be ineffective. It also does not build a case for change.
6. Effective—The clear expression of why the behavior is a problem would probably make this statement effective.

When to Be Assertive with Colleagues

Not only is it necessary for supervisors to be assertive with superiors, but it is also important for them to be able to be assertive with colleagues. The three main times for being assertive with colleagues are the same as with superiors: when getting what is needed to do the job, when representing employees, and when responding to requests and behavior that interfere with work.

Getting what is needed to do the job

There will inevitably be times when the cooperation of a colleague or of several people from another unit of the organization will be necessary in order to get a job done. In most modern organizations, every unit needs information or specialized work from other units in order to complete a task. In many organizations, there is a great deal of competition for the limited time available from some service groups. That means that a supervisor often has to develop a persuasive case for giving priority to his unit's needs.

> Leo had to deliver a proposal for funding a new teen-age pregnancy unit of a child welfare agency by a certain date. He needed the current head of the adolescent sexuality program to call a staff meeting to get input from her staff for the proposal. He needed to persuade her that funding was important enough to preempt the weekly case conference.

Representing employees

Sometimes supervisors will overstep their boundaries and treat employees in other departments in ways that undermine morale and productivity in that department. In order to have a strong commitment to their unit, employees need to know that their supervisor will protect them from unfair treatment by others in the organization.

> Mary Lee became aware that another supervisor was aggres-
> sively criticizing her medical technologists about their clo-
> thing, the organization in the lab, and a number of other
> issues. She went to the other supervisor and said, "When you
> criticize my workers or the lab, the workers are upset and
> therefore less productive. If you have complaints you feel need
> attention, come to me with the complaints but please do not
> criticize my technologists."

In meetings where organizational decisions are made by groups, a
supervisor may also need to represent his employees assertively
with his colleagues. In group decision making, nonassertive supervisors are poor spokesmen for the needs of their units. Effective
supervisors need to be able to speak out forcefully and clearly in
meetings. For example, when employee ratings are assigned in
group meetings of supervisors, assertive supervisors are often able
to make more convincing cases for their employees than nonassertive supervisors can. The nonassertive supervisor's employees may
be hurt because they do not get the recognition they deserve and
their motivation may ultimately be reduced.

Responding to requests and behavior
that interfere with work
When a colleague or another department asks a supervisor to do
things that interfere with priorities in his unit, he may have to say
no assertively. Just because someone in the organization asks a supervisor to have his unit do a job or make a particular job a priority
does not mean that it is in the best interests of his unit to do so.

> Tom worked in a city planning agency with a huge grant
> proposal due at the end of the week. A colleague pressed him
> to send two employees to a meeting on a joint project. Tom
> had to say no, although he reassured the other manager that
> he wanted to continue to work cooperatively on the project
> when the grant proposal was finished.

There are also times when the way things are done in one unit
seriously interferes with another unit's effectiveness and some assertiveness is required.

> Arlene was supervising an insurance claims processing office.
> The insurance agents saved all their claims forms and sub-
> mitted these forms to the claims processing office in large
> batches. This meant that her staff had periods with no work
> to do and periods with too much work to do. She needed to

say to the agents "When the claims forms arrive 50 at a time, it takes my staff almost a week to process all of the claims. We may then have another week with little work to do. If you could send forms over when you collect 10, we would be able to process claims much more rapidly and efficiently for you."

A colleague's behavior can also interfere with work in a supervisor's unit. In the simplest case, a colleague may drop by to talk when the supervisor has a great deal of work to do. In more complicated cases, an individual in another unit may be acting in ways that undermine the effectiveness of the supervisor's unit. An example of this would be criticizing a unit on the basis of distorted or limited information. Using calling the process or a script, a supervisor could say, "I understand that you have been telling people what a bad job my department is doing. I would like to correct any problems so I would appreciate your coming to me directly with any complaints. What problems have you had?"

How to Be Assertive with Colleagues

The same guidelines apply to asserting yourself with colleagues as with superiors. Again, the assertive message is made with persuasion and building an effective case, not from pressure you can exert. It is very important to be responsive to colleagues' potential resistance by acknowledging and taking into account their objections. Aggressive interactions are particularly damaging between units because aggressiveness that might be forgiven from a supervisor within a unit may be resented from a supervisor who has no authority in the unit.

Although there may be times when it is necessary to go through the chain of command when dealing with a colleague to enhance leverage, direct communication is faster, more efficient, and less subject to distortion. Many issues are simply not serious enough to merit management's intervention. Each supervisor needs to be able to assertively handle everyday interactions with colleagues. Management intervention is usually available as a consequence if a lower power intervention does not work: "If we can't resolve this, I'll have to speak to my manager about it."

Think of a situation in which you need to be assertive with a colleague in another department. What specifically is the problem? What do you want from your colleague in this situation? Why should your colleague do what you are asking? How could you build a case for change, and what documentation could you use? What is your colleague's resistance to your request likely to be?

Summary

This chapter examines when and how to be assertive with superiors and colleagues. A supervisor needs to be assertive with superiors to get what is needed to do the job, to represent employees, and to respond to requests and behavior that interfere with work.

Some of the things needed to do a job include a clear definition of goals, objectives, and priorities for the unit, resources, and leverage to confront problems.

Representing employees involves communicating employees' needs to upper management, getting recognition for employees, and maintaining a unit's visibility.

Responding to requests and behavior that interfere with work may involve saying no to tasks that are not appropriately the supervisor's or his employees' role or to tasks that cannot be done with the available time and resources. When the manager undermines the supervisor's authority, when a supervisor has to report to two managers with contradictory priorities, is being unfairly criticized by a manager, or is being treated in an aggressive, bullying way, it is also essential for him to be assertive.

It is important not to undermine the superior's authority, to build a strong case for change, and to recognize norms and power dynamics in the organization when being assertive with a superior. You can avoid undermining the superior's authority if you acknowledge this authority right from the start, are not aggressive, and start by working within the chain of command. When your direct superior is totally opposed to any assertiveness up the chain of command, it is necessary to weigh the risks and assert yourself anyway, or build a power base with upper management that can be used to make concerns known in an indirect way.

When building a case for change, you must be able to persuade your superior that what you are asking for is in the superior's or the company's best interest. Documentation to support a request will also motivate a superior. You can make a better case for a change if you take into account and work with the inevitable resistance to change. You also need to recognize when you should back off because it will be impossible to bring about change no matter how assertive you are. Recognizing norms and power dynamics in the organization, and communicating indirectly if you need to, is also important in being assertive with a superior.

Assertiveness with colleagues is necessary to get what is needed to do the job, to represent employees, and to respond to requests and behavior that interfere with work. Assertiveness with colleagues uses many of the same techniques as being assertive with superiors. Going through upper management can be used with colleagues if direct intervention does not work.

Bibliography

Bramson, R. M. *Coping with difficult people.* New York: Ballantine, 1981.

DuBrin, A. *Winning at office politics.* New York: Van Nostrand Reinhold, 1978.

French, J. R. P., & Raven, B. The bases of social power. In D. Cartwright (Ed.), *Studies in social power.* Ann Arbor, Mich.: University of Michigan Institute for Social Research, 1959.

Hegart, C. *How to manage your boss.* Mill Valley, Calif.: Whatever Publishing, 1982.

Kennedy, M. M. *Office politics/seizing power/wielding clout.* Chicago: Follett, 1980.

Lewin, K. Frontiers in group dynamics: Concept, method, and reality in social science, social equilibrium and social change. *Human Relations,* June 1947, pp. 5–41.

Orlando, M. Survival for counselors is possible. *The ASCA Counselor,* 1981, *19,* 1.

CHAPTER TEN

Questions and Answers about Implementing Your Assertiveness

In this chapter, you will learn how to deal with situations involving:
- Employees of different motivation and skill levels;
- The very timid and nonassertive, very aggressive and hostile, or troubled person;
- The employee who cries whenever you confront her;
- The employee who won't participate in a discussion;
- The employee who has the potential, but not the motivation, to be a top-notch worker;
- The employee who is genuinely limited or unpromotable;
- The employee who does his job but has a negative effect on the morale and productivity of others;
- The employee who knows that you have no real leverage over him;
- Maintaining a good relationship when you become a friend's supervisor;
- A personality conflict between two employees;
- Tension or a morale problem in your unit;
- Information from someone else about an employee's work;
- Union or minority employees;
- Supervising when you strongly disagree with the organization;
- Being assertive when you don't have much time or privacy on your job.

What has been covered in this book so far prepares you to apply assertiveness concepts to your supervisory job. Every supervisor, however, has questions about how to be assertive in some of the difficult situations she must confront in her job. This chapter tries to anticipate some of these questions and to provide some useful answers.

Maintain an experimental attitude toward your supervisory job and problems that you find difficult. Learn to observe yourself and your employees. When what you are doing works well, trust yourself and use what works. When it doesn't work well, examine the situation and your response to it. Ask yourself what you might have done differently. Try some new strategies and see how they work. Modify and alter the assertive approach of this book to make it work for you in your situation. The answers to the following questions are suggestions that you can use to formulate your own effective ways of responding.

My employees differ greatly in their motivation and skill. Should I treat them all the same?

Hersey and Blanchard (1982) have developed a model for helping supervisors to adapt their style to the "job-relevant maturity level" of their employees. They describe job-relevant maturity as the willingness and the ability to do a job. The job-relevant maturity level could vary across tasks with an employee. For example, an employee who was highly motivated but inexperienced at doing a job would be relatively immature for that job. An employee might be generally mature but immature on tasks that she particularly despises. An unwilling, unable worker would require a different amount and kind of supervision than would a very willing and able employee. In their model, called Situational Leadership, they define four types of supervisory approaches:

1. *Telling the employee how to do the job.* This style involves giving very specific instructions for how and when to do a task and asks for little input from the employee. The supervisor is very clearly in charge and follows up very carefully to see that work gets done. This style is best with very unwilling and unable employees.

2. *Telling the employee how to do the job and asking for input.* This style not only involves giving very specific instructions and following up to see that the work is done, but also asking for input from the employee about the job and giving positive feedback. This style is most effective with a moderately unwilling and unable employee.

3. *Developing a plan to do the job with the employee.* This style involves defining the parameters of the task and eliciting a plan from the employee through participatory decision making, positive feedback, and discussion. This style is best with moderately willing and able employees.
4. *Delegating the task to the employee.* This style involves assigning the task to the employee and leaving the decision making about how to do the job up to the employee. This style works best with highly willing and able employees.

Assertive interventions must be varied depending on the willingness and ability of an employee on a particular type of task. For example, a DESC Script delivered to a very unwilling and unable employee would specify the desired behaviors in terms of what the employee is to do, when she is to do it, and how she is to do it. Thus, although it is recommended to allow employees as much input into the solution of problems as possible, with very unwilling and unable employees, a style that is very participatory may be seen as weak. On the other hand, a very experienced and motivated employee may be insulted by overly explicit instructions about her responsibilities.

One technique that can be useful in helping employees to establish effective goals for themselves is a technique described by Blanchard and Johnson in the book *The One Minute Manager* (1983). In developing a goal, the supervisor and employee:

(1) Agree on goals, (2) See what good behavior looks like, (3) Write out each goal on a single sheet of paper using less than 250 words, (4) Read and re-read each goal, (5) Take a minute to look at performance and see whether or not the behavior matches the goal. (p. 34)

For example, the supervisor might say, "Bibi, what do you think that you need to do this week in order to finish the Pressman project?" After going over the employee's suggestions, the supervisor might say, "I agree except I think that you need to speak to the people in marketing also. Now, write down your goals and let's meet at the end of the week to see how it's going." The more unwilling and unable the employee, the more explicit and specific the explanation of what is expected must be and the more follow-up must be provided. An effective supervisor is aware of differences between employees and of an employee's need for supervision and can modify her assertive statements to respond to these differences.

SELF-TEST

Pick the most effective assertive statement for each of the following employees.

Employee A is a moderately skilled, experienced worker with good motivation.

Employee B has been your most difficult employee. She argues with you about every job assignment. She also has very poor skills on this kind of work.

Employee C is an eager worker and has been doing this kind of work longer than anyone in the department.

Employee D is generally quite skilled and experienced and is very motivated except in the area of paperwork. Since she dislikes paperwork, in this area of her job she can do poor work.

1. "I would like you to complete your report on the Jones project by Friday afternoon at 4:00. What specifically would you need to do to complete it by then?"
2. "I'm assigning you to complete the Jones project. I would like to sit down with you and decide together what should be done and what might be a reasonable schedule."
3. "I want you to finish the Jones report by 4:00 this afternoon. Specifically, I want you to collect the cost data from Nick, get the utilization figures from Helen, write a one-page summary, and deliver it to me by 4:00."
4. "I'm assigning you to the Jones project. Do what you think is necessary."

ANSWERS

Statement 1 would be appropriate for employee D. Generally this employee would not need a great deal of direction; however, on paperwork she will need more specific instructions because of her unwillingness to do that job.

Statement 2 would be appropriate for employee A. This moderately skilled and willing worker would respond very effectively to a participatory style.

Statement 3 would be appropriate for employee B. With an unwilling and unable employee, the instructions need to be very specific and a great deal of control is appropriate.

Statement 4 would be appropriate for employee C. This expert and motivated worker needs little direction or control.

**What can I do when I have to
interact with a very timid, nonassertive person?**
Although this book recommends a fairly forceful, assertive approach to others, there are some individuals who are very sensitive and easily intimidated. A relatively low-key assertive approach could be sufficiently intimidating to such a person that it leads to anxiety or withdrawal on his part. With this kind of person, two steps are necessary. First, it may be necessary to approach this person using a very low-key approach. Rarely would raising the muscle level be required. Usually a polite request will bring about change. Pointing up the person's positive qualities while giving criticism may be essential in order to avoid having him hear more criticism than you are saying. Even relatively nonassertive voice characteristics and body language, for example, a very gentle tone of voice, may be useful in making a point with this person. Second, you should very explicitly and actively encourage this person to become more assertive. One way to do this is to say something like "I would really like to hear from you when you disagree with me. I find your comments very helpful" or "What are your ideas about how to handle this situation?" Sometimes it may be helpful to call the process by saying something like "I notice that you don't say very much about what you think we ought to do, and I'm wondering if you're afraid that I'll jump down your throat if you don't say the right thing." Another way to encourage others is to acknowledge and reinforce all of their attempts to be assertive. When a very timid employee does speak up in a meeting, it may be useful to say "I really appreciate your speaking up. Your comments were very helpful." It is also extremely important not to further discourage open communication by becoming defensive or hostile when a person does finally manage to speak his mind. Encouraging assertiveness in all of the people you work with is very much to your advantage because nonassertiveness leads to many problems. The nonassertive employee stews over problems rather than bringing them to your attention so that they can be solved. She doesn't fully contribute her creativity and problem-solving ability to the organization because she is so reluctant to speak up. Therefore, it is to everyone's advantage to encourage others to learn to be more effectively assertive.

Chapter Nine discussed some of the problems associated with working for a nonassertive manager. These problems can be minimized if the manager has a very mature and motivated staff who are willing to take on a great deal of management responsibility.

When your manager is nonassertive, it may be useful to test to see how much management responsibility he is willing to relinquish. For example, some nonassertive managers are willing to allow supervisors in their departments to represent the department at some meetings with upper management. A nonassertive manager may happily support the supervisor's direct communication with upper management when asked: "I would like to talk to Don about this directly. Would you have any objections?" You can also support a nonassertive superior in becoming more assertive by preparing very well documented cases for requests that you want this superior to pass to upper management. Written proposals that can be passed on to management may prove quite useful in this situation. Force Field Analysis (see Chapter Nine) and some empathy with this manager's resistance to change make it possible to motivate him to take a stand on important issues. It may also be useful to try to train your manager to be more assertive by saying something like "I know that sometimes you are frustrated with my work. I'd really like to hear about it right away when you are so that we can correct the problem" or "I'm really glad you are going to talk to management about that problem. Your support is so important to our effectiveness in getting the job done."

When it is not possible to carry some of the assertive role in the organization for the manager or to train him to be more assertive, it may be possible to bypass that manager in order to bring about action. When you can't do that, it may be important to accept the manager's nonassertiveness as an organizational "given" and simply find ways to do your job as well as you can.

What can I do when I have to
interact with a very aggressive, hostile person?
As said in Chapter Nine, someone who is being aggressive from a bullying posture may respond positively to a very clear, assertive stand in the long run. However, if he does not, you may need to be aggressive. With a threatened, aggressive superior, it may be necessary to choose your battles very carefully, be aware of the other person's sensitivities, stroke that person, and approach him very carefully. It may help to inform the threatened superior about everything before you take any action to reassure him and keep him from getting anxious. With a highly aggressive individual, there may be situations in which some form of assertive withdrawal is the most appropriate response. With anyone whose angry, hostile reactions are interfering with constructive dialogue, it may be

possible to deliver a metascript (Chapter Seven), about how the other person's behavior interferes with dialogue.

With a very aggressive, hostile employee, it is very important not to either avoid all confrontations in order to prevent conflict or to consistently back off when hostility begins. If you stop being assertive every time someone is hostile, you are rewarding that person for his aggressiveness and training him to manipulate you. It may, however, be appropriate to temporarily back off to allow a person to calm down before trying to continue with a rational problem-solving discussion: "I still want to discuss this problem with you, but let's finish our discussion this afternoon at 3:00 when you have had a chance to think about what I said." Active listening to the other person's point of view may also serve to defuse hostile interactions: "So, from your perspective, I am being totally unreasonable in asking you to finish this project first. Can you tell me some more about why you feel that way?" It may be helpful to call the process to bring feelings into the open: "You seem to be getting angrier and angrier at me while we talk. What's going on?"

What can I do when I have to interact with a troubled person?
When you must supervise an emotionally disturbed employee, the supervisory job can become quite difficult. Family problems, personal crises, drug and alcohol abuse, and chronic psychological problems will inevitably interfere with full employee productivity. Experts have estimated, for example, that 20–30 percent of absenteeism is caused by emotional problems; 25–30 percent of any large work force needs mental health services; and 65–80 percent of firings are due to personal, not technical, factors (Weiner, Akabas, & Sommer, 1973). This kind of supervisory problem has been the impetus for the development of employee assistance programs in many organizations. In employee assistance programs, supervisors are trained to recognize signs of alcohol abuse or other personal problems that are interfering with work performance. When such a problem is recognized, the supervisor then has a conference with an employee in which she describes the performance problems she observes and refers the employee to the employee assistance counselor. This counselor then interviews the employee and either provides short-term crisis intervention counseling herself or refers the employee to an outside agency for counseling, alcoholism treatment, legal advice, or financial advice. The availability of this kind of program greatly simplifies your job when you have to deal with a troubled employee. It does require that you assertively describe

problems in performance and nonjudgmentally refer the person to the counselor.

When there is no employee assistance program available, you are in a much more difficult position, since you will not have the leverage to insist that a person get help. The first step is still to let the employee know that her performance is suffering. When you suspect a personal difficulty is the source of the problem, it may be more useful to call the process to find out what is happening than it would be to confront the employee with a request for change: "I've noticed that your performance has really been declining lately. What's going on?" It is not the supervisor's business to probe the intricacies of someone's personal life nor is it the supervisor's place to provide personal counseling. It may be appropriate to question enough to find out if there is a problem that is creating the performance deficit. Sometimes when the employee has been very effective in the past, it may be helpful to allow a temporary production lag in order to give the employee the space to settle a temporary personal problem. For example, there is no question that divorce can be extremely stressful. Expecting that an employee's divorce will have no effect on her work performance is unrealistic. Understanding and making allowances for the stress of this period in an employee's life can build a stronger supervisory relationship in the long run. Even with a "temporary" crisis like a divorce, the effects may linger for more than a year. For example, Wallerstein and Kelly (1980) have shown that the time of maximum stress may occur 1 year to 18 months after a divorce. At the same time that you make allowances for some decline in performance, it is important that you carefully consider the bottom line. What aspects of the employee's job can slide to some extent? What aspects of the job are essential to getting the work done? When productivity is below the bottom line, you may need to use a DESC Script with a "given that" statement to ask the employee to correct the problems: "Given that you have a great deal of stress in your life right now and it is bound to interfere with work performance to some extent, what could you do so that no contracts are submitted after the deadlines?"

You may need to refer employees with serious emotional problems to an outside source of help. In some cases, you might forcefully recommend counseling or some other assistance: "I know that you are grappling with some family problems right now, but they are interfering too much with your work performance. You need to get some assistance to keep these problems from affecting your performance."

When the emotionally disturbed person is a superior or a colleague from another department, the situation is more complex. Dealing with the emotionally disturbed superior was addressed in Chapter Nine. In such a situation, it may be important to make someone in upper management aware of the problem when it is possible to do that without jeopardizing your own position. When the troubled person is in another department, it may be helpful to pass the behavior description to your superior and let her pass the information on to someone who has direct authority over the person in question. This superior can then observe the individual and intervene to correct the problem.

What can I do when an employee cries whenever I confront her?

The most important thing to work on with an employee who cries is your own feeling of guilt. As said in Chapter Five, it is very easy to respond to someone else's tears as if that person is devastated. If you feel you should not hurt anyone else's feelings, you may believe that you have been terribly cruel when an employee cries. For many people, tears are an emotional release that occurs whenever they are under stress. It is true that any kind of confrontation may be painful and therefore will stimulate some hurt feelings. You are not necessarily being cruel if you hurt someone's feelings or make that person cry.

You can do several things when an employee begins to cry during an assertive interaction. Sometimes the most useful response is to hand the person a Kleenex and allow her to cry while you talk. It may even be helpful to say something like "It's OK to cry if you want. I understand that talking about this may be stressful." If the person seems very upset or if you as a supervisor cannot handle crying, it may be helpful to say "Why don't you take a few minutes to deal with your feelings and then we'll get back together and finish discussing the problem." It is important that you then follow up by continuing the discussion later until the problem is resolved. Avoiding confronting a person so she doesn't cry isn't good for you or her. When problems are not resolved, they may simply fester or grow until a much more upsetting crisis occurs. When an employee does seem very upset about a discussion, it may also be important to make sure that she understands what you are saying to her.

This can be done by clearly framing any criticism with reassurance and positive feedback when that is appropriate and by asking the person to let you know what she hears: "I'm not saying that you don't do anything right. I'm only saying that you need to improve this part of your proposal. What is your understanding of what I'm saying?"

What can I do when an employee won't participate in a discussion?

Since dialogue and involvement are ways to build teamwork, an employee who refuses to participate in a discussion can be a significant problem. For example, an employee may sit passively through a problem-solving session and when asked for suggestions for change, say, "I don't know what to do about it" or "Whatever you want is fine." Sometimes this person is sullenly withdrawn; at other times, the person seems very agreeable but uninvolved. There are several techniques that may be useful for dealing with this kind of problem. Often the first step is to call the process to see if you can discover the origins of the passivity: "I'm noticing that when I ask for your suggestions or involvement in solving the problem, you just say, 'I don't know.' What's going on?" You might discover, for example, that the employee is withdrawn because he is upset about something that needs to be brought into the open for frank discussion. You may even want to deliver a script to let the person know how important his involvement is: "When I ask for your suggestions or your involvement in the problem-solving process, you just say, 'I don't know.' That's a real problem from my perspective because I know that you are the one who will have to carry out any plan we come up with. If it all comes from me, it may be a plan that's hard for you to work with. I really want to hear some suggestions from you." It may be important not to accept full responsibility for devising the plan. Sometimes stroking the person's potential contribution can be very helpful. You could do this by saying "I know that you are the real expert on that job since you are the one doing it. Your involvement here can be really important."

What can I do when an employee has the potential, but not the motivation, to be a top-notch worker?

Sometime in your career, you will probably encounter at least one underachieving employee. This person may be doing a very good job relative to other employees, but you know that she could do a great deal better. Since this person may be doing a very adequate job, confrontation or punishment may be inappropriate or impossible. You would not, for example, threaten disciplinary action with a competent employee even if you thought that she could do better. The first thing to remember in confronting the competent but underachieving employee is that a person's involvement in her career is her choice. There may be some employees who will choose not to make a major investment in career advancement. This may be particularly true of part-time employees, who may work only part time to be able to commit themselves to personal goals such as raising children or going to school. It is their legitimate right to make that choice, provided they are doing their jobs competently. You cannot insist that a person feel the same about career advancement as you feel.

However, there may be some things that you can do to inspire an employee to invest more in career advancement. Discussion with the employee makes much more sense than confrontation. Calling the process may open dialogue about the person's feelings about her career: "I know that you are doing a very competent job, but I can't help but feel that you could do more if you were to make that choice. How do you feel about career advancement here?" Discussion may help the employee to sort out her values and priorities or to become aware of barriers to motivation that might be changeable. It is also appropriate for you to express your personal feelings of regret about the person's choice while at the same time recognizing the person's right to make that choice: "It sounds like what you are saying is that you want a job, not a career. You certainly have a right to make that choice, but I wish that you would reconsider. I really think that you have the potential to make a significant contribution here, and I hate to see that lost." The information you obtain by calling the process will help you to respond to any specific concerns the employee might have about investing more in the job. It may also be possible for you to gradually involve someone in a career through assigning challenging tasks, using her creativity, and giving positive feedback. However, there are some employees who will simply choose to do a very good job and will never choose to do more. There is nothing you can do but accept and appreciate what those employees do. An effective supervisor stimulates, encourages, and supports everyone in doing the best she can, but is also able to accept that others may have different priorities in life than she has.

**What can I do when
an employee is genuinely limited or unpromotable?**

Although an employee may be able to do a barely adequate job in her current position, she may be incapable of doing enough to match the work of more productive employees within the unit and may never be able to do sufficiently good work to be promotable. It is very difficult to deal with the employee who is, for one reason or another, limited in capacity. First, you must support and encourage this employee in doing the best she can without discouraging the employees who are capable of producing much more. In this case, you may need to let more capable employees know that what they do is valued while at the same time helping them to accept the fact that not everyone will produce at the same level: "I know that sometimes it is frustrating that you do more than May, but I believe that you are capable of doing much higher quality work, and I want you to do your best."

Another problem is finding ways to encourage an employee who will never receive promotions or merit raises. Sometimes supervisors have access to other less formal organizational rewards that can be made available to this employee or to the work group. For example, you may be able to have your company provide dinner tickets for all employees in a unit if the unit's productivity is high or employees may be eligible for awards for attendance. You may need to assert yourself with upper management to develop alternative forms of recognition. At the very least, you can verbally acknowledge that person's contribution while at the same time being sure to acknowledge more capable workers.

Sometimes you can encourage and support a person's efforts to find a job in which she can do better work. Since it may be very frustrating for an employee to be in a job that she has to struggle to do, a marginally capable employee may be willing to do different tasks or change jobs. For example, if you had a secretary who was very poor at typing, but was very friendly and comfortable dealing with people, you might want to encourage her to apply for a job as a receptionist.

It is important for a supervisor to recognize that people are different in talents and abilities. Not everyone will be able to perform as well as you can, nor at the level of your best employees. To be effective you must develop realistic demands that take into account individual differences.

What can I do when an employee does his job but has
a negative effect on the morale and productivity of others?
An employee may have a negative effect on the morale and productivity of others through a variety of behaviors. Constant complaining about the supervisor or the organization is one such
behavior. Complaining can encourage a negative work climate that
is discouraging to employees who might otherwise be quite motivated. In addition, complaining keeps both the complainer and
other workers away from their work. An employee may complain
to others because you have given him no other outlet for frustration; the most useful step is often to let him complain directly to
you. You could say, "I know that you are very unhappy with some
things around here. I'd like to sit down and talk about your complaints so that we can see if there is anything that can be done to
solve the problems." When this does not end the complaining, you
may need to deliver a script about the effect of the complaining on
productivity. It is important, however, to recognize that employees
do have freedom of speech. You cannot prevent them from complaining. You can ask them to complain in ways that do not disrupt
the work: "Chet, I know that you are very frustrated about some
things here. You certainly have a right to your feelings; however,
it is creating problems for you to spend time during the work day
at other people's desks complaining. I would like you to confine
your complaining to times when it will not interfere with other
people's work." It is also important to encourage other employees
to be assertive with someone whose complaining is disrupting their
work: "If Chet complains to you when you have work to do, you
need to say that you don't want to listen."

Other ways that employees may interfere with morale and productivity include having personality quirks that are disturbing to
others, having poor personal hygiene, and talking too much. Confronting some of these situations, such as telling an employee that
he needs to bathe more often, can be very ticklish. You need to let
the employee know in a tactful way the effect his behavior has on
others: "Jack, I think you would come across better both to co-
workers and customers if you showered more often or used a different soap. Any body odor can be very unpleasant for some people,
and I'd hate to have that influence people's perception of you."
Sometimes stating your own reactions to the behavior is helpful:
"I'm sure you are not aware how frustrating it can be when you

join in conversations between others without an invitation. I know that there are times when I want to talk to just one other person, and I would prefer it if you would ask if it's a private conversation before you join in."

What can I do when an employee
knows that I have no real leverage over him?

There are some situations in which you may have almost no leverage over a certain employee. This could be because an employee has a special relationship with upper management that gives him so much power that you have very little real leverage. Relatives, friends, or employees who are doing favors for upper management may all be able to ignore your attempts to raise the strength of consequences because they know that their upper management support system will protect them. This is one reason why it is so difficult to supervise in some family businesses. Everyone knows stories of the boss's incompetent relatives who are allowed to behave in ways that no other employees would dare to behave.

A second kind of employee who may be relatively invulnerable to supervisory authority is the employee with many years of good performance ratings. This employee may be able to get by on past accomplishments for many years. A classic case of this is the employee nearing retirement who stops producing. He knows very well that he will not be fired or even severely reprimanded no matter what he does.

Another situation that can create problems involves the employee with very rare skills. For example, a supervisor struggling to deal with an employee who is the only person in three states trained to repair a particular system could not muster any threat greater than that employee's threat to leave the organization.

Another employee who may be relatively invulnerable to leverage is the employee who has always managed to get his way by making such a fuss whenever there is a problem that he is very intimidating to upper management. The employee who files union grievances or storms into the vice-president's office or threatens to go to the papers every time there is a problem can create a situation in which his direct supervisor has very little leverage because upper management does not want to deal with the problems that this employee creates.

Another employee who may not be susceptible to leverage is someone who genuinely does not like or want a particular job. There are some employees who do not have the courage to look for more suitable or congenial work. For some of these employees, failure to perform when given very clear directives could be seen as an attempt to force termination.

When you are dealing with an employee that you have little leverage over, it is important to do everything possible to avoid getting into a power struggle. In a battle, the person with the biggest club wins. Since in this case you probably don't have the biggest club, you may lose if you start a war. Your best tactic with this kind of employee is to win his cooperation. Acknowledging your lack of leverage from the start sometimes helps you do this: "Both you and I are aware that I can't really force you to do the job. I would like, however, to find a way that we can work together more effectively, or we both are going to be frustrated. I am willing to do what I can to cooperate with you if you will work with me." Stroking the employee and listening to the employee's perspective can help to reduce resistance. For example, you could say, "Tell me some more about what you think you ought to be doing" or "John, I know that you can do very effective work for our organization because you have done so in the past. What could you and I do together to develop a better working relationship?"

Sometimes persistent and consistent follow-up over a long period of time may finally change an employee. Employees in these relatively invulnerable positions are used to having others back off when they refuse to correct a problem. A supervisor who very nonaggressively continues to pursue the employee and ask for excellence and productivity may eventually wear the employee down. It can be helpful to ask the employee to evaluate his own work on a regular basis. Asking the employee to describe specifically how he is being productive can create some pressure to do something worth reporting: "Peter, how do you think you're doing? What have you accomplished this week?" Sometimes you need to suggest that the employee find a more suitable job: "George, I get the sense that you do not like this job or working for me. Have you considered other positions where you will be less frustrated?" Sometimes it is possible to assert yourself with upper management by careful documentation of an employee's lack of productivity. It may also be possible to elicit management's involvement in the problem by asking your managers for advice on how to handle that particular employee. This protects you while making management aware of what that employee is costing the organization. Where the employee has the protection of a particular person in management, you may be able to elicit the support of other managers in bringing pressure to bear on the manager who is supporting the unproductive employee. Sometimes, however, you must simply accept the fact that you have little leverage over certain employees and find ways to minimize their detrimental effects on productivity.

What can I do to maintain a good relationship when I become a friend's supervisor?

Sometimes it is impossible to supervise someone and to maintain the same kind of personal relationship you had with the person before becoming his supervisor. It may be necessary to sacrifice the friendship in order to be effective as a supervisor. When it is obvious that your previous relationship with someone will cause problems in supervising him, it may be useful to discuss the problem with your manager and with the employee before the shift in roles occurs so that the possibility of promotion within a different department can be considered.

Often, however, it is possible to maintain a friendly personal relationship along with a strong supervisory relationship. The best way to work toward this kind of balance is to openly discuss the issue with the employee by calling the process: "Isaac, I'm concerned about how my promotion is going to affect our relationship. I know that I will have to disregard our friendship in order to provide fair supervision to all of the employees in this unit. I'm sure that there may be times when my sense of the best interest of the organization could conflict with what you want. How do you think we can work this out so that we can stay friends?"

What can I do when there is a personality conflict between two employees?

Supervisors often become the court of last resort for employees who have conflicts with each other. Even when the employees do not bring complaints to the supervisor, conflicts between employees may interfere with one or both employees' productivity and thus merit attention. There are several things you can do in this situation. First, it may be useful to call both people into your office and help them to clearly express their complaints to each other to see if a solution can be reached. Help each person express her complaints in a clear, nonjudgmental way: "Evita, specifically what is George doing that bothers you? Why is that a problem? What do you want him to do about it?" You can also help each person to understand and respond in a nondefensive way to the complaints: "George, Evita has told you some things that are bothering her. What do you think could be done to help the situation?" or "Rather than just telling me that the other person has no right to complain, I'd like to have both of you look at ways to get along better." You can also acknowledge nonnegotiable "given thats" by saying something like "I doubt that George will ever become a totally different person. Short of that, what would make the relationship between the two of you better?" When open discussion of the interpersonal problems with you as facilitator does not help, you still have a right to insist that both employees keep their conflicts from interfering with their work: "The two of you may never like each other, but you do need to find a way to keep your conflicts from interfering with your jobs."

What can I do when there is tension or a morale problem in my unit?

You need to be aware of the working relationships within your unit and to recognize and respond to signs of tension or morale problems like drops in productivity, much discussion between employees, complaints, verbal digs, and tense or withdrawn body language. Failure to acknowledge and confront morale problems can sap productivity. You should call the process when you sense tension or problems by calling a meeting or talking to individual employees and saying something like "I sense a lot of tension and resentment in the office right now, and I'm concerned about that. What's going on? Let's talk about it and see if we can find out what we can do to help."

What can I do when I get information from someone else about an employee's work?

Since peer pressure and observation can be an important force in promoting productivity within a work unit, it is important to respond when one employee gives you information about another employee. When someone complains about a problem and you fail to intervene in any way, that person may become discouraged and less motivated. She certainly will not take the risk of bringing another concern to you. Complaints about an employee's work may also come from supervisors, customers, or workers in other departments.

Complaints from a third party should prompt you to observe the employee's behavior more carefully so that you can gather data to use in a confrontation. For example, reports from other employees that an employee is spending a great deal of time on the phone can make you aware of a need to observe that employee's phone behavior for several days. With careful observation, you can confirm the problem for yourself before confronting the employee.

When you cannot directly observe the employee's behavior (as in calls on customers), you can still bring the employee's attention to a problem without getting involved in an argument about whether the behavior really happened. If, for example, the employee says, "You know how people are. They're always exaggerating things," you could say something like "That may be. Since I wasn't there, I have no way to know for sure what happened. I do know that whatever happened, it resulted in a complaint, and we need to do something to prevent further complaints." It is also difficult to monitor an employee's behavior when you are not normally at her work site. It may be necessary to make arrangements for someone else to watch an employee for a while and report back to you. In this case, you let the person know that you will be checking up on her work.

Sometimes one employee or customer becomes a tattletale. This person may constantly bring you information about employees. Although it is important to follow up on complaints made by workers or customers about others, it may be quite inappropriate to encourage this kind of tattletale behavior. With an employee, you may need to assertively say "I will observe others' behavior for myself. Please don't come to me with information about your co-workers anymore."

What can I do when I have
to confront union or minority employees?

Supervising union employees does not need to prevent you from working with employees to correct problems. Most unions do not support poor performance. They are mainly concerned about fair supervision. If you are assertive, you will be able to work more easily with a union, because your way of approaching employees will be thoughtful and fair. There are several things that you need to consider when asserting yourself with union employees. First, follow contractual obligations scrupulously. When a union steward is supposed to be included in a meeting, make sure that he is included. Second, make clear to the union representative that your goal is to correct a problem, not to undermine the union or the employee. Acknowledge the union steward's right to be involved in the case and his potential contribution to solving the problem. Sometimes the union steward can be a powerful ally in putting pressure on an employee to cooperate when the employee is clearly in the wrong. Remember, however, that in your presence the steward's job is to defend the employee. This means that he must provide at least token resistance. Third, clear documentation and specific description of problems is absolutely essential when a union is involved. So is equal treatment of all employees. If one employee is to be confronted about lateness, it is critical that other late employees are also confronted.

The management in some organizations has become very nervous about confronting women and other minority employees because of the many well-publicized discrimination cases that have reached the courts and been settled in the employee's favor. As in the case with union employees, working with minority employees does not require that you tolerate totally incompetent performance; it does require that you be scrupulously prepared and fair with employees. A willingness to listen empathically to employees and stroking the employees can reduce tension.

What can I do when I as the supervisor
strongly disagree with the organization in a given situation?
There are times when organizational constraints do make it much more difficult to do the supervisory job. You may feel that the company insufficiently rewards good employees or that some tasks you are asked to assign to your employees are unfair or that some policies are unjust. However, as long as you are working for that organization, you are contractually bound to carry out the organization's wishes (with the possible exception of times when you feel that policies will endanger you or your employees or are illegal or immoral). You also have a responsibility to do what you can to change policies or procedures that you think are unacceptable. When you need to confront an employee about a policy that you disagree with, you may want to state your feelings about the policy. For example, you might say, "I also believe that you shouldn't have to work every Saturday; however, until there is a change in this policy, both you and I are obliged to follow it. You will need to be here this Saturday" or "Regardless of our personal feelings about the case load, you need to meet with each client at least once every 2 weeks" or "I hear your objections and I'm doing everything I can to change the situation, but in the meantime you have to follow company policy."

What can I do to be assertive
when I don't have much time or privacy on my job?
It is true that the open dialogue between supervisor and employee that ideally follows an assertive interaction may not be possible in some settings at all times. A production supervisor, for example,

may not be able to take time to discuss a problem with an employee at a particular moment; however, he can still be aware of the assertive principles of eye contact, descriptive rather than judgmental criticisms, even voice tone, nonloaded language, and specificity and directness of expression. The book *The One Minute Manager* (Blanchard & Johnson, 1983) advocates a set of approaches very similar to assertive methods and delineates the 1-minute use of these techniques. You can still make an assertive initial approach to an employee even if there is no time for discussion. You don't have to be aggressive just because of time pressures. It is, however, helpful to follow up very quick assertive interventions with some problem-solving discussions in which employee opinions are solicited. Quality circles (Fitzgerald & Murphy, 1982) are a way some organizations have developed for soliciting employee input into problem solving. In some ways, these employee groups substitute for employee-supervisor dialogues that can occur in organizations where there is more time.

Another problem that you may encounter is the lack of privacy for employee-supervisor discussions. Some manufacturing, laboratory, or small office facilities are set up so that everyone works in one space. Even the supervisor may not have a private office. Although most organizations do have a meeting room where formal conferences can be held, making an appointment and taking an employee to the formal meeting room is a rather high-power transaction. If meetings are only scheduled when an employee is in serious trouble, the meeting room itself can arouse defensiveness and the employee may be subjected to harrassment from other employees when he returns from a meeting. One way to overcome this problem is to schedule periodic short meetings with employees just to discuss how things are going or to congratulate employees for good performance. In this way, a scheduled meeting can mean that something other than a reprimand is in order. For less serious interventions, it may be useful to pull an employee aside for an informal discussion rather than scheduling a formal meeting. In some cases, it may be very important for you to assert yourself to upper management to obtain a private office where you can meet with your employees.

The real key to applying assertive techniques on your job is *you*. As you learn to observe your behavior patterns, word choices, voice characteristics, and body language, you will begin to better understand some of your supervisory failures. Open dialogue with your employees will also help you learn from them how to be more effectively assertive. Clear, straight communication offers the potential to create an alive, vibrant organization in which conflict and problems can be resolved in a way that energizes rather than deadens. Respect and communication can contribute to a work environment in which both you, your employees, superiors, and colleagues feel self-respect, trust for others, and a deep sense of organizational commitment.

Good luck in developing your assertiveness.

Bibliography

Blanchard, K., & Johnson, F. *The one minute manager.* New York: Berkley Publishing Group, 1983.

Fitzgerald, L., & Murphy, J. *Installing quality circles: A strategic approach.* San Diego: University Associates, 1982.

Hersey, P., & Blanchard, K. *Management of organizational behavior: Utilizing human resources.* Englewood Cliffs, N.J.: Prentice-Hall, 1982.

Wallerstein, J. S., & Kelly, J. B. *Surviving the breakup.* New York: Basic Books, 1980.

Weiner, H. J., Akabas, S. H., & Sommer, J. J. *Mental health care in the world of work.* New York: Association Press, 1973.

APPENDIX

Using This Material
in Supervisory Training

The material in this book has been used in workshops with over 3000 participants from a wide variety of public- and private-sector organizations, such as hospitals, schools, banks, manufacturing plants, and social service agencies. Both nonassertive and aggressive supervisors have found these workshops helpful. Even supervisors who are already fairly assertive have found that the workshops helped them to better understand why what they did worked and how to apply it more effectively. Training with this material is relevant not only to supervisors but middle and upper managers and owners of small businesses who are involved with direct supervision.

Format of the Workshop

This material has been presented in a wide variety of formats depending on the time available and the type of learning expected. A workshop of 1 or 1½ hours can introduce people to the basic differences between the three supervisory styles, some assumptions about assertive supervision, and a few of the essential assertive techniques, and can provide time for questions. A 2- to 3-hour presentation can provide opportunities for participants to observe and discuss a demonstration of the three styles as well. It also allows for the introduction of additional assertive techniques and provides experience writing and getting feedback on a script. A 1-day workshop can allow for all of the activities previously described and also some simple training in listening skills, description of other assertive techniques, presentation of how to deliver criticism, and more practice of scriptwriting. The best presentation of the material, however, is in a 2-day workshop or a 2-day workshop with a ½-day follow-up about a month later. This allows time to cover all of the areas previously described and also information on how to respond to criticism, how to be assertive with superiors, and how to overcome difficulties in being assertive. It also allows for some roleplaying of assertive skills and for feedback from others on delivery style. The skill practice component of the training, which is very useful in behavior change, is time consuming and cannot be done effectively in less than several hours with a group of any size.

Schedule of the Workshop

The following step-by-step outline describes the lecture material, demonstrations, and exercises that can be used in a 2-day workshop. This is not to imply that this is the only reasonable way to conduct a workshop; the schedule presented will provide a useful framework for you to design your own workshop in assertive supervision. The tables mentioned in the text are located at the end of the appendix and may be copied for workshop use.

Day one

Generally, the initial step in an assertive supervision workshop involves introductions and assessment of needs. Asking participants to describe themselves, their expectations for the workshop, and their supervisory frustrations helps you and the participants to get acquainted, establishes a climate of personal involvement, and allows for the uncovering and discussion of unrealistic expectations. A warm-up exercise like the Name Game (in which each participant says his own name and someone else's, and the person named then says his name and another person's name) may also be useful as a way to establish a more relaxed climate.

Participants also need to know the assumptions about assertiveness the workshop is based on (Table 1) and what will be covered in the workshop. Discussing participants' reactions to the assumptions can provide opportunities to start restructuring their beliefs. An exercise in which participants are asked to write down words that describe supervisors who have been particularly motivating or discouraging for them can help to focus attention on the implications of supervisory style.

Giving participants an opportunity to see the nonassertive, aggressive, and assertive supervisory styles in action can lead to a deeper discussion of these styles. The three styles can be demonstrated with videotapes or by setting up examples with a workshop participant playing the employee. The "employee" is instructed to simply react to whatever you do as the "supervisor." In the first roleplay, put particular emphasis on lack of eye contact; pleading or questioning voice tone; downtrodden posture; and unclear negotiation and compromise. Emphasize "looking-through-you" eye contact; sarcastic, judgmental, overbearing voice tone; tense, impatient posture; blaming criticism; and unwillingness to listen in the second roleplay. And emphasize good eye contact; even, powerful voice tone; erect, relaxed posture; descriptive instead of judgmental criticisms; a willingness to listen; and good assertive problem solving in the third roleplay. You can then ask for observations about what happened in each roleplay, how well each approach would work, and how the employee responded to the supervisory style. It seems to be particularly helpful in highlighting the effects of each style to emphasize the different reactions of the employee. The person roleplaying the employee may look like three different people because he inevitably reacts differently to each style.

After the demonstration has elicited many of the characteristics of the styles, it is useful to provide a straightforward summary of the characteristics of each style (Table 2). Participants can be asked to experiment with the three styles by saying the same sentence to a partner in a nonassertive, aggressive, and assertive way. They are to change the style of the sentence by using body language and voice characteristics rather than changing any words. Trying several sentences that focus on different supervisory issues can be useful. Good sentences to use include "I need your report by Monday," "I'd like to be kept informed about this issue," "This part of the project needs to be redone," "No. I won't do that for you," and "You did a good job with Mrs. Jones." Asking participants which styles feel comfortable and which styles are difficult to express helps each person to identify and discuss his typical style and his partner's style.

At this point, participants are prepared to begin to learn some assertive techniques. The first technique to teach is active listening (Gordon, 1977) because unless participants learn how to listen effectively they have difficulty remaining assertive in later exercises. Describing the communication process and demonstrating active listening provides a good foundation for listening skills practice. Then the participants can be asked to think of a problem they are having with someone and to find a partner to discuss this problem with for 7 minutes. The listening partner is instructed not to give advice, not to tell the person what he would do, and not to give his reaction. He is to use the technique of active listening, supplemented by clarifying questions to understand how his partner sees the problem. After each person has had a chance to listen, the partners are asked to discuss how it felt to listen and to be heard. What the partners learn can be shared with the larger group.

To lead into giving criticism and problem solving, participants need to learn to take a more objective look at their problems. A presentation on the differences between facts and assumptions (Table 3), which includes some examples of how negative assumptions affect objectivity, can help them to do this. An exercise that develops objectivity requires that participants think of a supervisory situation in which someone is doing something that creates a problem. They write down the facts of the situation and then write down assumptions they are making about the behavior in this situation. Then they meet in groups of three or four to decide whether the facts are really facts and to develop alternative sets of assumptions that would explain the same facts. Discussion of the exercise focuses on benign versus negative assumptions and the rigidity of assumptions.

The next step is to help participants recognize that in order to be effectively assertive it is necessary to know what they want (Table 4). Conducting an exercise in which participants are asked to write down answers to the questions on Table 4 for the situation they just described focuses attention on goals. The final presentation on the first day of training can focus on skills for giving criticism to solve problems (Table 5). Outlining the techniques of the DESC Script (Bower & Bower, 1976) and then having participants critique examples from Chapter Seven will prepare them to write their own scripts at home to be reviewed on the second day of the workshop. They are asked to make sure that the person receiving the script would know what he is doing, why it is a problem, and what the critic wants him to do instead. They are also asked to make sure that the script is neutral so that it will not put the person being criticized on the defensive.

The following schedule gives the approximate lengths of time necessary for the activities on day one. These activities can easily be expanded to an 8:30 to 4:00 workshop.

9:00–9:30   Introductions, assessment of needs, Name Game exercise

9:30–9:45	Assumptions about assertiveness, what will be covered in workshop, exercise describing supervisors
9:45–10:30	Demonstration of the three supervisory styles
10:30–10:45	Break
10:45–12:00	Characteristics of the three styles, exercise saying sentences three ways
12:00–1:00	Lunch break
1:00–1:30	Listening skills, listening exercise
1:30–2:15	Objectivity, exercise on facts and assumptions
2:15–2:30	Break
2:30–2:45	Goals for assertive action, exercise on goals
2:45–3:45	Writing a script
3:45–4:00	Questions

Day two

A good way to start the second day is to go around the group and ask participants what they learned the day before and what questions they still wish to have addressed. This serves as a warm-up and also provides information that helps to shape the agenda for the day. Participants then form groups of three or four in which to share and critique their scripts for clarity and neutrality. After this, the large group reassembles and discusses questions and observations about the scripts. At this time, the problem solving process can be reviewed (Table 4) and participants can be provided with information about how to deliver criticism (Table 6), other assertive techniques (Table 7), and special considerations in being assertive with superiors (Table 8).

Although participants may resist practicing assertive skills, roleplaying is essential in encouraging participants to make use of the training received in the workshop. Getting full participation in this part of the workshop seems to require selling the group on the value of roleplaying by emphasizing how difficult it is to get good feedback about word choices, voice characteristics, and body language in real supervisory situations. It can also be pointed out that most new skills require some coaching and practice during the learning process. Although many participants would rather roleplay situations that are provided for them, they may learn more when they practice either their scripts or some other situation that they want to learn to handle more effectively. It is not important in the roleplays that the person playing the problem employee or the manager do or say exactly what the real person would do or say. What is important is only that he presents the same kind of problem that the real person would. It is also important to emphasize the need for group members to give each other good specific feedback. Giving feedback on the roleplay helps the person giving the feedback to learn to be clear as well as helping the person receiving it to sharpen his assertive skills. After each person has had a chance to roleplay and get feedback, the large group reconvenes for discussion. This part of the workshop may take up to 2 hours with groups of four since each roleplay and feedback session will take at least 20 minutes. Since some groups will finish sooner than others, they will need to be instructed to discuss supervisory concerns, roleplay new situations, or roleplay the same situations incorporating the feedback given while other groups finish.

The material on overcoming difficulties in being assertive (Table 9) can be presented next. After this presentation, participants can find a partner and share one situation in which they were nonassertive or aggressive when they wanted to be assertive. The partner's task is to help uncover the feelings that interfered with assertiveness and to help develop some ways to deal with these feelings.

Next, the styles of responding to criticism (Table 10) and how to respond to different types of criticism (Table 11) are presented. Participants can be asked to list three criticisms that others have made of them and to give his list to a partner. The partners should give each other a piece of criticism, but do it poorly. The partners can use the techniques previously described to respond to the criticism and give each other feedback on how well they were able to respond without sounding defensive.

It is a good idea to present the importance of positive recognition (Table 7) at the close of the workshop. This not only introduces participants to the characteristics of good specific positive recognition, but also leaves them with positive feelings. Participants are asked to get together in small groups and each person in the group is asked to give everyone else one piece of genuine, specific positive recognition. The person who receives the recognition is instructed not to say anything but "thank you." Either before or after this exercise, participants can be asked to give feedback and comments about the workshop.

An approximate schedule follows for day two of the workshop. Again, these activities can be expanded for a longer workshop.

9:00–9:30	Rounds and questions
9:30–10:30	Critiquing of scripts
10:30–10:45	Break
10:45–11:30	Problem solving review, delivery of criticism, other assertive techniques, assertiveness with superiors
11:30–12:00	Skill-practice roleplays
12:00–1:00	Lunch break
1:00–2:15	Skill-practice roleplays
2:15–2:30	Break
2:30–3:00	Overcoming difficulties in being assertive, exercise on difficulties in being assertive
3:00–3:30	Responding to criticism, exercise on criticism
3:30–4:00	Positive recognition, exercise on positive recognition, closure

Structure of the Training Group

This material has been used in workshops with anywhere from 10 to 100 participants. Generally, 2-day workshops in which there will be a great deal of small group and roleplay practice should be limited to 30 people. With groups of about 30, you can have participants form small groups and you can circulate to the small groups during practice sessions for feedback and coaching. In a smaller group, you can work with each person in practice sessions in front of the whole group. For some supervisors, however, practice in front of the whole group can be very threatening. For this reason, dividing the group into small groups of three or four people seems to work better.

Open-enrollment groups have included first-line supervisors as well as managers or owners of small businesses. The diversity of this type of group allows for a great deal of sharing of experience and also allows people who have come from the same organization to choose whether to work with each other or with strangers. In-house training serves two functions: to teach supervisors something about effective supervision and to build teamwork among supervisors by developing a shared framework for what supervisors do and encouraging mutual support in supervisory problem solving. Unless an organization has an open and comfortable climate, the inclusion of managers in the same training sessions with supervisors can create problems; however, even this composition can work if managers and supervisors are separated during small group activities.

Unless you can model good assertive communication, this training will not be effective. This means that you must listen nonjudgmentally to others, give good assertive feedback, respond in a nondefensive way to criticism directed at you, be able to formulate good scripts on the spot, and present assertive word choices, voice characteristics, and body language. By encouraging sharing and observations in the group, you have the opportunity to uncover potential misunderstandings and can elicit involvement in the training process. The more you can develop examples and demonstrations relevant to the participants and their work settings, the more effective the training will be. Enthusiasm and involvement on your part will create a much more stimulating learning climate.

There are certainly many ways to use this material in assertive supervision training. I have shared my workshop model and the thinking that has gone into the design in hopes that you will find it useful in designing your own assertive supervision sessions. If you develop creative ways to use the material that I haven't considered, I would love to have the opportunity to share your experiences. Thank you very much.

Bibliography

Bower, S. A., & Bower, G. *Asserting yourself.* Reading, Mass.: Addison-Wesley, 1976.

Gordon, T. *Leader effectiveness training.* New York: Wyden Books, 1977.

Smith, M. *When I say no I feel guilty.* New York: Dial Press, 1975.

Table 1. Basic assumptions about assertiveness.

1. Effective supervisors get the job done and solve problems in a way that builds involvement and teamwork.
2. Assertive supervisors respect themselves and others.
3. Others' reactions depend on how you choose to act and on your word choices, voice characteristics, and body language.
4. People want to do a good job.
5. People have a powerful need to save face.
6. Failing to tell someone about a problem is not doing him a favor.
7. No one can force anyone else to change.
8. Assertiveness will not always work right away.
9. Assertiveness is not a "do your own thing" philosophy.
10. Asserting yourself doesn't guarantee you will always get what you want.
11. Assertiveness is not an invitation to be rude, obnoxious, and unpleasant.
12. You don't have to be assertive all of the time.
13. Learning to be assertive is awkward at first.

Table 2. Comparison of the nonassertive, aggressive, and assertive supervisory styles.

	Nonassertive	Aggressive	Assertive
Behavior Patterns	No expression of expectations and feelings	Critical expression of expectations and feelings	Clear, direct, nonapologetic expression of expectations and feelings
	Views stated indirectly or apologetically	Blaming and judgmental criticisms	Descriptive instead of judgmental criticisms
	Complaints made to the wrong person	Negative intentions attributed to others	Persistence
	Problems not confronted soon enough	Muscle level too high	Willingness to listen
	No persistence	Problems acted on too quickly	Negotiation and compromise
	Unclear negotiation and compromise	Unwillingness to listen	
		Refusal to negotiate and compromise	
Word Choices	Minimizing words	Loaded words	Neutral language
	Apologetic statements	"You" statements	Concise statements
	Statements made about people in general instead of to a specific person	"Always" or "never" statements	Personalized statements of concern
	General instead of specific behavioral descriptions	Demands instead of requests	Specific behavioral descriptions

	Statements disguised as questions	Judgments disguised as questions	Cooperative words Requests instead of demands No statements disguised as questions
Voice Character-istics and Body Language	Pleading or questioning voice tone Hesitation Lack of eye contact Slumping, downtrodden posture Words and nonverbal messages that don't match	Sarcastic, judgmental, overbearing voice tone Interruption "Looking-through-you" eye contact Tense, impatient posture	Even, powerful voice tone Eye contact Erect, relaxed posture Words and nonverbal messages that match

Table 3. Facts and assumptions.

Facts

Specific behaviors that you can see or hear

Assumptions

What you think behaviors mean

Attributing negative intentions on the basis of irrational beliefs, labeling, mind-reading, magnifying, personalizing, and rigid "shoulds" and "shouldn'ts"

Table 4. Goals for assertive action.

What behaviors would you like yourself to stop doing, start doing, or keep doing?

What behaviors would you like the other person to stop doing, start doing, or keep doing?

What is the minimum behavior change you would settle for?

What is it costing you not to be assertive?

What are the risks of asserting yourself?

Table 5. Steps in giving assertive criticism and solving problems.

1. Call the employee's attention to the problem with assertive criticism. (What is the problem? Why is it a problem? What do you want the person to do instead? What are the benefits for changing behavior or the negative consequences for not changing?)

2. Discuss the causes of the problem with the employee and elicit his perspective on the problem.

3. Develop a plan of action to solve the problem.

4. Get a commitment from the employee to the plan.

5. Follow up to see that the plan is working.

Table 6. How to deliver criticism.

1. Use assertive word choices, voice characteristics, and body language.
2. Deal with your anger before beginning the criticism.
3. Describe the problem, why it is a problem, and what you want the employee to do instead before allowing the employee to interrupt.
4. Realize that an initial negative reaction does not mean the criticism won't work.
5. Make sure the other person understands.
6. Confront only one or a few issues at a time.
7. Give the employee a frame for understanding where the problem fits in his overall behavior.
8. Choose the time of the confrontation carefully.
9. Recognize that changing long-term habits will require a number of confrontations.

Table 7. Assertive techniques and their uses.

Technique	Uses of the Technique
Active listening (Gordon, 1977)—summarizing and repeating the speaker's message	1. Clarify the message when the listener may be distorting it because of cultural differences or strong emotional reactions or when the message is unclear or confusing 2. Make a statement that the listener respects the speaker enough to really make the effort to listen 3. Create a climate where people feel free to express themselves and problems can be solved 4. Reduce conflict in tense situations 5. Help others change their attitudes and behavior
Techniques for stating expectations clearly—telling employees what to do, how to do it, when it should be done, and the priority of the task	1. Get the job done as desired 2. Avoid confrontations 3. Motivate employees
Saying no—saying no clearly and forcefully	1. Deal with inappropriate requests 2. Deal with requests that conflict with present priorities 3. Deal with requests that demand more resources than are available

Giving positive recognition—acknowledging employees' contributions and good intentions and superiors' authority	1. Motivate and encourage others 2. Establish a climate conducive to teamwork and problem solving 3. Reduce tension when being assertive with superiors
"I" statements—describing your view (I think . . .) without making judgments about the other person's point of view	1. Encourage an open discussion of differences of opinion 2. Express an opinion clearly and recognize others' rights to their opinions
Calling the process—making an observation, then asking a question, stating a hunch, or using an "I" statement	1. Respond to interruptive behavior and return focus to task 2. Check out assumptions 3. Diagnose cause of a problem and resolve it 4. Uncover and discuss hidden conflicts and tensions
"Given that" statements—acknowledging handicaps while still seeking to solve problems	1. Eliminate unproductive discussions about how bad things are and whether the employee is justified in being frustrated 2. Put responsibility on employee to try to improve performance in spite of handicaps
Broken-record technique (Smith, 1975)—acknowledging what the employee says but going right back to the point	1. Avoid being sidetracked in a discussion
Selective ignoring—refusing to respond to certain styles of interacting or certain topics	1. Close discussion on a topic 2. Deal with someone interacting in an unacceptable way

301

Table 7 (cont.)

Assertive withdrawal—giving a clear nonverbal signal of the desire to postpone or terminate a conversation	1. Buy time for a thoughtful response 2. Avoid lengthy discussions when the supervisor is too upset to do effective problem solving 3. Indicate unwillingness to continue a particular discussion
Techniques for leading meetings—keeping everyone working for the same purpose, focused on a topic until closure, and moving to new topics, summarizing to make issues clear, and intervening in destructive processes	1. Contribute to a climate of open communication, cooperation, and productivity

Table 8. Asserting yourself with superiors.

1. *Don't undermine the superior's authority.*

   Acknowledge his authority from the start.
   Don't be aggressive.
   Work within the chain of command.

2. *Build a strong case for change.*

   Develop a good explanation of reasons for change.
   Document when possible.
   Take into account and work with resistance.
   Know when to back off.

3. *Recognize norms and power dynamics in the organization.*

   Understand the need for an indirect approach.
   Be aware of unspoken rules about how to be assertive.
   Recognize who has power and build a power base.

Table 9. How to overcome difficulties in being assertive.

Difficulty	How to Overcome It
Guilt	1. Become aware of guilt feelings and guilt triggers. 2. Uncover irrational beliefs, cognitive distortions, and parent messages and decide if the guilt is appropriate. 3. Develop an antidote statement.
Fear of Consequences	1. Uncover your catastrophic fantasy and exaggerate it. 2. Ask yourself "What's really likely to happen?" and be alert for irrational beliefs and cognitive distortions. 3. Weigh the risks of being assertive and the costs of not being assertive. 4. Assess what you need to do to protect yourself from negative consequences.
Fear of Being Taken Advantage Of	1. Recognize your fear and the assumptions behind it. 2. Dispute your assumptions.
Anxiety	1. Realize you can still act rationally when you're anxious. 2. Practice relaxation techniques. 3. Use deep breathing or a short meditation before confrontations.
Doubt	1. Do your homework—know what you want to accomplish and the facts of the situation. 2. Substitute positive pep talks for negative pep talks. 3. Focus on supervisory rights and responsibilities.

Anger	1. Examine negative assumptions and look for more benign alternatives.
	2. Look for and dispute irrational beliefs and cognitive distortions.
	3. Watch for anger triggers, especially red-flag people.
	4. Empathize—put yourself in the other person's shoes.
Inflexible Self-image	1. Realize that one or a few interactions will not make or break your image.
	2. Remind yourself that you can act in opposing ways and still maintain your image.
Negative Self-image	1. Identify and dispute ways that you undermine yourself.
	2. Give yourself credit for your strengths.
	3. Forgive yourself for your flaws.
Sexual and Racial Blocks to Assertiveness	1. Dispute internal programming that keeps you from being assertive.
	2. Define negative reactions as inevitable responses to changes in the traditional distribution of power.
	3. Build a power base to support your assertiveness.

Table 10. Styles of responding to criticism.

Nonassertive	Aggressive	Assertive
Is apologetic, hurt, frightened, guilty, defensive, and self-critical	Is angry and attacking	Is calm, self-accepting, not angry or guilty.
Accepts all criticism	Rejects all criticism	Sorts criticism and accepts accurate criticism
Takes criticism personally	Takes criticism personally	Uses criticism as information
Reacts to general information	Reacts to general information	Questions to get specific information
Avoids criticism	Punishes criticism	Works toward open dialogue and problem solving
Ignores tension and conflict	Escalates tension and conflict	Defuses tension and conflict
Ignores hidden conflict	Ignores hidden conflict	Uncovers hidden conflict

Table 11. Responding to different types of criticism.

Mistakes in responding to criticism

1. Not distinguishing the other person's problem from your problem
2. Seeing criticism as a personal attack
3. Distorting criticism
4. Seeing criticism as a reflection of worth
5. Believing that everyone must have a good opinion of you

Techniques for responding to teasing

1. Humor
2. Ignoring
3. Fogging
4. Saying stop it
5. Using a script
6. Calling the process, questioning, and problem solving

Techniques for responding to blowing off steam

1. Correcting misperceptions
2. Using listening and asking for details to allow the person to release tensions and to calm down
3. Being alert for problems that need to be solved
4. Acknowledging the other person's right to be angry
5. Setting limits when the person is violent or abusive, when the time or place is inappropriate, or when you are not willing to listen to the person blow off steam

Techniques for responding to criticism that attempts to solve problems

1. Eliciting good describe, express, and specify portions of a script
2. Evaluating the criticism for accuracy
3. Deciding whether you accept the criticism as your problem and are willing to change and, when appropriate, clearly disagreeing with the criticism
4. Exploring mutually acceptable solutions if you agree with the need to change

Table 11 (cont.)

Techniques for uncovering hidden conflict
1. Being aware of nonverbal cues of conflict
2. Calling the process
3. Having a regular mechanism for discussing problems within your unit

Index

About the Author

Susanne S. Drury has an A.B. in Chemistry from Earlham in Richmond, Indiana and Ph.D. in Clinical Psychology from the University of Chicago. She has been a human resources consultant since 1967 and has taught full or part time at the University of Delaware for 8 years. All of her clinical consulting and teaching focuses on helping people to develop concrete interpersonal skills that they can use in their work and their personal lives. She has conducted workshops on topics such as problem solving and goal setting, dealing with anger, stress management, and time management for individuals and for staffs of agencies and businesses. She has been conducting assertiveness workshops since 1975. The assertive supervision workshops on which this book is based evolved when she incorporated assertiveness concepts into an ongoing supervisory training program and found that the concepts were of real use to supervisors. She has provided training in assertive supervision to over 3000 people in open-enrollment workshops and in training programs for organizations such as Delaware Trust, Du Pont, and Rollins Leasing. She is currently Coordinator of Professional Development and Training for Tressler Center for Human Growth in Wilmington, Delaware, a consultant trainer, a private practitioner in clinical psychology, and a part-time university faculty member. Susanne lives in the woods in Arden, Delaware with her husband and her three teen-age children.